'The increasing professionalisation of organisational and leadership coaching is supported by academics and practitioners, providing models and evidence with well-thought-through and practical research gravitas. Dr Lloyd Chapman's work is an excellent contribution to this development. He covers and integrates an extensive array of theoretical and practical views, stimulating deep (and sometimes surprising) reflection about the essence and practice of, as well as the way of being in, the coaching relationship. This book acts as a must-have desk reference for coaching practitioners and academics.'

Frans Cillers, *Department of Industrial and Organisational Psychology, University of South Africa*

'Through his wide-ranging research, Lloyd takes us on a revealing journey into the evolving discipline of executive coaching. He thoroughly understands how the coach's presence contributes to the coaching experience, and the physiological basis of that presence. Underpinned by the theories of Kolb, Wilber, Moustakas, Stacey, Freire and Almaas, his focus is on how integrated experiential learning enhances personal growth and development. He encourages practitioners to develop their own coaching model within the context of the experiential learning cycle, so any coach wishing to enhance the potential of individuals and teams should read this book.'

Sunny Stout-Rostron, *Stellenbosch Business School, University of Stellenbosch, Cape Town, South Africa; Founding President of Coaches and Mentors of South Africa (COMENSA)*

'Lloyd Chapman is a respected expert in the field of experiential learning, both academically and as a seasoned executive coach. In this text he advances his previous work with the latest thinking for the field, arguing that the best of us act continuously as researchers of our own practice. I particularly enjoy the way he synthesises complexity theory with areas of learning theory in his elegant Integrated Experiential Learning Process model. Highly recommended!'

Marc Simon Kahn, *Chief Strategy Officer, Investec Plc and Visiting Professor, Middlesex University, London*

'This book offers a unique and yet important contribution to the world of coaching. Kurt Lewin wrote 'there is nothing as practical as a good theory' and Chapman's book is living proof of this statement. Drawing on the work of such eminent people as Ralph Stacey, Paulo Freire, David Kolb and Ken Wilber, Chapman provides a theoretically-grounded evidence base to support and inform experienced coaches, executives and HR managers about coaching and its relationship with experiential learning. This book needs to go on the must read list!'

Bob Garvey, *Emeritus Professor at Sheffield Business School and Visiting Professor at Leeds Business School, UK*

'Research shows that the efficacy of coaching is undeniable, yet we don't quite know why or how. Lloyd brings together seemingly unconnected theoretical worlds in a thought-provoking synergy that provides a foundation from which to critique, understand and practise coaching, and being a coach. This is a timely and welcome addition to our growing understanding of the profession.'

Nicky Terblanche, *Programme Head: MPhil Leadership Coaching, Stellenbosch Business School, University of Stellenbosch, Cape Town*

'Combining practical experience and detailed research, this book is indispensable to coaching practitioners, and all those who want to understand the psychological and physiological responses to learning that could guide coaching in a business context. It contains new and thought provoking insights into the ever-evolving coaching field, especially related to the evidence-based model. It is really insightful for the coaching practitioner to consider the science involved and to understand the physiological impact of coaching on the mind and body! Highly recommended!'

Colin Archery, *Executive: Transformation, Gijima.com, Midrand, South Africa*

'Chapman attempts to provide scientific underpinnings to a profession so easily filled by practitioners who reduce coaching to common sense or intuition. This book clarifies various dimensions coaches should consider in their practice, placing particular emphasis on the major impact on the coaching experience of the physiological states of both the practitioner and the client, so easily overlooked. Chapman's work provides useful insights into what a coaching approach should look like, while deliberately steering away from prescribing a rigid model.'

Morné Weyers, *Chief Information Officer, Curo Fund Services, Cape Town*

The Evidence-Based Practitioner Coach

The Evidence-Based Practitioner Coach gives a descriptive, phenomenological understanding of human development through the lens of the Integrated Experiential Learning Process, and how it can be applied in coaching.

Aimed at coaches who would like to ground their experience in an evidence-based practitioner model, it synthesises evidence and theory from a range of disciplines, exploring how we learn through a complex process involving brain, body and social relationships, and facilitated consciously and unconsciously through the central and autonomic nervous systems. It applies this understanding to a range of settings, contexts and environments. The book notably combines the fascinating knowledge produced by cutting-edge research with useful, practical methodologies developed by some of the wisest observers of humanity. Its sheer readability, in an engagingly down-to-earth and warmly human way, helps make the contents readily accessible to coach practitioners and others from non-academic backgrounds.

Rigorous and erudite, this book would be suitable for business coaches, corporate executives, senior managers, and human resource specialists, and provides an invaluable contribution to what it means to be a scientist-practitioner within the evolving profession of coaching.

Lloyd Chapman is an executive coach with business experience in managing and implementing strategy, organisational change, mergers and acquisitions, and IT projects. He specialises in executive coaching and team coaching, work-based learning, and stress management. He holds a Professional Doctorate in executive coaching and an MBA.

The Professional Coaching Series

This series brings together leading exponents and researchers in the coaching field to provide a definitive set of core texts important to the development of the profession. It aims to meet two needs – a professional series that provides the core texts that are theoretically and experimentally grounded, and a practice series covering forms of coaching based in evidence. Together they provide a complementary framework to introduce, promote and enhance the development of the coaching profession.

Titles in the series:

Internal Coaching: The Inside Story
By Katharine St John-Brooks

Coaching in Education: Getting Better Results for Students, Educators, and Parents
By Christian van Nieuwerburgh

Coaching in the Family Owned Business: A Path to Growth
By David A. Lane

Integrated Experiential Coaching: Becoming an Executive Coach
By Lloyd Chapman

The Art of Inspired Living: Coach Yourself with Positive Psychology
By Sarah Corrie

The Evidence-Based Practitioner Coach: Understanding the Integrated Experiential Learning Process
By Lloyd Chapman

For further information about this series please visit www.routledge.com/The-Professional-Coaching-Series/book-series/KARNPROFC

The Evidence-Based Practitioner Coach

Understanding the Integrated Experiential Learning Process

Lloyd Chapman

Routledge
Taylor & Francis Group

LONDON AND NEW YORK

Designed cover image: © Getty Images.

First published 2023
by Routledge
4 Park Square, Milton Park, Abingdon, Oxon OX14 4RN

and by Routledge
605 Third Avenue, New York, NY 10158

Routledge is an imprint of the Taylor & Francis Group, an informa business

British Library Cataloguing-in-Publication Data
A catalogue record for this book is available from the British Library

Library of Congress Cataloging-in-Publication Data
Names: Chapman, Lloyd, author.
Title: The evidence-based practitioner coach : understanding the integrated experiential learning process / Lloyd Chapman.
Description: Milton Park, Abingdon, Oxon ; New York, NY : Routledge, 2023. |
Series: The professional coaching series | Includes bibliographical references and index. |
Identifiers: LCCN 2022054339 (print) | LCCN 2022054340 (ebook) |
ISBN 9781032411361 (paperback) | ISBN 9781032411354 (hardback) |
ISBN 9781003356424 (ebook)
Subjects: LCSH: Executive coaching. | Executives–Psychology.
Classification: LCC HD30.4 .C48328 2023 (print) | LCC HD30.4 (ebook) |
DDC 658.4/07124–dc23/eng/20221114
LC record available at https://lccn.loc.gov/2022054339
LC ebook record available at https://lccn.loc.gov/2022054340

ISBN: 978-1-032-41135-4 (hbk)
ISBN: 978-1-032-41136-1 (pbk)
ISBN: 978-1-003-35642-4 (ebk)

DOI: 10.4324/9781003356424

Typeset in Times New Roman
by Newgen Publishing UK

To my father, Reg, and my mother, Joey, for their continuous love and support.

Contents

Figures

Tables

Foreword

With his first book in our *Professional Coaching Series*, Lloyd Chapman provided arguably the primer for thinking about executive coaching as a serious discipline which combined an understanding of business with adult learning. He put together a text that explored both his own journey and the ideas that underpin a genuine business or executive coaching model, rather than one derived from a counselling perspective. As reviewers at the time commented, it offered a rich and robust theory, and a truly integrated experiential coaching model. It represented the starting point in the next evolution of coaching, and moved executive coaching from a set of tools to a solid, academically based discipline. He appealed to his readers to look at their own work and build a model of practice that was founded in an evidence base.

That was in 2010; the field has since moved on, and so has Lloyd's work and practice. In revisiting the field, he has continued to argue for practitioners to become researchers into their own practice and adopt a scientist-practitioner model. In looking at the field again, he has identified a number of areas that are now essential components of the understanding of anyone either working as an executive coach or using the services of such practitioners. Experiential learning remains at the centre of his approach, but this is now informed by an understanding of complex responsive processes. Our understanding of the physiology of learning, particularly the impact of developments in neuroscience, is now a necessary part of the perspective coaches bring. He explores this emerging field in some detail. Perhaps an unusual set of ideas brought to the table include the relationship between movement and learning. His ideas on the importance of this area may cause some readers to pause, but having done so, his observations will then certainly give rise to useful reflection and hopefully action. As in his first book, he turns to both Kolb and Wilber for an understanding of human development models, and makes a strong case for their continuing importance.

These ideas provide the grounding for an exploration of how to become an evidence-based practitioner, which is the story of this book. He explores research methodology and how we might use it to understand practice. The Integrated Experiential Learning Process he has developed is then explored in relation to working through each of the stages within a coaching framework. Its application in the business context is further explored before considering its use in a team context. This leads naturally to a consideration of what it means to be present as a coach, and coaching as a complex responsive process.

He concludes by reminding the reader of the importance to our field of being a scientist-practitioner, and appeals to each of us to develop our own approach based on experience and evidence. The book is, as he says, an ongoing response to the *Dublin Declaration on Coaching*, which in 2008 noted the importance of evidence to coaching and the crucial role of practitioners in conducting their own research. He has provided a personal account of how he responded to that call, which provides an inspiration for coaches to do the same. He does not set out a definitive model of coaching, but rather implores each of us to become active consumers of emerging evidence, and researchers into our own practice.

The call is timely, and once again I am delighted to introduce Lloyd's latest addition to our series. It is a well-written and important contribution to building coaching as an evidence-based profession.

Professor David A. Lane
Professional Development Foundation
Series Editor: Professional Coaching Series

The author

Lloyd Chapman is an executive coach, with 21 years' experience coaching individuals and teams in a wide range of organisations in 21 countries. Prior to that, he spent 14 years in corporate life gaining experience in leading, managing and implementing strategy; large-scale organisational change; mergers and acquisitions; business process re-engineering; and workflow implementations and other IT-related projects.

Lloyd completed a doctorate in professional studies in executive coaching through Middlesex University and the National Centre for Work-Based Learning in the United Kingdom. (He was the first person in the world to qualify with a DProf in executive coaching.) He also holds an MBA degree, degrees in marketing and theology, and a diploma in personal fitness training. He is a faculty member at the University of Stellenbosch Business School.

Lloyd lives in Cape Town, South Africa with his wife, and has a daughter and son.

Acknowledgements

The writing of this book would never have happened if it were not for the continuous support and encouragement of Professor David Lane. I am also thankful to David for once again arranging a publisher for this book, and for his guidance and recommendations.

To Russell George and Katie Randall at Routledge for their help, guidance and support with this project.

To my colleague Nick Wilkins who edited and re-edited drafts of the book before it went to the publishers. What I appreciate most is his attention to detail, and his absolute professionalism. Secondly, for project-managing me throughout the entire process. This book was a true team effort.

My wife Pamela, my daughter Ashley, my son Sheldon, and my mother and father for their love and support.

Lloyd Chapman

Introduction

As was the case with my previous book (Chapman, 2010), if you are hoping that this is another publication which will provide you with a basic five-step or seven-step coaching model, please put it down, as you would be wasting your money. This book is not aimed at the novice coach; it is aimed at those coaches who have extensive experience and would like to anchor their practice on a theoretically grounded, evidence-based scientist-practitioner model. Senior executives and human resources management practitioners who have an interest in using and sourcing executive coaches will also find this book helpful, in that it will give them an idea of the kinds of question they should be asking of prospective coaches. Can the prospective coach make their model explicit? What philosophy, theory, application and experience underpins the coach's work? Has their work been researched; if not, what evidence do they have to substantiate their claims about their work?

This book is the result of an ongoing journey towards trying to master the art of executive coaching. In July 2008 a number of coaches from around the world met at the Global Convention on Coaching (GCC) in Dublin to discuss the development and professionalisation of coaching. The GCC's Working Group on a Research Agenda for Development of the Field noted in the Research Appendix to the Dublin Declaration on Coaching that "Research is critical to the development of the emerging profession of coaching", that "Every practitioner has the responsibility of doing research in their own practice", and that "Practitioner and academic research are considered to be of equal value to the coaching community and its developing body of knowledge" (GCC, 2008:11). This book is a continuation of that call. Since my first book was published in 2010, I have continued to research my own practice and refine my coaching methodology in light of new thinking and research that have emerged. At the same time, this work is an attempt to produce what Argyris (2010) calls Model II reasoning, which aims to:

- seek valid information (i.e. information which is testable);
- develop informed choices; and
- vigilantly monitor to detect and correct error.

DOI: 10.4324/9781003356424-1

In this way, knowledge can be produced that makes its reasoning transparent and open to public scrutiny, where the claims can be robustly tested. The more fundamental aim of the book is, however, to share a thought process with you that will enable you, the reader, to further develop your own coaching model and practice within the scientist-practitioner framework.

In their book *The Modern Scientist-Practitioner: A Guide to Practice in Psychology*, David Lane and Sarah Corrie (2006) argue the case for reformulating what it means to be a modern scientist-practitioner within the profession of psychology. I believe that their reformulated scientist-practitioner model is a very good basis on which to establish and define the profession of executive coaching. They suggest that the scientist-practitioner organises their reasoning skills around three domains, namely purpose, perspective and process (Lane and Corrie, 2006:48–49):

1   *Purpose.* In undertaking any psychological enquiry, it is vitally important to be clear about the journey's fundamental purpose. What is it that the practitioner and client are hoping to achieve? In other words, what are the outputs or results that the client wants to achieve? In defining a clear purpose, clear boundaries can also be established. It helps to define with whom the practitioner will and will not work, and when it will be important or necessary to refer the client to another professional.

2   *Perspective.* Part of the agreed purpose would include being able to define what the practitioner brings to the encounter. This would include all their models, values, beliefs, knowledge and philosophies, as well as a sense of their competence limitations.

3   *Process.* Having defined the purpose and perspective underpinning the work, it then becomes possible to structure a process to undertake it. So what method or tools can be used to help achieve the desired purpose within the constraints of the specified perspective?

Lane and Corrie's (2006) three domains for the scientist-practitioner are analogous to Mouton's (2001:137–142) "three worlds" framework for research, comprising:

1   *World 1.* The world of everyday life and lay knowledge, of ordinary social and physical reality. This is where we spend most of our lives, and we use lay knowledge (i.e. common sense, experiential knowledge, wisdom, insight and practical know-how) to solve problems and gain insight into everyday tasks and problems. It is here that social and practical problems arise which require interventions, action, programmes or therapy. Lane and Corrie's (2006) "purpose" will be formulated in, and address problems encountered in, World 1.

2   *World 2.* The world of science and scientific research, in which scientists select phenomena from World 1 and turn them into objects of scientific

inquiry. World 2 involves the research process in terms of its problem statement, design, methodology and conclusions. This of course takes place within certain defined theories, models, typologies, concepts and definitions. World 2 is the context of Lane and Corrie's (2006) process domain.

3 *World 3.* The world of meta-science, in which we reflect on the reasons and justifications for certain actions. More importantly, it is the world of critical reflection, deciding which theory, indicators, measurements and research design to choose. Over time, this has led to various meta-disciplines, theories and paradigms, including paradigms in the philosophy of science and in research methodologies. This is the perspective domain covered by Lane and Corrie (2006), a critical component which I believe is often neglected by coaching practitioners.

As coaching continues to develop into a fully fledged profession, I believe it is vital for us as coaches to develop our critical reflection skills and apply these to the world of meta-science, metaphysics and meta-theories as it pertains to coaching. I am therefore in agreement with Lane and Corrie (2006) that scientist-practitioners must be able to make their perspectives explicit – because only if we make them explicit can they be held up for critical reflection.

This book does not offer a causative, mechanistic understanding; it is instead a synthesis of various disciplines and scientific writings to offer a descriptive phenomenological understanding and theory of human development through the lens of the Integrated Experiential Learning Process. This includes making the Integrated Experiential Learning Process explicit, so that it can be held up for critical reflection. It is my sincere hope that this work can contribute to the continuing dialogue on what it means to be a scientist-practitioner within the evolving and emerging profession of coaching.

The structure of this book

Chapter 1: Complex responsive processes and experiential learning

Chapter 1 explores the complex world in which we all live and participate daily. More specifically, I discuss the work of Ralph Stacey on complex responsive processes and what that means for each of us. According to this theory, we all contribute to and co-create the complexity in which we live, whether we choose to or not. Both our conscious or unconscious actions and inactions are continually contributing to complex responsive processes. The danger in such an environment is that we tend towards acting like victims. To counter that danger, the work of Paulo Freire (2005), the Quaker Persuasion Model (Nielsen, 1998) and David Kolb's (1984) experiential learning theory are explored as ways to live and act more proactively and counteract victimhood.

Chapter 2: The physiology of learning

Chapter 2 explores the physiology of learning. Stacey (2003, 2009) and Stacey and Griffin (2005) believe that it is due to the evolution of the central nervous system that humans can reflect on their actions, become aware of themselves and know what they are doing. Through experience they can therefore learn to act in expectation of particular responses from other individuals; it is about making sense of lived experience. The self and the mind are actions of the whole body; they are not just cognitive aspects. The experiential learning cycle is possible only because of the evolution of the central nervous system. Furthermore, understanding the physiology involved will help us to understand what physiological states are optimal for learning to take place, and what physiological states hinder learning. And it is the physiology underpinning experiential learning that we will explore in this chapter. This will be done with special reference to polyvagal theory, regulation theory, the brain lateralisation work of McGilchrist (2019) and the work of Hannaford (2005, 2011) on learning and movement.

Chapter 3: Movement and experiential learning

Chapter 3 explores how the development of the nerve networks (the central and autonomic nervous systems), and ultimately learning, depend on movement. Our nerve networks grow out of unique transactions and sensory experiences in our environment. It is through our senses that learning first starts to happen. It starts with our initial sensory experiences, which lay down intricate nerve networks and patterns serving as the foundations for higher-level brain development and our free-form information system. And the intricacies of these patterns are shaped by all the activities we experience and by our environmental circumstances. It is these internal and external sensory experiences that continuously modify, change and create more complex images of ourselves and the world, resulting in new and continuous learning. This is because each new and novel experience contributes to us updating our free-form information system and causing it to become more elegant. All of which is dependent on movement.

Chapter 4: Human development models

In Chapter 4, I turn to human development and explore three meta-theories that have influenced, and are an integral part of, the Integrated Experiential Learning Process. The first meta-theory is the Integral Model of Ken Wilber. I want to make it clear from the outset that I believe Wilber's theory is *a* theory and not *the* theory. I have, however, found it to be a very useful conceptual framework within which to think and do my work.

The second meta-theory explored briefly in Chapter 4 is the Diamond Approach developed by A.H. Almaas. I do little justice to the depth and excellence of Almaas's work, but in the context of this book it is necessary only to make the reader aware thereof. I would highly recommend his publications to any person exploring a more integrative approach to life.

The last meta-theory explored in Chapter 4 is the experiential learning theory of David Kolb. The more I work with his theory, the more respect I gain for the depth involved therein. Sadly, I believe that many people use Kolb's work very superficially. Finally, I end Chapter 4 with an integration of Wilber (1995) and Kolb (1984). This new synthesis is the Integrated Experiential Learning Process, the key hypothesis of which is that human development is a function of lifelong experiential learning.

Chapter 5: Research methodology

Chapter 5 deals with research. Having a philosophy and working hypothesis is all good and well, but a working hypothesis without a methodology to research it is of no practical use whatsoever. This chapter deals with the further enhancement of the Integrated Experiential Learning Process by adding a research methodology. This is achieved by integrating it with the transcendental phenomenology of Moustakas (1994), and briefly discussing my original research findings.

Chapter 6: Applying the Integrated Experiential Learning Process to coaching

Chapter 6 deals with how the Integrated Experiential Learning Process is applied to coaching, and the stages that are involved. It proposes that coaching is about facilitating integrated experiential learning in individuals in order to enhance personal growth and development. It is "integrated" in that it caters for Schumacher's (1978) four fields of knowledge, and for Wilber's Integral Model, which analyses personal development through various levels of consciousness, especially in the personal and transpersonal levels. It is "experiential" in that it uses Kolb's Experiential Learning Model as the paradigm or injunction, and Harri-Augstein and Thomas's (1991) concept of learning conversations as the primary learning tool.

Chapter 7: Applying the Integrated Experiential Learning Process in business

In Chapter 7, I explore how the Integrated Experiential Learning Process can be applied in the messy and complex world of managerial leadership. The chapter takes the theoretical Integrated Experiential Learning Process and adds a business context thereto. This is done by incorporating the work of Ralph Stacey on complex responsive processes, and the work of Galbraith, Downey and Kates (2002) and Rehm (1997) on organisational design principles. All of this has to happen within a world of managerial complexity which can overwhelm executives.

Having set out the business context, Chapter 7 then explores the individual leadership competencies of Jaques and Clement (1997), and how those competencies could help an executive cope with managerial complexity. What becomes clear is that within the business context, coaching is not therapy. Using the work of Peltier (2001), a distinction is made between coaching and therapy.

Lastly, referring to the work of Oshry (1999) and Kilburg (2000), it is shown that behavioural problems manifested by individuals within an organisation could be intrapsychic, or due to systemic organisational design problems, or even the result of a combination of both. Hence it is argued that an executive coaching intervention should be aimed at working with cognitive potential, values, knowledge, skills and wisdom within the system in which the individual operates. In the Integrated Experiential Learning Process, executive coaching is therefore about facilitating integrated experiential learning in individuals in order to enhance personal growth and development, with the aim of improving individual and organisational performance. It is not therapy.

Chapter 8: The Integrated Experiential Learning Process in a team context

Chapter 8 explores how team coaching using the Integrated Experiential Learning Process is about facilitating experiential learning within the context in which the team finds itself. Its major assumptions are that we are all unique, with inherent strengths and weaknesses, and that we can all learn effectively. Experiential learning is a natural process with which we all identify once it has been made explicit. Combined with our natural talents, it yields strengths that should be harnessed with the greatest of ease to improve team performance. And it does so by consciously making a choice to identify strengths and to use them. It is about harnessing the natural potential of individuals and teams, rather than focusing on what is wrong. It draws on the work of Rehm (1997), Stacey (2003, 2009), Stacey and Griffin (2005), and Kline (1999, 2005, 2015).

Chapter 9: Coaching presence

In Chapter 9, I explore the concept of coaching presence by drawing on polyvagal theory and regulation theory, and how these theories have contributed towards the understanding of presence within a therapeutic context. This understanding is then adapted to the coaching context to explore how the coach's presence can contribute to or distract from the coaching experience. I then explore how the Integrated Experiential Learning Process is in fact a complex responsive process between the coach and the coachee.

Chapter 10: Being a scientist-practitioner

In conclusion, I give some recommendations on a process that can be followed in order to develop your own coaching model and methodology within the context of the experiential learning cycle.

Chapter 1

Complex responsive processes and experiential learning

Introduction

In this chapter, I explore the complex world in which we all live and participate daily. More specifically, I explore the work of Ralph Stacey on complex responsive processes, and what that means for each of us. According to Stacey, we all contribute to and co-create the complexity in which we live, whether or not we choose to do so. Both our conscious or unconscious actions and inactions are continually contributing to complex responsive processes. The danger in such an environment is that we tend towards acting like victims. To counter that danger, the work of Paulo Freire, the Quaker Persuasion Model and David Kolb's experiential learning theory are explored as ways to live and act more proactively and counteract victimhood.

This book was written during the third year of the global COVID-19 pandemic. One would have thought that by such a late stage the whole pandemic would have been under control, because we knew we needed to wear masks, maintain social distancing and get vaccinated. Yet each time we thought we were getting on top of the disease, a new variant of the COVID virus evolved somewhere and spread rapidly all over the world. To make matters worse, while governments encouraged people to get vaccinated against the disease, we saw riots breaking out in some of the biggest and most modern cities in the West, as people protested in support of their supposed "right" not to be vaccinated. The scientific data had shown us how we could break this pandemic, yet somehow conspiracy theories spread by social media seemed to have greater impact on societal thinking than scientific evidence.

At the same time, we have been seeing and experiencing the impact of climate change. When one watched the news during the past few years, all one heard were people blaming these disasters on one of the most nebulous concepts in the world, a lack of good leadership. We all seemed to be waiting for some great messianic leader, all-knowing and very clever, who would lead us out of the various messes we had gotten ourselves into. Even worse, conspiracy theorists on social media sat back and complained about how we are all the victims of a conspiracy by a few very powerful people, who have

DOI: 10.4324/9781003356424-2

developed an entire world system to control us so they can become even richer. Chris Argyris (2010), a professor at Harvard, agrees that we are all trapped in systems that seem overpowering and make us feel like victims. As he points out, however, people

> are not trapped by some oppressive regime or organisational structure that has been imposed on them. They are not victims. In fact, people themselves are responsible for making the *status quo* so resistant to change. We are trapped by our own behaviour.
>
> (Argyris, 2010:2)

The sad reality is that we have all co-created the system we are in, and then we act as if we are the victims of some oppressive system or regime. The truth is that we as humans are social beings, and it is through our interactions that we co-create the systems and societies in which we live. In fact, we even co-create each other's identities and who we are. The first step out of this mess is to realise that we are not the victims of some bizarre conspiracy of very rich people, but that we are all co-creators of the world in which we live:

> The processes to begin to reduce Traps will become activated if the participants focus on their personal responsibility in creating the Traps and examine the validity of their claim that they are helpless victims.
>
> (Argyris, 2010:24)

Complex patterns and lack of control

There is no doubt that we live in a very complex world. According to Ralph Stacey (2010), a professor of management, part of our problem is that we tend to build theories on assumptions or abstractions that we try and apply across populations. The reality, however, is that most of the time we interact with each other on a local level. Despite this, we continue to perpetuate the stories, fantasies and narratives of these strong individuals who are or were major change agents. The truth is that most of these narratives are generalisations, oversimplifications and idealisations that have been abstracted from experience. In addition, there is a very real difference between what Argyris (2010) calls our "espoused theories" and the theories that we apply in praxis, the "theories-in-use" – in other words, between what we say we do and what we actually do.

For example, when Stacey studied the financial market crash of 2008 to try and understand what happened and who caused it, he observed the following:

- Organisations are patterns of interaction between people brought about by their responsive acts of communication. Organisations are therefore not actual things; they are imaginative constructs like "this company" and "the market". The way the story is told, however, is that some impersonal forces are at work in and between these imaginative constructs and abstract institutions. The real people who do the interacting are often left out of the story.

- An organisation comprises groups of interacting people who are interdependent. And it is this interdependence that is the source of power, in that their interdependence both enables and constrains them.

- These interdependent groups of people reflect on their current experience, form intentions, make choices and come up with strategies to respond to their current situation. At the same time, however, there are other groups of interdependent people doing the same things. And what happens in or evolves out of this situation is determined by the interplay between all these groups of interdependent people – not simply by one group alone.

- As a result, nobody can be in control of what happens, because nobody can control the intentions, choices and actions of all the other people in all the other organisations. The interplay of all these intentions, choices and actions produce emergent patterns, in this case the pattern known as the "credit crunch". This is not what everybody wanted or intended; in fact, they wanted the complete opposite, endless growth. Further, Argyris (2010) argues that the policies, rules and structures put in place to prevent such crises were not enough, because individuals learn to protect themselves by denying any personal responsibility, blaming others or the system instead. The espoused theories were that they are victims, when in reality, the theory in praxis was that they actively contributed to the crisis. The same dynamic was playing out within various groups.

- Ideologically based choices, power relations and local interactions of communication, ethics and self-interest are all examples of the forms that the interplay of intentions can take between people.

- The interplay of local intentions and actions which produce small local changes can easily escalate across national and international populations, and in so doing they can generate widespread patterns of change. These patterns we tend to call technological innovations, industrial revolutions, globalisation and recessions.

- Given that nobody controls how these changes escalate, uncertainty is fundamental to human reality. And because nobody knows with confidence what is going to happen, there are high levels of unpredictability inherent within this uncertainty. This, of course, raises the question of whether we know what is going on right now; even the present moment is always open to different interpretations. This is because every individual and group will try and make sense of, and discover their own meaning within, the current situation. Stacey (2010) sees this as a paradox, in that we cannot predict with certainty what will happen, but because there is some repetition in human affairs, we can speculate about what can happen. It is only with hindsight that we tend to recognise what has happened. Hence, we can know some things, but because they are always open to radical change we can never know with certainty. At best, every one of us has a hypothesis about what is going on.

- Every individual is consciously or unconsciously involved in co-creating what is happening within organisations, the system and in the wider world. For example, the "credit crunch" of 2008 could not be blamed only on bankers or politicians. The people who took out mortgages knowing they could not repay them helped to co-create the financial crisis – along with the staff of lending institutions who sought out riskier borrowers in order to increase revenues, profits and bonuses; and the politicians who had relaxed the regulation of financial markets, and then struggled to understand and deal effectively with the crisis.
- These patterns of interaction between people contain paradoxes with inherent tensions. Paradoxes like knowing and not knowing; forming patterns of interaction, while at the same time being formed by them; and continuity and novelty (Stacey, 2010:8–9).

Reflecting on the COVID-19 pandemic, it becomes clear to me that the observations Stacey (2010) makes about the 2008 financial crisis are just as meaningful in explaining why we battled to get COVID under control. All the above observations were at play during the global pandemic, which spread via human interaction. And yet in response, we all cried out "Where is the leadership?" In other words, who or where were the messianic leaders who were going to solve this pandemic for us? The bad news was that they did not exist; all of us had co-created the situation, and somehow we all eventually co-created our way out of it. It seems to be just another paradox of human existence.

Immersion and abstraction

Another paradox, with which all humans seem to wrestle, is that human life is an act of immersion and abstraction at the same time. Humans have the capability to reflect on their experiences and to think in rational, simplified and objective ways. Stacey (2010) argues that we immerse ourselves in our local interactions with other human beings to help us accomplish our activities. At the same time, we abstract ourselves from this experience and create narratives and philosophies by generalising, simplifying and categorising the experiences as first-order abstractions. In the modern world, we tend to create second-order abstractions by creating models and theories that are idealisations and even more generalised categories of the actual experience. Hence our modern understanding of the abstract as a theory, as something that is the opposite of practical. However, the Latin root of the word "abstract" literally means to "draw away from". All thinking about experience therefore involves an element of drawing away from the experience, and as a result it involves a first order of abstraction. Theoretical thinking that is not practical is of no help to anybody; our first-order abstracted thinking must still be practical.

The opposite of abstract in this case is immersed. The Latin root of the word "immerse" literally means to "plunge into". To be immersed therefore means to be absorbed in the situation. For Stacey (2010), immersion means to devote oneself fully to some interest or situation; to be completely immersed in the experience, to the point that there is a strong connotation of unconscious processes. For humans to live in a completely immersed way would, however, mean that there would be no reflection, thought or meaning-making. Humans tend to seek meaning in life, and as a result we have always been involved in immersion and abstraction of experience. We immerse ourselves in the experience of life, and abstract ourselves to reflect and create narratives and philosophies about that experience.

For us to make sense of the complexity in which we live, Stacey (2010) suggests that we need both immersion and abstraction, yet we need to be careful not to slip into the trap of allowing second-order abstractions to be split off from our immersion in local interactions. By second-order abstractions, he means the following activities:

- Objectifying and categorising. All phenomena are placed in well-defined, bounded groups, where differences in categories are obliterated. This applies as much to celestial bodies as to human modes of thinking.
- Using standardised measures to gauge the quantitative aspects of these categories.
- Averaging out the differences in categories.
- Using mathematical and statistical techniques to analyse the data.
- Forming hypotheses about relationships, entities and some causal relationships.
- The building of models to forecast specific probabilities and distributions.
- Setting targets for planning and monitoring.
- Prescribing rules, be they laws or moral norms (Stacey, 2010).

These second-order abstraction activities have helped us develop the scientific method and advanced technology. And as the economist E.F. Schumacher (1978) reminds us, the knowledge that second-order abstraction produces can be divided into two broad groups: descriptive knowledge, which is primarily about what can be seen, observed or otherwise experienced; and instructional knowledge, which is primarily about how certain systems work and how predictable results can be produced. Without this knowledge there would be no modern world, states or policies on how to continuously improve, and humanity as a whole has experienced many benefits therefrom.

There is no denying that second-order abstractions have helped to change the world and bring about our modern society. The problem, according to Stacey (2010), is that this second order of abstraction removes diversity, which is its actual aim. The net result is that real people are replaced with simplistic averages of and generalisations from the whole population. This is a similar concern to the one raised by Field Marshal Jan Christian Smuts, the person who developed the concept of "Holism". Smuts (1973:262) argued that psychology does not "materially assist" in the study of personality, since psychology deals with the average or generalised individual; and in so doing, it ignores the individual uniqueness of the personality. What is more, these generalisations can be idealisations of hypothetical wholes which we then believe to be reality. David Bohm, the physicist who worked out many of the mathematical formulae used in the Manhattan Project, was also the person who reintroduced dialogue as a means of communication in our modern world, and he reminds us that we have to be alert to "the fact that our theories are not 'descriptions of reality as it is' but, rather, ever-changing forms of insight, which can point to or indicate a reality that is implicit and not describable or specifiable in its totality" (Bohm, 1995:17).

Stacey (2010) suggests that Western thinking originally abstracted from immersion in experience of the natural world by categorising it (first-order abstraction). Over time, however, Western thought evolved into an increasing focus on second-order abstraction, in which first-order categories of experience were used to model not only the natural world, but also the social world:

> Thought came to focus so heavily on second-order abstraction of systems and models understood as science, that when it was applied to human organisations, the ordinary reality of the experience of local interaction between actual human bodies disappeared from view.
>
> (Stacey, 2010:118)

The reality is that the ordinary everyday experience of people interacting with each other changes the world, and it needs to be taken seriously. What Stacey is calling for is to develop modes of thought which allow for a tension between being immersed in the ordinary daily experience of local interaction, and abstracting from that experience both on a first and second order of abstraction. Hence his call for us to understand the immersed world of everyday experience, the experience of interacting every day on a local level to get things done and to achieve what we need to achieve. It is in this interplay of intended and unintended actions, as we relate and respond to each other, that we co-create our futures. The future evolves out of these responsive patterns because, as he argued, human relating is inherently pattern-forming. Human action and doing is a responsive process of relating to each other in order to survive, which results in patterning processes. And it is these processes that he referred to as complex responsive processes. It is these complex responsive processes that drive human action, and not psychological concepts like the personal dynamic unconscious, archetypes, the collective unconscious, common pools of meaning and transcendental wholes.

Complex responsive processes

According to Stacey (2003, 2009) and Stacey and Griffin (2005), complex responsive processes constitute a way of thinking in which the individual mind and society are patterning processes that evolve out of the interactions between human bodies. This theory is heavily influenced by the dialectical thinking of Hegel, Norbert Elias and George Herbert Mead, and includes the following assertions:

- Complex interactions between humans as they relate to each other lead to the emergence of individual and collective identities. These interactions also lead to the emergence of meaning and knowledge. In this way of thinking, one assumes that mind and social interactions are aspects of the same process. As a result, attention is focused on the ordinary experience of people relating to each other.
- People learn to cooperate in sophisticated ways through responding to each other's intended actions. Actions in this context means physical movements of the body constituting gestures to and responses from others. These include the visual gesture–response of facial expressions, the vocal gesture–response of sound and the felt gesture–response of changes in bodily rhythms that are feelings or emotions. This is fundamentally a communicative process because each gesture will evoke a response in others (Stacey and Griffin, 2005:14–15). Stacey (2003) makes the point that humans are dependent on each other's physiology to regulate their bodies. This is because the biochemical mechanisms for arousal and calming are linked to the actions of separation from and attachment to others. At a physiological level, humans are fundamentally social beings who continuously relate to each other through various processes.
- People interweave their actions so that they can go on being and operating together. It is a circular social process where they act selectively in relation to each other in such a way that they evoke selective responses from each other.
- Each person is a unique individual, part of which is the individual's unique self-conscious mind. This mind reflects on itself so that it can call forth the appropriate responses similar to the actions it has directed to other individuals. This response that the individual calls forth is therefore selected and acted upon by the individual's history of relating to others. Thanks to the evolution of the central nervous system, humans can reflect on their actions and become aware of themselves, to know what they are doing. Therefore, through experience they can learn to act in expectation of particular responses from other individuals. The self and the mind are actions of the whole body, and not just cognitive aspects. It is about making sense of lived experience.
- The individual self or mind comprises actions privately directed back at the body, while actions that are publicly directed at other individuals constitute the social.

- Human action therefore consists simultaneously of private and social responses. The social comprises the public actions directed between individuals, while the private comprises the private actions directed back at the individual self or mind. More importantly in this view, self and the social are the same process of bodily action. Human consciousness, social interaction and self-consciousness are the same process. Here the individual mind or self, and the social, form each other at the same time – in other words, they co-create each other. The individual and society are therefore evolving patterns of interaction. As a result, human interdependence is a fundamental reality of human experience.
- All human action is enabled by and constrained by the actions that preceded it; it is therefore history-dependent. All actions are always in the "living present" and based on future expectations, yet future expectations arise on the basis of past experience. In each present moment we reinterpret and/or reconstruct the past based on future expectations. That means that previous history, the current context and future expectations all pattern human actions. As a result, the future emerges as both a continuity of the past and containing the potential for transformation at the same time. The actions, however, always happen in the present, now.
- We therefore have vast numbers of continually iterated interactions between human bodies. Most of these interactions are local, in that each of us can interact with only a limited number of other individuals. When these interactions between people are diverse enough, it is possible for novelty to emerge and develop intrinsic pattern-forming properties. For example, global patterns of collective power and economic relations emerge when a vast number of local interactions become widespread. These patterns can become highly repetitive and iterated over long periods of time to become durable social values. As a result, societies evolve out of this interplay of individual and social actions. These patterns evolve naturally and cannot be designed or controlled by anybody.
- Individuals can reflect, in that they can make themselves an object to themselves as subject, and they can take on the attitude of the other. As a result, they can form intentions as to their next actions, and choose between their actions or desires. Sophisticated cooperative activity is therefore possible between people, because communication happens via the medium of symbols. Symbols like norms and values provide the criteria for choosing between actions and desires. Once again, the evolving patterns of self and society emerge as spontaneous choices of individuals as they respond to each other. Nobody is designing or controlling those patterns; they evolve out of lived experience. Reality is therefore the experienced reality of people cooperating and conflicting with each other. As a result, they are continuously constructing and negotiating what is real for them, by trying to make sense of the experience in that moment.

- The biological evolution of the hands has enabled humans to develop tools as extensions of the body that allow them to cooperate in their activities. These tools are technology, artefacts and designed systems that allow them to cooperate collectively.
- The physiological need to belong, as well as the physiologically based communicative interaction with the addition of tools, are not automatic, instinctual genetic responses. Rather, they are learned responses to environmental stimuli. This is because the human brain has evolved to be highly plastic, and is shaped by the body's experiences within and in response to the environmental stimuli. And in humans a large part of those experiences are social experiences, shaped by attachment and separation interactions between bodies. Although genes play a part in forming the body, they do not directly form the actions of the body; the latter are learnt from experience. Hence, according to Stacey (2003), the brain is simultaneously shaped by and shapes the actions of human interactive patterns and relationships. These relational interactive patterns are nonlinear and iterative processes that contain the potential for transformation. As a result, the social is essential to human survival and the individual learns through experience how to function with it, so that people both enable and constrain each other.
- These interactive patterns can settle into habits that can be largely unconscious. These habits can have social and individual aspects at the same time. It can be unconscious in that the response has not been formulated yet, due to a more primitive physiological response, or because habit over time has made it automatic.
- For Stacey (2003), complex responsive processes are intimately linked to human physiology, and as a result human physiology is central to an understanding of groups and individuals. Hence human emotions like love, anxiety and hating are all social processes that the individual experiences as variations in body rhythms.

Stacey (2003:130–131) sums it up as follows:

> I am arguing for ... a move away from psychoanalytical and systemic meta theories ... for a move to process thinking ... which understands human identities ... The advantage of such a move ... is a way of thinking that is ... far closer to ordinary, everyday human experience.

Rethinking social research

Some of the paradoxes with their inherent tensions that Stacey (2003) refers to involve:

- individual minds simultaneously forming and being formed by the social;
- conscious and unconscious patterning taking place at the same time;

- the patterning of mind and social emerging as both continuity and novelty; and
- creative and destructive patterns of interaction emerging.

Hence Stacey (2010) has some doubts about objectivity when it comes to social research, which involves local participation. Instead, he argues that we need to focus our attention more clearly on the subjective nature of experience in organisations. And I would add to that, not just in organisations but in life as a whole. In other words, the method of research involves making sense of one's own experience, by exploring and reflecting on the complex responsive processes involved as humans relate to each other. It is an individual reflective research method, in that the individual makes explicit their way of thinking, why they chose that focus and how past experience is shaping their interpretation of events. Yet even though the individual is reflecting on their own experience, it is also a social process:

> Taking one's experience seriously, through articulating the narrative themes organising the experience of being together, is an essentially reflexive activity and in its fullest sense, this is a simultaneously individual and social process, including the social patterns that are much wider than our own immediate interaction.
>
> (Stacey, 2010:221)

Stacey is therefore arguing that we make sense of what is going on by reflecting on our experience (what is going on for me and what is going on for the other), and then trying to make sense of that experience, which enables us to decide on the next action going forward. In essence, what he is calling for is to learn from our own experience; in other words, it is experiential learning. Whatever the current complex responsive process of which we are trying to make sense, it always consists of individuals who bring their entire human developmental histories into the current situation. And those individuals have become what they are as a result of what they have learnt from experience in all their previous environments. We are what we are because of what we have learnt from our experiences. And it is our continuous learning from experience that continuously forms us as individuals, and at the same time we form the social, and *vice versa*. The mistake we make is to think that some smart individuals plan and control the process, when in fact it is a complex organic, unfolding evolutionary process that we all co-create through our local interactions, reflection and action.

As Argyris mentions, when people feel unsafe or threatened or face any potentially embarrassing situation, they will act in such a way as to protect and defend themselves. They are protecting their sense of self and self-worth. Upon reflection, they will develop a defensive mind-set to explain their actions, and at the same time use that defensive mind-set to plan and implement their future actions. The theories that they use will lead to what Argyris (2010) calls Model I reasoning, the objectives of which are to:

- behave rationally (normally the rationalisation is based on reflection on actions or behaviour that has already taken place and used to justify the behaviour);
- be in unilateral control;
- suppress negative feelings; and
- win at all costs and do not lose.

When we read about this kind of behaviour and reasoning, there is always the temptation to believe that other people act and do that, not us. Yet given certain physiological conditions we all act and behave in that way, and in so doing, we protect ourselves and the groups to which we belong. Those very actions defend us from change, or at least we tend to think they do; and that adds to the inherent complexity within complex responsive processes. The aim is to develop more responses based on Model II reasoning, which aims to:

- seek valid information (i.e. information that is testable);
- develop informed choices; and
- vigilantly monitor to detect and correct error (the theory of complex responsive processes shows that it is very easy in such a complex environment to get things wrong) (Argyris, 2010).

In so doing, knowledge can be produced that makes its reasoning transparent and open to public scrutiny where the claims can be robustly tested. I suppose the temptation for all of us is to act like victims when we are challenged to reflect on these complex problems, to throw our hands in the air and to say, "That is just how it is and I am only an individual, what can I do?" The theory of complex responsive processes highlights the fact that whether we do nothing or do something, the choice of action will involve certain behaviours, and those behaviours and actions will contribute to co-creating something. The very fact that we are alive and interacting with other human beings means that we are co-creating the system in which we live. It ultimately comes down to a choice: whether we are going to unconsciously help co-create, or at least consciously try to co-create, the environment and systems in which we live. It is through the social process of co-creating that we develop as human beings and keep becoming who we are.

The question then becomes: Is it possible to do this co-creation at a more conscious level, and how? Are there models we could look at that might help us feel less like victims and try to consciously co-create the environments and systems in which we live? Fortunately for us, there are some practical models and examples that understand the reality of complex responsive processes and how we can learn to act locally.

The work of Paulo Freire

One individual who seemed to understand the complexity of the systems in which we live and how we tend to co-create them was the Brazilian educationalist Paulo Freire. His most famous work, *Pedagogy of the Oppressed*, first published in 1968, was an attempt to understand how the oppressors and the oppressed co-create the systems in which they live, but more importantly what and how ordinary people can bring about change within that system.

Freire (2005), a Christian socialist, believed education is never neutral, and by that he meant that it serves the purpose of somebody. As a result, he was against what he called the "banking" concept of education. This is the belief that the educator or teacher is the expert and that the students are empty vessels that must be filled with knowledge stemming from the expert. In this model, the expert deposits knowledge into the naïve or uneducated students. The question then is, who determines what type of knowledge needs to be deposited into these naïve students? Well, the experts; and in this case, the experts are usually serving the interests of those in power.

The danger with the banking concept of education is that the more the students accept this passive role imposed on them, the more they simply adapt to the world and the environment in which they find themselves. As a result of accepting and storing these knowledge deposits, the less they develop the critical consciousness that would enable them to question the existing system and actively try to transform their world. Instead, even the very well-educated tend to passively accept, adapt to and live within the system. And being an adapted person, the individual is a good "fit" within the current system and world. It was in the interest of the powerful to keep the poor illiterate, and to develop a system of education that reinforced the very social system that kept the oppressors in power. In Brazil at that time, the illiterate were not allowed to vote. As people are born into this system, they are socialised into believing that is just the way it is, and that is the fate to which they are born. In so doing, several myths are co-created between the oppressor and the oppressed to keep the system in place. One of those myths is the belief that the objective social reality is one of chance.

Freire was at pains to point out that social reality is a product of human thinking and action. And he saw it as the historical task of humanity to transform the social reality. This transformation would be brought about by praxis, which he saw as "reflection and action upon the world in order to transform it" (Freire, 2005:51). More importantly, he called for critical reflection on the objective reality. The problem with just reflecting is that it runs the danger of not critically questioning the assumptions and beliefs that are in place and that keep the current system working the way it does. The aim is to critically reflect on that objective reality, with the goal of coming up with actions that aim to change the objective reality. And it was this critical reflection on the objective social reality that turned Freire into such a threat to those in power.

He realised that there was a dialectical tension between the oppressed and the oppressor. Firstly, through critical reflection the oppressed had to realise that because they were under the oppressors, they were dependent on them, and as a result they had started to become emotionally dependent on the oppressors. Secondly, if the oppressed did not critically reflect on the system that oppressed them, if they did overthrow the oppressors through a revolution, the danger was that they would do it with the mind-set of the previous oppressors. That is, they would have reflected on the system as it currently is and just imposed the same system on the previous oppressors. In other words, the oppressed now becomes the oppressor. In reality, nothing would have changed, the only change being that the power relationship would have shifted from one group to the other. The problem with replacing the old system with the same system, just with reversed power roles, is that it dehumanises all the people involved.

Freire therefore totally rejected the banking concept of education, which saw it basically as just a transference of information. Rather, he saw liberating education as consisting of acts of cognition. And by that he meant that men and woman cognitively start to understand the system in which they find themselves and see it as a "problem to be solved". A problem that humans can collectively tackle together:

> Authentic liberation – the process of humanisation – is not another deposit to be made in men. Liberation is a praxis: the action and reflection of men and women upon their world in order to transform it … the posing of the problems of human beings in their relations with the world.
>
> (Freire, 2005:79)

This problem-posing education denies that humanity is isolated, independent and abstracted from the world. At the same time, it denies the idea and belief that the world exists as a reality apart from human beings. Problem-posing education sees consciousness and the world as simultaneous, that is, it considers people in their relations with the world. It gets people to critically reflect and perceive how they exist in the world and how they interact within that world. As they do that, according to Freire (2005), they become aware that the world is not a static reality, but reality in process.

This is very much in line with the concept of complex responsive processes, which suggests that all human action is enabled by and constrained by the actions that preceded it, and therefore history-dependent. All actions are always in the "living present" and based on future expectations, yet future expectations arise based on past experience. In each present moment, we reinterpret and/or reconstruct the past based on future expectations. That means that previous history, the current context and future expectations all pattern human actions, and that the current system was patterned in this case by the oppressors who co-opted the oppressed.

Problem-posing education turns people into critical thinkers who realise that reality is not a given, but a process that can be transformed. With that comes the realisation that humans are in the process of becoming, that we are unfinished beings, and hence the same applies to reality and our environment. The task of humans is to humanise oppressive systems by transforming them in the dynamic present. For Freire (2005), this transformation and the pursuit of full humanity cannot be carried out by an individual in isolation – it can be done only in solidarity and in fellowship via interactions with other individuals. Once again, his thinking is very much in line with the theory of complex responsive processes, which believes that societies evolve out of this interplay of individual and social actions.

For Freire (2005), this co-creating interaction between people must happen via dialogue. Using dialogue to facilitate learning is the opposite of the banking concept of education. When it comes to dialogue, no one individual or group of individuals has the answer which they try and deposit into others. Rather, it calls for humility, faith and love. Humility in that there is the realisation that the problem the group is wrestling with is far too complex for one individual to understand and have the answers on how to transform it. Instead, it is an attempt by the entire group to explore the problem, realising that every individual has some piece of the puzzle that they can contribute. It is having faith and love in other people to realise and recognise that their experience is valid, and that their knowledge of the system and the environment is legitimate.

For Freire (2005), this was especially important for revolutionary leaders to remember. Yes, the leaders and the educators who worked with the illiterate brought with them certain knowledge. But the peasants, even though they could not read or write, had experiential knowledge of the land they worked and the conditions under which they lived. For Freire (2005), any attempt to transform society by telling people what their true condition was and telling them what they needed to do to change it was doomed to failure. Leadership and education which assume the leaders are the messiahs who will lead the poor and illiterate to the promised land is based on the banking concept. It is the belief that some are the experts, while others are the idiots that just need to be filled with the right knowledge which is provided by the experts. For Freire (2005), true transformation, liberation and humanisation cannot be done for and to the people. It is only through dialogue, where everybody's experience and knowledge are valid, that true transformation, liberation and humanisation can be co-created by everybody involved. Yes, there is the recognition that everybody has different knowledge and different experiences of the problem. And yes, there is the recognition that there are different power roles at play. Despite that, dialogue honours all that diversity, and wants to incorporate all that experience into a possible solution to the problem.

Freire (2005) therefore restores the diversity that the second order of abstraction removes (where real people are replaced with simplistic averages of and generalisations from the whole population). It is not about individuals or groups trying to convince the others that theirs is the right view and manipulating them into accepting their point of view. Unlike the banking concept, dialogue is not an argument to be won, so that it is a win–lose situation; dialogue strives for a co-created win–win situation. Given what dialogue demands of all the people involved, Freire (2005) was therefore realistic enough to boldly speak about the need for love, humility, faith and hope. Those are the behaviours and qualities needed to humanise those who had been dehumanised, and for dialogue to succeed in transforming objective reality:

> Dialogue cannot exist … in the absence of a profound love for the world and for people. The naming of the world … is not possible if it is not infused with love. Love is at the same time the foundation of dialogue and dialogue itself.
>
> (Freire, 2005:89)

It calls for a continuous faith in humankind, and for Freire (2005) that meant having faith in mankind's ability and power to create, co-create, make and remake their objective reality. Yet it is critical enough to know that even though humanity has these capabilities, in times or situations of alienation, the power and ability to do that can be impaired. The point is never to lose faith in humankind despite the impairment and setbacks. It is this faith, hope and love which create the environment for all those involved in dialogue to learn to trust each other and partner in trying to transform society.

It is through this interaction of dialogue that the people together critically reflect on their situation and their environment. Collectively they explore their combined experiences of the environment and critically reflect on how the system was created, how it was formed, what keeps it in place and what makes it work. What is their concrete experience of living in the system, what myths and beliefs have they bought into and co-created to keep the system in place? What limiting assumptions do they have that they believe make it impossible to challenge and change the system? What are the dehumanising themes that emerge as they explore the situation in dialogue? Freire (2005) referred to this as "thematic investigation" and believed that this becomes a common striving towards self-awareness and towards awareness of reality. And for him this was the starting point of the educational process and cultural action for liberation. Thematic investigation is the discovery of meaningful themes, in that the people start to create meaning of their experience, which they can then use to pose as problems to be solved within their cultural and historical context:

> investigation of thematics involves the investigation of the people's thinking – thinking which occurs only in and among people together

seeking out reality ... it is only as they rethink their assumptions in action that they can change. Producing and acting upon their own ideas ... must constitute that process.

(Freire, 2005:108)

For Freire, critical reflection is, however, not enough. Reflection without action just becomes empty words and is mere "verbalism" or idle chatter: "there is no transformation without action" (Freire, 2005:87). On the other hand, action for action's sake without reflection is merely "activism". Dialogue requires both critical reflection and action to develop a true praxis. And by praxis, Freire meant directing reflection and action at the structures that needed to be transformed. And to do that, the dialoguing people had to develop a theory of transforming action – a theory of how the people were going to collectively bring about that change. Freire was very clear that the theory of transformation could not assign the thinking to the leaders and the doing to the people. The leaders cannot think for the people, nor can they think without the people. They need to think with the people, because critical reflection and thinking moves everyone from a naïve knowledge of reality to perceiving and understanding the causes of their reality. The critical reflection that is brought about in dia- logue integrates the empirical knowledge of reality of the people and the crit- ical knowledge of the leaders, which evolves into a collective knowledge of the causes of reality. Hence everybody, both the leaders and the people, had to be involved in reflecting and acting.

That is why for Freire, as in complex responsive processes, the individual and the social are one and the same process through their interaction. This theory cannot speak of an actor or actors, it can only be "actors in intercom- munication" (Freire, 2005:129). It is dialogue (intercommunication) with reflection and action, and a transformation theory, that in his view separated an authentic revolution from a military coup. Yet he was realistic enough to realise that, at times, certain actions could not immediately be undertaken:

Action and reflection occur simultaneously ... Those who through reflec- tion perceive the infeasibility or inappropriateness of one or another form of action (which should accordingly be postponed or substituted) cannot thereby be accused of inaction. Critical reflection is also action.

(Freire, 2005:127)

In Freire's work, we see a realistic and very practical way in which change can be brought about, while inherently recognising and honouring the principles involved with complex responsive processes. It is realistic in that it recognises that all the people involved are working within a very complex environment and social reality, which have evolved through the historical actions of people interacting with each other to try and achieve their objectives. It is realistic in that it includes the altruistic human ideals and emotions of love, hope and faith, while at the same time recognising all the power positions at play. It honours and uses the everyday experience of the people on a local level to address the problem of their reality, which is what the theory of complex responsive processes calls for. Freire's work believes that change happens at a local level through the interaction of these people sharing their experiences to try and develop a common understanding or meaning of the social reality they have co-created, and how they can collectively transform it.

It is practical in that it starts by exploring people's everyday experience. It uses dialogue to explore and honour people's experience, to come up with the major themes that make up their current social reality. Collectively, they then critically reflect on that experience to try and understand the history of how that current reality was created through human thought and action. The critical reflection includes how all the role-players in that system have helped to co-create it and kept it in place. All the role-players together then come up with a theory or plan of how they are going to change the current social reality into a more humanised social reality. Of critical importance is that they must then collectively act on their theory or plan. There are no separate thinkers and doers, there are only collective thinkers and doers.

This critical reflection on experience, combined with theory and action, is the praxis that brings about change. This critical reflection on experience, development of a theory and acting on that theory is a continuous inter-active process of dialogue. And it is this interactive process of dialogue that brings about the change to which the theory of complex responsive processes refers. No individual has come up with the idea, plan and management for this change. Rather, the change evolves out of the interaction brought about through the social dialogue of all the individuals involved. The individuals, the social and the interaction are one unified process. This social co-creation process is aimed at changing the social reality, and in so doing each indi-vidual is re-humanised and develops as an individual. And the best environ-ment to enable that, according to Freire (2005), is one based on love, faith and hope.

The Quaker Persuasion Model

The second example of how to act locally through interaction comes from the "Friendly Disentangling" method or persuasion model. Nielsen (1998) refers to the persuasion model used by the Quakers John Woolman (1720–1772) and Robert K. Greenleaf (1904–1990). The methodology was first developed by the Philadelphia cloth merchant John Woolman in the mid-eighteenth cen-tury. Woolman could never reconcile the facts that the Quaker community in Pennsylvania held a fundamental belief that the "Divine Spark" exists in every human being, while as a community Quakers accepted the institution of slavery, and many of them owned slaves. For him, this was a fundamental contradiction in beliefs and behaviours with which he could not live. In order to address the issue of slavery among the Quakers, he developed and used the method of friendly persuasion with individuals and small groups, and within a period of 20 years he almost singlehandedly rid the community of slavery. Due to his tireless efforts, the Quakers were the first religious group in the United States to formally denounce and forbid slavery among their members.

The method that Woolman developed consisted of four principles:

- *There is good in everyone.* The basic assumption is that there is some good in all of us. This good in everyone serves as the foundation for action and learning. For him it would appear that it was better to start from what we have in common, that is the good, rather than starting from what is not so good and how we differ. The important thing was to try and find common ground on which to build a constructive relationship.
- *Traditional customs and structures as causes of the problem.* This is the belief that individuals are social constructions of the traditional systems and structures within which they are born and socialised. That is, individual behaviours and values are greatly influenced by the traditional system within which people are born and socialised. In this regard, it has some commonality with the post-modern perspective as well as the theory of complex responsive processes, which recognises that any abstract concept will be influenced by the individual's concrete experience and the cultural context in which they have developed. Secondly, there is the recognition that a system can and is able to produce certain predictable behaviours despite the individuals involved. So, for example, Woolman found that the Quakers' children accepted slavery in part out of love for their parents and community, who in turn had become entangled in slavery and implicitly and explicitly accepted the teaching that slavery was acceptable. This was a very similar situation to what must have happened in Germany with anti-Semitism and in South Africa with apartheid.
- *Friendly and cheerful.* For both ethical and effectiveness reasons, act in a friendly and cheerful manner towards those with whom you are in actual and potential conflict. For ethical reasons, it is important to be friendly because it is important to respect and care not just for those with whom you agree, but also with those who have a totally different view, values and ethical standards. In so doing, it helps to create a more enabling learning environment.
- *Continuous, experimental action-learning.* John Fox, who was one of the founders of Quakerism, started his journal with the phrase "This I knew experientially". For Fox, Woolman and Greenleaf, the emphasis was on experimental learning, towards action preceding learning and towards learning through experimental action. Critical to their method was the idea that experimentation needs to be continuous. On closer inspection, however, one can soon see that they were using a form of experiential learning. This is very much in line with the theory of complex responsive

processes that calls for the honouring of everyday experience (Nielsen, 1998:126–138).

So how does the persuasion model work?

- It is important to frame oneself in a "we" fellowship with others, and to look for the source of the current problematic behaviour within the biases of an embedded tradition system, rather than solely within the behaviours and governing values of the individual. This basically means that we must look at how the prevailing culture, structures and procedures contribute to the individual's behaviour, all the time remembering that there really is some good in every individual. Basically, it means accepting the person for who they are, and accepting that, for the most part, they are basically good people. At the same time, recognise that some cultural or system-level bias might be entangled with the individual behaviour, and we usually co-create those cultures. This is in agreement with the theory of complex responsive processes and the thinking of Freire (2005).
- Approach those involved in a friendly manner. Your approach to the people involved should be friendly and respectful, not adversarial or critical. Again, very similar to what we see in Freire, when he states that the essence of the interaction in dialogue should be love, faith and hope. It is about openly exploring another person's experience, all the time remembering that any view is not "the truth" but a partial truth.
- Ask for help in disentangling a problematic behaviour from potential biases within "our" embedded tradition system. Remember that you share the situation with the individual. It is not an "I versus you" situation. Coming from a lofty position does not help; people simply become defensive and close up. Rather, ask for help in trying to understand where they are coming from, and which cultural biases are at play. Once again, this is very much in agreement with the approach we find in Freire and his "problem-posing" education.
- Work with alternative behaviours and/or governing values that do not rest on the troublesome biases of the tradition system. This involves asking the other person to experiment with different behaviours or actions. This is where active experimentation comes into action. You do not ask them to do everything in a new way. All you do is ask them to experiment with a new possibility. Woolman, for example, found it intolerable that Quakers, who have a fundamental belief that God is in every individual, could support an unjust system like slavery. Their experience was that they supported slavery through their actions, yet their fundamental belief system confessed something else. This was a classic case where the theory in practice was not the espoused theory. Woolman asked them to help him disentangle a problematic behaviour (supporting slavery) from potential biases within their embedded tradition system. This is

very similar to Freire's idea of problem-solving education: what problem do we need to solve collectively? Woolman was asking them to participate in critical reflection. What they discovered through the reflection was that most Quakers believed blacks were very lazy and would not work as hard as free white labourers. He then got them to reflect on this experience and assumption even further. What they hypothesised was that blacks were fundamentally demotivated because they had nothing to work for: no matter how hard they worked, they would always be slaves; they could never improve their lot in life. Free whites, in contrast, could become wealthier through working harder. So, the working hypothesis they developed was that slaves would work harder if they were freed and able to own their own property. This hypothesis became the activists' theory of change. To test this hypothesis, Woolman asked his fellow Quakers to perform an active experiment, which they did. He asked Quaker farmers to free their slaves and provide them a piece of land that they could work as sharecroppers; any produce produced on this land the tenants could sell, and accumulate the profits. As a result of this experiment, the Quakers became the most profitable farmers in the region, because the former slaves worked much harder as free sharecroppers. The Quakers started to realise that their assumptions about African Americans were false, and that they had internalised those false beliefs through the process of socialisation. The remarkable thing was that Woolman achieved this one farmer at a time, asking each farmer to repeat the experiment. As a result, the Quakers started to free their slaves and grant them sharecropping opportunities. Within 20 years, many farmers had adopted this ethical and political-economic reform; by 1770, Quakers were forbidden to own slaves, and by 1800 slavery had been made illegal in Pennsylvania.

Robert K. Greenleaf used exactly the same principles and approach to create and bring about equal employment opportunities for women within the giant US telecommunications corporation AT&T. Prior to employing this approach, women could not do technical work in the company because they were not strong enough to carry 50-pound rolls of telephone wire. In adopting this approach, the company experimented with 25-pound rolls of wire, and it was found that women could comfortably carry them. As a result, more women were hired to work in the technical field. Greenleaf did the same with African American management development at AT&T. By using the same approach between 1955 and 1964, even before the passage of the landmark Civil Rights Act of 1964 in the United States, AT&T managed to increase its proportion of black managers from about 0.5 per cent to about 4.5 per cent of total employed managers (Nielsen, 1998).

The beauty of the persuasion model is that, like Freire's approach, it can empower the individual to work towards their own cognitive insight, the experience of emotional meaningfulness and taking of responsibility for their own growth through experimenting with alternative cognitions and behaviours within their social context. In both cases, the knowledge is not forced on the individual. Both models actively engage the individual to explore their own assumptions, to try and understand their behaviour, to ask the individual to come up with a hypothesis of why that is the case, and then to explore and experiment with alternative assumptions and behaviours. In so doing, new cognitive and behavioural patterns are established over time. And all of this happens within the context of the social reality in which the individuals find themselves. It is in dialogue with others that this individual process unfolds and happens. Both approaches recognise that the individual, social and social reality are part of one integrated process. There is a recognition that the individual forms and is formed by the social, and *vice versa*. It is interesting that both these approaches used a methodology that is very similar to David Kolb's experiential learning cycle, while at the same time specifying the human emotions and behaviours that would facilitate the process more effectively. I believe that Kolb's (1984) experiential learning cycle and experiential learning theory give us a very practical theory, model and methodology on how to learn to create meaning, develop theories and act in the situations and environments in which we find ourselves. And in so doing, we can make conscious decisions that help co-create the systems in which we live, and at the same time facilitate and co-create our own development.

Kolb's experiential learning theory

Stacey (2010) calls for us to be completely immersed in our lived experience. For humans to live in a completely immersed way would, however, mean that there would be no reflection, thought or meaning-making. Humans tend to seek meaning in life, and as a result we have always been involved in immersion and abstraction of experience. We immerse ourselves in the experience of life, and abstract ourselves to reflect and create narratives and philosophies about that experience. It is the same point that Freire (2005) makes, that dialogue requires both critical reflection and action to develop a true praxis.

The question is, how do we do that? I believe this question can be answered by one of the most well-researched learning models, namely David Kolb's (1984) experiential learning theory. A quick search on Google Scholar for this theory or model returned about 71,900 published papers. Apart from it being so widely researched by both supporters and opponents, over the years I have found it to be a very practical theory to apply. Furthermore, given that things seem to be changing so fast in the modern world, the modern war cry seems to be that we "need to be more agile". But what does agile or agility mean? The Cambridge Dictionary defines agility as "the ability to move your body quickly and easily" or "the ability to think quickly and clearly" (Cambridge University Press, 2022a). Interestingly enough, the definition has both physiological and mental or conceptual components. Both the physiological and conceptual components imply the ability to learn quickly and to react appropriately to the environment, be that physically or mentally. In my mind, agility therefore has to do with our ability to learn quickly from our environment. For us to be agile, we need to understand what we mean by learning and how we learn.

Kolb's Experiential Learning Model

Kolb (1984) developed his Experiential Learning Model by drawing on the work of John Dewey, Kurt Lewin and Jean Piaget, among others. In effect, his model is a synthesis of their work. In their later book *The Experiential Educator*, Alice and David Kolb (2017) mention the influence that people like William James, Carl Rogers, Carl Jung, Len Vygotsky, Paulo Freire and Mary Parker Follet have also had on their philosophy of experiential education. Based on the work of all these scholars of experiential learning, the Kolbs developed six principles which form the foundations of experiential learning:

- *It is best to conceive of learning as a process, and not in terms of an outcome.* Learning is a never-ending process, and does not end with an outcome. The reason is that our experiences never stop; they are a continuous flow of sensory input. Furthermore, ideas and thoughts are continuously formed and re-formed through experience, and therefore no two thoughts are ever the same. We live with the fallacy that thoughts and ideas can be fixed, and in so doing we tend to define learning in our modern society in terms only of outcomes and performance.
- *Learning is a continuous process grounded in our experience.* All knowledge is derived from the experience of the individual, who tests the knowledge against that experience. It is not a process whereby some expert deposits knowledge onto a blank slate. It is a process of making explicit the existing beliefs and theories that the individual has, examining and testing them and then integrating the new ideas into the individual's belief system. It therefore implies that all learning is relearning, and is a dynamic, dialectical process.
- *There are dialectically opposed modes of adaptation to the world, and learning requires the resolution of these conflicts.* By its very nature, learning is a process filled with tension and conflicts, because the individual must resolve the tension and conflict between action, reflection, feeling and thinking through iterations of movement between these opposing experiences. It involves solving polar opposites, and choosing which ability to use in each particular situation.
- *Learning is a holistic process of responding to the world.* Thinking, feeling, perceiving and behaving are all involved in experiential learning as integrated functions. To respond to the environment effectively, learning cannot be limited to any one realm of human functioning. For example, we

cannot survive in the world by relying only on cognition, we need to think and act. We adapt to the world and our environment through the learning process.

- *Learning involves transactions between the individual and the environment.* We are all born into a unique culture which has its own social knowledge that evolved over time. At the same time, individuals have their own subjective experiences, which constitute their personal knowledge. It is the interaction between this social and personal knowledge that creates knowledge through the learning process. So not only are we formed by our environment, but we form it in return through the process of learning.
- *Learning is the process of creating knowledge.* Each discipline or field of inquiry has unique assumptions about truth and the nature of knowledge, and as a result knowledge is structured differently in each of those disciplines. Consequently, each knowledge system has content and a learning process that is unique. For example, learning how to use and apply statistics is a very different process to learning how to listen effectively (Kolb and Kolb, 2017).

These principles underpin Kolb's four-stage experiential learning cycle that involves four adaptive learning modes. The four adaptive learning modes are:

- *concrete experience (CE)* – the ability to involve oneself fully and openly and without bias in new experiences;
- *reflective observation (RO)* – the ability to reflect and to observe the experience from many perspectives;
- *abstract conceptualisation (AC)* – the ability to create concepts and to build logically sound theories from the observations; and
- *active experimentation (AE)* – the ability to use the constructed theories to make decisions and experiment with new behaviours and thoughts (Kolb, 1984:68–69).

Kolb and Kolb (2017) mention that there is a strong need to integrate these four adaptive modes into a creative synthesis. Within this synthesis of the four adaptive modes, there are two distinct dimensions representing two dialectically opposed adaptive orientations:

- concrete experience versus abstract conceptualisation; and
- active experimentation versus reflective observation.

The important thing to remember is that these dimensions are independent but mutually enhancing, and each makes a contribution to the learning process. Learning requires the resolution of conflicts between these conflicting dialectical orientations, between feeling and thinking, and between reflection and action. How do you achieve this in a real-life situation? How can you reflect and act at the same time? How can you be both theoretical and centred in your concrete experience at the same time? Effective learning involves all these polar opposites that the individual must choose from to apply to specific learning situations. This is similar to the dialectical tension that Stacey (2010) sees as a paradox of human life, that thought is an act of immersion and abstraction at the same time. He argues that we immerse ourselves in our local interactions with other human beings to help us accomplish our activities. At the same time, we abstract ourselves from this experience and create narratives and philosophies by generalising, simplifying and categorising the experiences as first-order abstractions. By its very nature, therefore, learning is a conflictual and tension-filled process for Kolb (1984).

The first dialectical dimension, concrete experience versus abstract conceptualisation, Kolb (1984:43–51) refers to as the prehension dimension, as it represents two different and opposing ways of experiencing the world:

- The reliance on symbolic representations or making use of concepts, which he calls "comprehension". In Stacey's (2010) terms, this would involve the act of abstracting oneself, "drawing away from" experience and forming abstractions.
- Another which is more tangible and makes use of the directly felt experience, which he calls "apprehension". In Stacey's (2010) terms, this would involve the act of immersion, or literally "plunging into" experience.

There are therefore two distinct modes of grasping experience, which is the process of taking in information. When I walk outside on a very cold morning, for example, I will feel the cold directly. That is, I will have experienced the cold via direct apprehension. This direct apprehension I cannot pass on to my family or colleagues; the best I can do is to describe to them that it is cold. To do that, I need to convey the concept that it is cold. They, in turn, can grasp the reality via comprehension. I have passed on my experience via a concept. I can never, however, pass on the actual experience. As pointed out by Almaas (2002), the problem with grasping via comprehension is that it is very much governed by my past experience and the level of my development. My concept of coldness as a South African will be very different to an Alaskan's concept of coldness. Concepts can pass on only so much of experience; it will always be limited. That is why it is preferable to have both apprehension and comprehension. Herein lies the dialectical tension: there is a difference, for example, between a consultant who knows all the theory on how to run organisations (grasping via comprehension), and managers who actually have the hands-on experience (grasping via apprehension). In Kolb's (1984) view, you need both.

The second dialectical dimension, active experimentation versus reflective observation, Kolb (1984) calls the transformation dimension, which is the process of interpreting and acting on information. It represents two opposed ways of transforming experience, either by reflecting on it, which is called "intention", or through "active external manipulation of the external world", which is called "extension". It is this dialectical dimension that is responsible for the creation of meaning. It is in the transformation dimension that we see the connection between experiential learning and Victor Frankl's logotherapy. It was in the Nazi concentration camps that Frankl developed logotherapy, which is built on three pillars: the freedom of will, the will to meaning and that all of life contains meaning. By freedom of will, he meant the freedom of the human will. Humanity is not free from conditions or experiences. Rather, people have the freedom to choose the stand they take in response to those conditions and experiences and to find meaning in them. More importantly, Frankl (1988), like Kolb, emphasises that there is no universal meaning; instead, there are only unique meanings that are discovered through each individual and unique situation or experience.

For Kolb (1984), the transformation dimension is also responsible for the awareness of consciousness. In addressing the transformation dimension, Kolb is honouring the call by many to integrate the inner and outer domains of human existence. Interestingly, Kolb (1984) believes that the Eastern traditions have been stronger on transformation by intention, while the West's pragmatism has led it to place more emphasis on transformation via extension. The real power in Kolb's (1984) model is that he recognises and honours this dialectical tension, and reminds us that both are required for learning and growth to take place within the individual. This need for tension is inherent in logotherapy and the theory of complex responsive processes as well: "A sound amount of tension, such as the tension which is aroused by a meaning to fulfil, is inherent in being human and is indispensable for mental wellbeing" (Frankl, 1988:47–48).

Intention on its own is mere escapism or fantasy, while extension on its own can be very dangerous and meaningless. Almaas (2002) mentions that the test of true mysticism has always been that the journey inward is always the journey outward. Mother Teresa of Calcutta expressed the transformation dimension very eloquently when she said, "The fruit of silence is prayer. The fruit of prayer is faith. The fruit of faith is love. The fruit of love is service. The fruit of service is peace" (quoted in Vardey, 1995:39). The transformation dimension is an integrated whole.

According to Kolb (1984), learning is a dynamic process and happens as a result of the transaction between these four adaptive modes and the way in which the dialectical tension gets resolved. The resolution of this dialectical tension, which is a combination of the grasping and the transformation of experience, leads to the creation of knowledge. Kolb and Kolb (2017) are of the opinion that the failure to recognise the dual dialectics often leads to a simple step-by-step interpretation of the four adaptive modes of the learning cycle, and in so doing misses the foundations of the learning styles typology.

There are four forms of knowledge, as presented in Figure 1.1. (Those familiar with Kolb's model will realise that the order of the four forms has

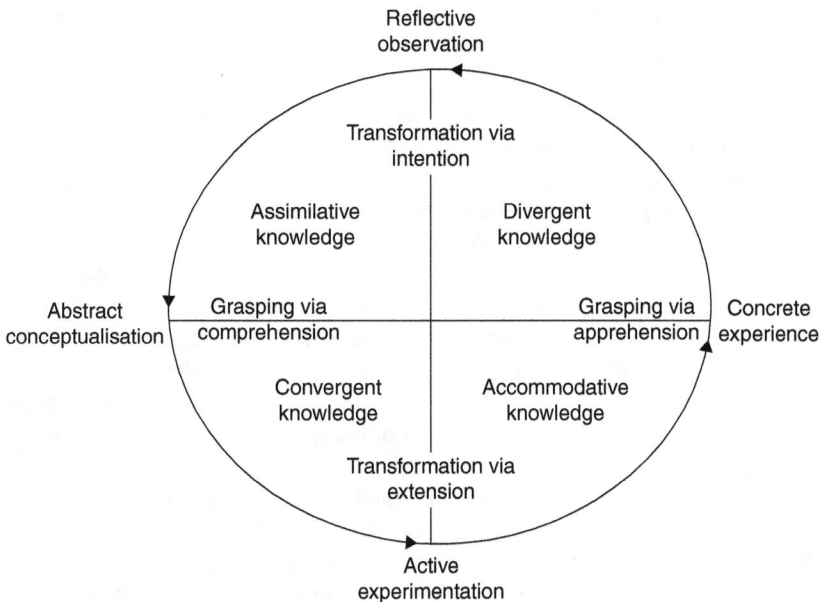

Figure 1.1 Kolb's Experiential Learning Model.
Source: Adapted from Kolb (1984:42).

been altered. Instead of moving clockwise around the cycle from the top-right quadrant, the order has been reversed to anti-clockwise. The reason for this adaptation will be made clear later.) The four forms of knowledge are defined as follows:

- *Divergent knowledge* is the result of grasping experience through appre-hension and transforming it via intention.
- Experience grasped through comprehension and transformed via intention results in *assimilative knowledge*.
- *Convergent knowledge* is the result of experience being grasped through comprehension and transformed via extension.
- When experience is grasped through apprehension and transformed via extension the result is *accommodative knowledge* (Kolb, 1984:42).

Kolb's (1984) point is that grasping knowledge is not sufficient for learning. For learning to take place it has to be acted on; in other words, the grasping has to be transformed via either intention or extension. At the same time, transformation on its own is also meaningless. There has to be something, an experience or concept, which is to be transformed. Kolb (1984) points out that all adults are capable of using all four modes. The learning processes are not, however, identical for all human beings. As a result, individuals tend to empha-sise and use some adaptive orientations over others. It is not that they cannot use all four; they just prefer certain orientations to others. This can lead to people getting stuck in those orientations. The important thing to mention here, as Kolb and Kolb (2017) point out, is that this is not an independent personality trait. Rather, it is a habitual process of learning that the individual uses, which emphasises some learning modes as opposed to others. It should be seen as a dynamic state that can respond to the demands of the environment, and can therefore change and develop. The way that individuals apply the opposing learning modes and the inherent dialectic dynamics between the modes, as well as the differences in learning styles, means that the learning cycle is not a rigid four-stage process that starts with concrete experience and moves through the other stages. Where the experiential learning cycle starts is dictated by the context; it could start in any of the stages. For as Kolb and Kolb (2017) point out, learning usually happens in partial or numerous small cycles, it does not happen in one big cycle.

As somebody who has coached and facilitated learning using this learning cycle for over two decades, I can agree with the Kolbs that learning does not happen in one big cycle. Action, for example, can be put on hold for some time while thinking and reflection are being refined. Similarly, there can be a tremendous amount of experiencing and reflection going on before it is crystallised into a working concept or hypothesis which leads to the relevant actions. At times, it might be better to start with abstract concepts, because the individual is much more comfortable working with theories than being prac-tical. Each of the stages can be an entry point into the learning cycle, as well as an exit point. For example, if an individual, upon reflection on some experi-ence, suddenly gains a new insight or has an "aha" moment, does that mean they have not learnt anything because they did not go through the entire cycle and come up with some action plan that resulted in some actions? Of course not; it is just an example of an individual going through a partial cycle at that point in time within the context of a never-ending bigger learning cycle. This is the same point Freire made:

> Action and reflection occur simultaneously. A critical analysis of reality may, however, reveal that a particular form of action is impossible or inappropriate at the present time ... Critical reflection is also action.
>
> (Freire, 2005:127)

The philosopher Christian de Quincey (2005) stated that the world (the phys-ical universe) consists of things plus experience of things. What does he mean by that? The physical things are made up of matter, energy flows, vibrations and vortices; things like trees, stones, lightning, thunder and buildings. At the same time, there are nonphysical things like mental concepts and ideas. Experiences are what know these physical and nonphysical things. If we agree with that, then it soon becomes apparent that all the modes of the learning cycle are experiences. Concrete experience, reflective observation, abstract conceptualisation and active experimentation are all experiences; they are just different kinds and manifestations of experience. As we will discover in the next chapter, pure concrete experience is stimuli and sensations that our nervous system picks up from the environment and responds to at either an unconscious or conscious level. It becomes conscious only when we make this flux of sensations explicit and hold it up for reflection, create concepts and then decide to act or not act thereon. It is one unbroken flow of experience, a continuous process. The whole experiential learning cycle is experience, and not just concrete experience. We grasp experience through concrete experience and abstract conceptualisation, and we transform experience through reflective observation and active experimentation. As a result, I for one have never understood the criticism that Kolb's model is a purely cognitive model and deals only with things in the past. It is one of the reasons why I started to explore the physiology of learning, which will be covered in the next chapter.

It is through experiential learning that we respond to and make sense of the world in which we live, including the social environment. I would argue that it is through the process of experiential learning that complex responsive processes evolve. Experiential learning accommodates modes of thought which allow for a tension between being immersed in the ordinary daily experience of local interaction and abstracting from that experience both on a first and second order of abstraction. It is how we understand the immersed world of everyday experience, the experience of interacting every day on a local level to get things done, and to achieve what we need to achieve. It is in this interplay of intended and unintended actions, as we relate and respond to each other, that we co-create our futures. The future evolves out of these responsive patterns because, as Stacey argues, human relating is inherently pattern-forming, because humans act and interact in the ways they do in order to survive. Therefore, human action and doing is a responsive process of relating to each other, which generates patterning processes.

Not only do we learn how to respond to our environment (including the social environment) through experiential learning, but experiential learning theory holds that we develop intuitive affective knowing by immersing ourselves in our concrete experience, which allows for ontological development (the nature of our being). And we create generalised knowledge through abstract conceptualisation, which allows for epistemological development (the theory of knowledge). It allows us to explore who we are and to try and develop the theories to explain what we experience. Individual and social development in this model is characterised by adapting to the world with increased complexity and relativism, and by increased integration of the dialectic conflicts between concrete experience and abstract conceptualisation, and between active experimentation and reflective observation. And all of this happens as a result of transactions with the environment, including the social. Given all the complexities involved in this process, there is a recognition that learning can be faulty and that we can get it wrong. Therefore, when it comes to experiential learning, I would agree with Freire (2005) that, as with dialogue, we need to undertake it with love, humility, faith and hope.

Summary

Yes, we all live in a complex world, in which we all actively contribute to creating the complex responsive processes that lead to the evolution of the reality we currently find ourselves inhabiting. And yes, the bad news is that there are no messianic leaders who are going to lead us out of this situation to some promised land of milk and honey. The good news, however, is that we are not helpless victims. Through the process of experiential learning we can learn to co-create alternative futures for ourselves and our communities.

Chapter 2

The physiology of learning

Introduction

In the early version of his theory, Kolb did not focus on the physiology under-pinning experiential learning. Fortunately, in his later work he does turn his attention to the physiology. I believe it is essential to understand the physi-ology underpinning experiential learning theory in order to understand that it is not just a cognitive, constructionist model of learning. And I am not alone in thinking that this is important. Stacey (2003, 2009) and Stacey and Griffin (2005) believed that it is due to the evolution of the central nervous system that humans can reflect on their actions, become aware of themselves and know what they are doing. Therefore, through experience they can learn to act in expectation of particular responses from other individuals. The self and the mind are actions of the whole body; it is not just a cognitive aspect, it is about making sense of lived experience. For them, the experiential learning cycle is possible only because of the evolution of the central nervous system. Furthermore, understanding the physiology will help us to understand what physiological states are optimal for learning to take place, and what physio-logical states hinder learning. And it is the physiology underpinning experi-ential learning, especially the central nervous system, that we will explore in this chapter.

Polyvagal theory

In my previous book (Chapman, 2010), I started to explore the connection between stress and learning, to explain how our physiological states impact learning. At the same time, I looked at how heart rate variability (HRV) could be used to measure levels of stress via the autonomic nervous system. At that point in time, I was using the widely accepted definition of the autonomic nervous system and its two subsystems, the sympathetic and parasympathetic nervous systems. Over years of working with executives and senior managers, it became even more apparent that stress continues to be a major problem, and that it impacts the quality of the learning and decision-making of these

DOI: 10.4324/9781003356424-3

individuals. As a result of my continuous interest in trying to understand this connection even better, I came across the work of Stephen Porges (2011). He was one of the pioneers in working with, and developing methods to measure and quantify, HRV.

In Chapman (2010:222), I referenced the research of the Institute of HeartMath and their work on HRV; their research looks at how stress impacts HRV, and how HRV in turn impacts cognition. HRV, as measured with an electrocardiogram (ECG), measures the beat-to-beat changes in heart rate. Many of us have become so used to wearing heart rate monitors when we exercise that we mistakenly assume the heart beats monotonously and regularly. In reality, the rhythm of a healthy heart under resting conditions is surprisingly *irregular*. These moment-to-moment variations in heart rate are easily overlooked when average heart rate is calculated with a heart rate monitor. Traditionally, it was thought that the normal variability in heart rate is due to the synergistic action of the two branches of the autonomic nervous system: the parasympathetic (vagus) nerves, which slow heart rate, and the sympathetic nerves, which accelerate it.

In 1992, however, Porges (2011) had already proposed an estimate of vagal tone, derived from measuring respiratory sinus arrhythmia, as an index of stress vulnerability. The ventral vagus nerve influences heart rate, by slowing it during exhalation of the breath and speeding it up during inhalation of the breath. These beat-to-beat changes in heart rate, the rhythm of the heart during spontaneous breathing, is called respiratory sinus arrhythmia. He presented a quantitative approach that applied time series analysis to the amplitude of respiratory sinus arrhythmia to gain a more accurate index of ventral vagal activity.

Porges arrived at this contribution after years of working with HRV, especially in his work with infants. He was, however, eventually confronted with a paradoxical dilemma, in that the traditional definition of the parasympathetic nervous system slowing the heart rate down was seen as a good thing. That was until one of the paediatricians he was lecturing confronted him on this issue, asking whether it was at all possible that the slowing down of the heart could be a bad thing. As is the case with bradycardia (abnormally slow heart action), for example, where the heart rate slows down so much that the infant dies, which happens in the case of cot deaths.

As a result of this parasympathetic paradox and further research, Porges (2011) developed polyvagal theory, which is informed by neuroanatomy, neurophysiology and evolution. The basis of polyvagal theory is that the parasympathetic nervous system consists of two vagal pathways that developed through the evolutionary process: the dorsal vagal nerve, which is an evolutionary relic of amphibians and reptiles; and the ventral vagal nerve, an evolutionary modification unique to mammals. Furthermore, these two systems are programmed with different response strategies to environmental challenges, which in turn regulate heart rate in response to novelty and to a variety of stresses.

Vagus nerve

The vagus nerve is therefore central to polyvagal theory and warrants some discussion. It is the tenth cranial nerve or CN X, the longest nerve in the human body, and interfaces with the parasympathetic control of the heart, lungs and gut. It travels upward from the brainstem at the base of the skull to connect with nerves in the neck, throat, ears and eyes, and downwards through the lungs, heart, diaphragm and stomach. Although the vagus nerve is often referred to in the singular, it is not one nerve but two distinct pathways (hence the term "polyvagal"), the dorsal vagus and the ventral vagus. Both originate in neighbouring parts of the medulla oblongata, the part of the brainstem that connects to the spinal cord. The dorsal vagus arises from the dorsal nucleus of the vagus, while the ventral vagus originates in the nucleus ambiguus. Because the nucleus ambiguus is in front of the dorsal nucleus of the vagus, it is called "ventral". The dorsal and ventral vagal fibres exit the brainstem together and travel their individual routes above and below the diaphragm.

More importantly, the vagus is a motor pathway, or a pathway that not only conducts information away from the brain but towards the brain as well. Approximately 80 per cent of the vagal fibres are conducting pathways from the body towards the brain. In other words, the vagus conducts more information towards the brain than away from the brain. Not only is the vagus lateralised with nerve trunks originating in the left and right sides of the brainstem, but it is also asymmetrical. What that means is that the left and right sides perform different tasks and may have oppositional outputs to the same target organ. In other words, they are programmed with different response strategies to environmental challenges. We know that the right or ventral vagus is myelinated (i.e. enclosed in a sheath formed from a fatty deposit called myelin to insulate it), which increases the efficiency of electrical transmission, and is most potent in the chronotropic regulation of the heart. By contrast, the left or dorsal vagus is unmyelinated. Porges (2011) goes on to suggest a typology in which the ventral vagus is involved in more conscious, voluntary, flexible, and often social activities, while the dorsal vagus deals with unconscious reflex or vegetative functions.

Because primary emotions are related to the autonomic function of the nervous system and are often linked to survival, they must be integrated into cardiopulmonary regulation. The connection between emotions and the heart is not a new idea. As far back as 1872, Darwin noted that when an emotional state occurred, the beating of the heart changed instantly. This change in cardiac activity influenced brain activity, and the brainstem structures through the cranial nerves stimulated the heart. He speculated that there were neural pathways that provided the necessary communication between specific brain structures and the heart to promote unique patterns of autonomic activity associated with emotions. And this communication happened via the vagus nerve, independent of the sympathetic nervous system and the spinal cord. More importantly, it showed that the heart not only receives information from the brain, but also sends information (including emotional information) to the brain via the vagus nerve. This functional relationship between the brainstem and the heart is known as cardiac vagal tone.

Vagal tone fulfils two roles. First, during states of low environmental demand (sleep or quiet states), vagal tone fosters physiological homeostasis to promote growth and restoration. It is important to point out that in this context, homeostasis is not meant to reflect a static state. It is rather a dynamic feedback and regulation process necessary to maintain internal states within a functional range of the individual. It manifests itself as rhythmic physiological variability. And the healthier the individual, the greater the amplitude of oscillation of these rhythms will be. According to Porges (2011), the amplitude of the rhythmic physiological process may be a good indicator of the state of the individual's nervous system and capacity to respond, as well as their range of possible behaviours. The greater the amplitude, the greater the response potential and possible range of behaviours.

Secondly, when confronted with environmental challenges, the ventral vagal system (neomammalian, which is myelinated) is responsible for rapid withdrawal of vagal tone by removing the vagal brake. The role of the vagal brake is to keep the heart rate slow (around 72 beats per minute) by increasing vagal output to the heart and actively inhibiting the sympathetic nervous system. When the vagal brake is released, it reduces vagal inhibition to the cardiac pacemaker, the sinoatrial node, and heart rate increases. This is because the intrinsic rate of the heart's pacemaker, the sinoatrial node, is naturally higher. At the same time, mechanical reflexes and sympathetic influences increase to mobilise energy resources for the classic fight-or-flight response.

In other words, cardiac vagal tone is increased by applying the vagal break and slowing down the heart rate to support homeostatic functions and functionally calming the individual. Or in response to environmental challenges, cardiac vagal tone is decreased by withdrawing the vagal brake and increasing the heart rate to increase output, to support specific motor behaviours like the fight-or-flight response. According to Porges's (2017) model, response strategies for homeostasis and environmental demands are interdependent. During homeostasis or no environmental demands, the vagal system services the needs of the internal environment (e.g. the heart, lungs, stomach and intestines) to enhance growth and restoration. In contrast, if the homeostasis process is compromised or in response to environmental demands, the vagal system supports increased metabolic output to deal with these external challenges.

This dynamic interplay between internal and external needs is continuously monitored and regulated by the central nervous system. Fortunately for us, this continuous trade-off can be monitored via the dynamic regulation of the heart by the vagus and the actions of the vagal brake. As was previously mentioned, the functional output of the vagus on the heart may be measured by monitoring respiratory sinus arrhythmia. The output from the ventral vagus nerve which terminates on the sinoatrial node of the heart conveys a frequency common to both respiratory and cardiac systems. In contrast, the output from the dorsal vagal nerve conveys a respiratory rhythm. That is because the dorsal vagal nerve is unmyelinated and appears to have little impact on cardiac output in most conditions. The hypothesis does, however, exist that under conditions of low oxygen availability this system conserves resources by stimulating massive bradycardia and apnoea.

Neuroception

Central to polyvagal theory is the concept that Porges (2017) calls "neuroception", whereby the nervous system is continuously scanning and taking information in from the environment through the senses. Every living moment of our lives we experience the world through our varied sensory systems, and these experiences contribute to the organisation of our thoughts and emotions, which in turn drive our behaviour. The mistake we make is to think that this is always a conscious meaning-making process. The reality, according to Porges (2011), is that via neuroception the autonomic nervous system, in response to an assessed situation, has initiated a response before the brain has understood and created meaning from the experience. The nervous system tries to navigate, negotiate or trigger a neural response that fits the context without conscious awareness. It does this through the process of exteroception and enteroception. Exteroception is any stimulus that is located outside the body and is detected via hearing, vision, touch, pressure, cold, heat, pain, taste or smell. Enteroception includes both the unconscious monitoring of our bodily processes and our conscious feelings of those processes. Porges (2011) points out that, like sensory systems, enteroception has four components:

1   Various internal organs have sensors located in them to sense internal conditions.
2   Information about the internal conditions is conveyed to the brain via sensory pathways.
3   The sensory information is interpreted by brain structures to organise systems to respond appropriately to the changing internal conditions.
4   The brain communicates back to the internal organs via motor pathways to change the state of the internal organs concerned.

Enteroception combines with our five exteroceptors of sight, hearing, touch, smell and taste to direct our thoughts, emotions and behaviours in response to environmental challenges. As a result, the nervous system, through neuroception, is continuously evaluating the risks in the environment. The nervous system quickly works out whether the situation in the environment or the people in the environment are safe, dangerous or life-threatening. According to Porges (2011), neuroception happens without our conscious awareness because it takes place in the primitive parts of the brain. It is therefore different to perception, which involves a degree of conscious awareness. In other words, without us even being aware of it at the cognitive level, as soon as the nervous system has determined that it could be unsafe, our body has already started a sequence of neural processes that triggers defensive behaviours such as fight, flight or freeze on a neurophysiological level.

As Dana (2018) puts it, the physiological state shapes the response, and neuroception shapes the physiological state. In unsafe situations, humans (like all other mammals) will react from the more primitive neurobiological defence systems. This happens because the neuroception of danger has made the ventral vagal pathways biologically unavailable. Humans do, however, need to override these more primitive defensive reactions if they want to create lasting social bonds. Physiological responses that are associated with the fight-or-flight response, like an increase in heart rate and rising cortisol, are dampened through metabolic adjustments as soon as our nervous system works out via neuroception that it is safe again. At the same time, other physiological states involving big drops in heart rate and blood pressure thereby causing fainting, which are associated with freezing and shutdown behaviours, are also stopped. So as soon as the nervous system has worked out that it is a safe environment or that the individual is safe, it overrides more primitive defensive strategies.

The big question is how does the individual's nervous system determine whether it is dealing with a safe person or not? Modern technologies such as functional magnetic resonance imaging (fMRI) have identified areas of the brain that detect and evaluate features such as body and face movement and vocalisation as cues for safety. Activation of what Porges (2017) calls the social engagement system depends on how well the individual can regulate the muscles of the head and face via pathways that link the brainstem and the cortex. These muscles give expression to our faces, help us to gesture with our heads, direct our gaze and permit us to distinguish background noise from human voices. The process is reciprocal, in that it is possible for us to derive the state and intention of other individuals from their facial expressions, their gestures, the tone of their voice and their posture. The important thing to note here is that it is only after the physiological response has occurred that the conscious brain tries to make sense of the response. According to Porges (2017:178), the conscious mind uses the experience of the physiological response to build "a plausible personal narrative". Here we start to see the physiological basis of experiential learning.

Polyvagal theory therefore links affective experience, facial gestures, vocal communication, emotions and social behaviour with the evolution of the neural regulation of the heart, which in turn is neuroanatomically linked to neural control of the muscles of the face and head. Further, through neuroception these neural and neuroanatomical processes are triggered unconsciously in response to dynamic internal and external environmental demands and challenges. Even though humans are not usually aware of the cues that trigger neuroception, we do become aware of the changes in our physiological state. That would include changes in our heart rate, pounding of the heart and sweating, for example. Becoming aware of our physiological state and the changes that take place as a result of neuroception is very important, because as Porges (2017) points out, neuroception is not always accurate. Neuroception can get it wrong, in that it can identify cues of safety when there is a risk involved, or identify a risk when there is no risk involved. As a result, polyvagal theory sees clinical disorders "as difficulties in neural regulation of specific circuits associated with turning off defensive strategies and enabling social engagement to spontaneously occur" (Porges, 2017:45). This is very different to models which assume that atypical behaviours are learnt and can be unlearnt.

Evolutionary development

Polyvagal theory suggests that the nervous system evolved and developed hierarchically. Moshé Feldenkrais (2019), the nuclear physicist who became a scholar of human movement, agrees that the nervous system evolved hierarchically, and that it is among the most complex structures in existence. What this means is that the nervous system has very old layers, covered by less old ones, followed by more recent layers. The older layers are primitive, and abrupt in the all-or-nothing way. Newer-evolved layers check the older ones and supersede them, and each new layer is finer in its function. As a result, it makes action more graded, more differentiated. The older structures need less learning, and function faster and more reliably. Under emergencies, the older layers take over and assure survival, while the newer layers switch themselves off. Once the emergency has ended, the finer and more varied newer parts will take over. The old structures are therefore not destroyed; they are latent, less obvious but essential in an emergency. The older formation will take over and produce a regression when the situation cannot be dealt with at leisure. The newer neural structures are slower than the older structures. If you slip on a banana peel, for example, the body must correct itself before it falls. Thinking about all the options and then deciding what to do relies on the newest brain structures that take far too long, with the result that you will fall. The older layers of the nervous system can deal with this situation without thinking and do what needs to be done to correct your posture before you fall.

Dorsal vagal system

Polyvagal theory agrees that each of these developmental layers and stages are preserved in the higher stages, meaning that all these stages are present and preserved in humans. The dorsal vagal system was the first to develop (500 million years ago), and is the oldest branch of the vagus nerve. It is responsible for immobilisation, feigning death, behavioural shutdown, bradycardia and apnoea. It is the unmyelinated portion originating in the brainstem known as the dorsal motor nucleus of the vagus, and it evolved with the reptilian brain. Reptilian behaviour is mostly focused on foraging, stalking and feeding. Reptiles spend limited time and energy on social interactions such as parenting and reproduction. They have smaller metabolically active body organs and different metabolic mechanisms than mammals. As a result, reptiles are less dependent on oxygen and can go for long periods without it, which means that their physiological status is not compromised by a very slow heart rate when they freeze as a defensive strategy. This behaviour is seen, for example, when a lizard is under threat; it will freeze up and act dead, which could prevent predators from eating it out of fear of being poisoned. Immobilisation or freezing is one of the most ancient defence mechanisms, which works fine for reptiles with small, developed brains. Combined with this freezing of gross motor activity is a limited repertoire of behaviours characterised by a focus of exteroceptors (sensory receptors that receives external stimuli).

Thomas Hanna (1988), the founder of the field of Somatics, refers to this as the "startle response or Red Light Reflex" which aids all animals to avoid or evade a threat. In humans, the withdrawal is very quick in response to a threat; as a result, the body moves into a flexed and crouched position, almost as if it is going to fall and go into the curled-up foetal posture. This is counter-intuitive, and as Feldenkrais (2019) mentions, one would expect that the individual would try to get away from the danger as quickly as possible. When the threat is too near or too violent, however, it produces this general contraction of the flexor muscles, which enables the individual to freeze or even simulate death. The cascading of the response starts in the face, then moves down the neck, then arms and trunk, and finally the legs and toes. The reason is that these impulses, as noted from polyvagal theory, originate in the lower-level reptilian brainstem, and arrive at the facial and head muscles first; they then need time to travel down to the rest of the body. The primitive reptilian brain is much faster than the later-developing parts of our brain that control our voluntary actions. This protective response can be triggered in response to any negative stressors, and is recognised in a forward stooped posture.

The interesting thing is that in lower animals this reflex is an all-or-nothing response; it is either there or it is not. In mammals, and especially in humans, there are levels of gradation. As Hanna (1988) points out, the startle response varies from very low to very high. And the degree of gradation can be calibrated by measuring the degrees of muscle contractions during this process. He refers to research done in Canada, where it was found that electromyographic tension (measuring muscle response to a nerve stimulating the muscle) increased when individuals are involved in a task involving fear or failure. What was even more interesting was that the muscle tension built up while working on the task, and did not dissipate on completion of the task if the individuals concerned did not feel a sense of completion. If people were praised for doing a good job, the tension dissipated; but if they were criticised, the tension remained.

Continuously being in some gradient of this state can lead to physiological and psychological issues.

Dana (2018), a trauma therapist who uses polyvagal theory in her work, mentions that an individual in this state will experience the world as dark, empty and dead. Because the body and mind have moved into conservation mode, the individual can be too tired to think or act. As a result, the individual can feel hopeless and abandoned. Lack of energy, isolation, memory problems, dissociation and depression could be some of their problems in daily living. Chronic fatigue, stomach problems, Type 2 diabetes, fibromyalgia and low blood pressure are among some of the health consequences.

Sympathetic nervous system

As evolution progressed, however, and the brains of vertebrates became bigger, it was a dangerous defensive strategy to completely freeze up, because a bigger brain needs more oxygen. The next defensive strategy that mammals developed involved fight-or-flight responses. This, in turn, necessitated an increase in metabolic output to foster these fight-or-flight behaviours. Prolonged periods of reflexive neurogenetic bradycardia in response to environmental threats or challenges would reduce oxygen resources and metabolic output, and compromise the fight-or-flight potential of mammals. More than that, extended periods of low oxygen would impact the functioning of the central nervous system, reduce behavioural complexity, damage vital organs, induce unconsciousness, and finally, could lead to death. Thus, a physiological response that does not compromise the oxygen-needing nervous system of mammals had to replace the more primitive physiological response.

The next physiological response to develop was therefore the mobilisation system (fight-or-flight behaviours), which is dependent on the functioning of the nerves of the sympathetic nervous system. This occurred about 400 million years ago. The sympathetic nervous system originates in nerves that arise from the thoracic and lumbar regions of the spinal cord. The sympathetic nervous system prepares the body for action through two mobilisation systems. The first system to be activated very quickly (within 100 milliseconds) via a shot of adrenalin is the sympathetic adrenal medullary system. It is a short, rapid response, and is quickly followed by a return to regulation. If that does not solve distress, the slower system that takes minutes to take effect kicks in. The hypothalamic–pituitary–adrenal axis then releases cortisol (the stress hormone) into the body. This new system was able to increase metabolic activity and cardiac output (by increasing heart rate and giving the heart greater ability to contract), thereby introducing movement as a survival strategy. In other words, when the animal was in danger it would either fight or it could run away to save its life. Hanna (1988) refers to this as the "Green Light Reflex"; it is assertive, and its function is action, to make us go. It is the opposite of the Red

Light Reflex of the dorsal vagal state; the body is therefore hyper-extended, ready to fight or run away.

Dana (2018) mentions that in this state the individual will feel the rush of adrenalin. They could feel angry or anxious, which makes it hard for them to keep still. The world feels like an unfriendly, dangerous and chaotic place. As a result, the individual cannot hear friendly voices. There is the added complexity of misreading cues in this state; for example, a neutral face can appear angry and be experienced as being dangerous. (This is a very good example of how and when neuroception could be faulty by misreading the cues.) Physiologically, the breath has become short and shallow, and the heart rate speeds up to get the body ready for action. This is why a negative emotion like anger and/or frustration produces an erratic and chaotic pattern in HRV. If this becomes a chronic state, inability to focus or follow through, panic attacks and relational issues can become problems in daily living. The individual will experience a negative impact on cognition, known as cortical inhibition. As a result, the individual is inclined to experience less ability to think clearly, less efficiency in decision-making, less ability to communicate effectively and reduced physical coordination. This in turn can lead to the following health issues: stomach problems; sleep problems; memory impairment; chronic back, shoulder and neck tension; and high cholesterol, high blood pressure and heart disease.

The ventral vagal system

The next step in the evolutionary process with mammals (200 million years ago) was the development of the ventral vagal system, which Porges (2017) refers to as the social engagement system. This evolutionary step involved the source nuclei of vagal pathways shifting from the phylogenetically older, unmyelinated vagal pathways to the myelinated vagal pathways, thereby creating the face–heart connection. An anatomical and neurophysiological connection was created between the special efferent pathways that regulate the striated muscles of the face, head and neck and neural regulation of the heart via the myelinated vagus. These muscles help to create facial expressions (how we look) and gestures with our heads, and help us to distinguish between human voices (how we listen and speak) and the noises in the background. Collectively, therefore, these muscles act as filters for social stimuli. According to Dana (2018), a genuine smile involves the eyes closing a little, there are wrinkles around the eyes, and the cheeks move upward, all of which contribute to a neuroception of safety, and send out an invitation to approach to other individuals. If those cues are absent, the nervous system sends out a message of warning. Similarly, our vocal intentions are revealed by the intensity, sound patterns, rhythm, duration and frequency of speech, and not merely by the words we speak. With the development of the social engagement system, due to more optimal myelinated vagal regulation, more adaptive social behaviour starts to emerge. Porges (2017) points out that this is because the facial nerve in mammals not only regulates facial muscles but also engages the vagal system. This is due to the integration of cranial nerves V, VII, IX, X and XI, which means that the eyes, ears, voice and head now work in concert with the heart.

For example, emotion, which is defined by shifts in the regulation of facial expressions and vocalisation, will bring about changes in cardiopulmonary functions. Moreover, the neurophysiological regulation of heart rate happens primarily along the right ventral vagus to the sinoatrial node in the heart. This means that heart rate is under the control of higher, right-hemisphere structures in the brain. Porges (2017) refers to studies of individuals with unilateral brain damage conducted in 1987 which demonstrated that heart rate responses are reduced in individuals with right-side brain damage. The right hemisphere of the brain is predominant in regulating autonomic function and emotion, because it is responsible for regulating homeostasis and modulating physiological states in response to both internal and external environmental feedback. The predominance of the right brain hemisphere in processing emotions based on facial cues is central to Allan Schore's (2019) regulation theory that will be covered later.

Dana (2018) points out that in this state, the individual is connected to their experiences and the world, and they can reach out to others because they can see the "big picture". Descriptions of this state include being interested, the world is safe and peaceful, fun, active, happy, joyful, relaxed and being in the flow. Having a general feeling of being organised and a sense of management, taking care of myself, being productive at work, playing and doing things with others is an integral part of daily lived experience. Research by the Institute of HeartMath (2001) shows that in this state, there is improved mental performance and achievement, more creativity and problem-solving, better decision-making, more flexibility in the way we think and improved memory. All because physiologically the heart rate is regulated, the breath is full, the eyes are softened and there is a kind tone in the voice. As a result, there is an overall sense of wellbeing, regulated blood pressure, a healthy heart and immune system, quality sleep and good digestion. In this state, heart rhythm coherence develops into a stable, sine wave-like pattern in the HRV waveform.

According to polyvagal theory and regulation theory, the ventral vagal system or the social engagement system is activated when the individual feels safe and secure. And we get the cues for safety from each other's facial expression and tone of voice. One of the central tenets of polyvagal theory is, therefore, that individuals co-regulate each other's nervous systems, and this happens via the ventral vagal system and the right hemisphere of the brain. It is only when we are in a calm physiological state, however, that we can send out cues of safety to other individuals. Co-regulation is a biological imperative, a necessity to sustain life, and when we feel safe, it allows us to move into connection and create trusting relationships. When this happens, the more primitive defensive strategies, mediated by the sympathetic nervous system (fight-or-flight mobilisations and tantrums), and the unmyelinated dorsal vagal system (shutdown behaviours) are regulated more effectively.

According to Porges (2017), the human nervous system retains the three neural circuits, which are organised in a phylogenetic hierarchy. In this hierarchy of adaptive responses, the newest circuit is used first. In other words, whenever an individual comes into a situation, the first system that will be activated if the individual feels safe and secure is the ventral vagal system. In this state, individuals try to co-regulate by using strategies of social engagement and social communication. As Dana (2018) points out, this is because humans as social beings need reliable, reciprocal relationships for both physical and emotional wellbeing. If that circuit fails to provide safety, the older circuits are recruited sequentially. If the individual is unsuccessful in using connection and communication to partner with others, they move out of the safety of the ventral vagal state and engage the sympathetic nervous system's fight-or-flight response. To resolve the danger and return to the safety of ventral vagal regulation, strategies of fight, flight, confrontation or avoidance will be employed. And if that does not work, the nervous system will trigger the dorsal vagal system, which leads to total freezing. This is the case when people experience severe trauma like combat, in which some people totally freeze up. The other extreme case where we see this happening is where individuals have experienced rape and freeze up, are immobilised because of the extreme traumatic experience. Freezing in this case can be physical and/or psychological. It is the primitive defence response triggered by the dorsal vagal system to protect and keep the individual alive. In less extreme cases, as Dana (2018) mentions, individuals are disconnected from themselves, from others, and from their internal and external resources. There is a feeling of being lost and unable to find their way back into connection.

Intertwined states

These three states of the autonomic nervous system therefore co-regulate and regulate our states and behaviour dynamically, depending on our environment. And as we have mentioned, these states are also graded according to intensity. There are, however, experiences in life that involve the complex interaction of more than one of these three autonomic states. Dana (2018), drawing on Porges's work, mentions a few examples, such as the act of lovemaking between lovers. This experience needs the interaction of the ventral vagal system (social engagement system) and the more ancient dorsal vagal system. This is an example of where the immobilisation system has been modified through evolution to support intimate needs. Lovemaking allows for immobilisation without fear, where the dorsal vagal system is enlisted to support social behaviours that require stillness and some immobilisation. Another example, which is critical for development, is play. Play is possible only when the ventral vagal and sympathetic systems work together. Given that play often involves some rough and tumbling movements and actions, it can soon degenerate into an act of danger or survival if one of the participants no longer feels safe. It is only while the ventral vagal system keeps working with the sympathetic nervous system that it remains an act of play. This happens due to the vagal brake being relaxed via the ventral vagal system, which allows the sympathetic system to be engaged.

Unconscious behaviours

Another tenet of polyvagal theory is that the nervous system triggers our behaviours unconsciously, and that it controls our behaviours rather than us doing so consciously. This is a liberating idea for anyone who has experienced a traumatic event. In the case of rape, for example, the survivors must deal with that intense trauma as well as the possible shame associated with it. The shame we are talking about here is that imposed on the survivor if people ask them why they did not fight back or try to stop the attacker. Polyvagal theory offers survivors a new paradigm in trauma counselling, in that it helps them understand that instead of feeling shame they should be thankful that their nervous system worked out very quickly what was needed to protect them and keep them alive. In a situation like rape, where the perpetrator is often much stronger than the survivor, an attempt to fight back could have led to the latter being killed.

In her work as a trauma therapist, Dana (2018) mentions that the autonomic nervous system simply acts to manage risk and seek safety; the nervous system does not make value judgements. In her experience, polyvagal theory helps trauma survivors reduce the shame and self-blame they so often feel, by learning to appreciate the protective intent of their autonomic responses. They become more compassionate with themselves as they become curious about the cues of safety and danger their nervous systems are sensing. Survivors learn to appreciate their reactions as courageous survival responses generated by the autonomic nervous system, which evolved over millions of years to keep us alive and help us respond appropriately to our environment. It does this by taking information in from the external and internal environment and determining the most appropriate behaviour. At the same time, Dana (2018) points out that experience shapes the autonomic nervous system, which builds up autonomic patterns over time. In other words, the individual builds up habitual reaction patterns in response to experiences of connection and challenge.

Unique to polyvagal theory is the assumption that complex behaviours, including social interactions, depend on physiology and how appropriately the nervous system regulates the dynamic autonomic states. And as Dana (2018) points out, it provides a physiological and psychological understanding of how and why individuals move through mobilisation, disconnection and engagement on a continuous basis. Furthermore, that recognition can then be used in therapy or any helping profession to help a client recognise the autonomic state they are currently in, respect the adaptive survival response, learn to regulate or co-regulate into a ventral vagal state, and learn to tell the story differently.

Like Kolb (1984) and Chapman (2010), Dana (2018) believes that humans create meaning through the experiential learning process. In my experience, there is a tendency to believe that the experience Kolb (1984) speaks about is purely conscious, but what polyvagal theory adds to the equation is a form of experiential learning that is preconscious. It is through neuroception that the nervous system has learnt from experience to scan the environment for cues of safety or threat and to trigger the most appropriate behaviour without involving the conscious thinking brain. And this process is often triggered by non-conscious emotions. In unpredictable environments, non-conscious emotion processing provides rapid modulation of behaviour. From an evolutionary per-spective, emotions provide a modulatory control system that facilitates sur-vival and reproduction. Reflex-like reactions to emotional events can occur before attention is paid to them. And as Schore (2019), McGilchrist (2019) and Hannaford (2005) show in their research, this unconscious response seems to happen in the right hemisphere of the brain. These unconscious responses by the nervous system can then drive the creation of the stories that shape our daily lives, thereby contributing to the uniqueness of every individual, whose nervous system has been shaped by experience and has developed its own unique response patterns.

If we truly understand this process, we can appreciate why it is so easy to fall into the traps and Model I reasoning that Argyris (2010) talks about. And given the right conditions, we will all fall into these traps because uncon-sciously our nervous system has already worked out that it is an unsafe envir-onment and triggered the appropriate behaviours to protect us. At the same time, we can start to understand why complex responsive processes are so complex, because one of their characteristics is that these interactive patterns can settle into habits that can be largely unconscious. These habits can have social and individual aspects at the same time. It can be unconscious in that the response has not been formulated yet, due to a more primitive physio-logical response, or because habit over time has made it automatic.

Fortunately for us as humans, as Schore (2019), McGilchrist (2019) and Hannaford (2005) point out, we have a left brain hemisphere that can make this unconscious neuroception process conscious, so that we can interrupt responses if necessary and make sense of them. Although neuroception is an unconscious process that has evolved over millions of years to help us survive in a very complex environment, we are not helpless victims of this process. Dana (2018) mentions that bringing conscious awareness to the autonomic response brings the influence of perception to neuroception. Conscious per-ception enables us to interrupt the ingrained response pathways. We do this by using the brain's right-hemisphere bias by feeling an embodied sense of the autonomic state and embodied sense of the self, and then using the brain's left-hemisphere bias to make things explicit by adding language to the experience.

Regulation theory

Schore (2019) and Hannaford (2005) suggest that the human brain develops according to an evolutionary hierarchy similar to the evolutionary hierarchy in polyvagal theory. Neurological maturation evolved from the subcortical to cortical structure. The subcortical structure consists of the reptilian brain and the limbic system. Nerve nets are first developed in the reptilian brain, because it is the first to develop and the oldest part of the brain in evolutionary terms. The reptilian brain (or basal ganglia as it is known in humans) consists of the brainstem, cerebellum, pons and medulla oblongata and is responsible for autonomic functioning, arousal and pain. The next to develop is the limbic system, which processes emotions and motivation. It is the area of the brain that lies between the reptilian brain and the cerebral cortex, and it is where most of our emotional processing occurs. Every sensory experience we have therefore starts in the brainstem or reptilian brain. It then moves through the limbic system (thalamus) which monitors the sensations and incorporates emotions. Finally, it is consciously realised in the last part of the brain to evolve and develop, the most plastic part, the neocortex. The neocortex consists of two hemispheres, left and right, with each hemisphere containing four lobes. The right hemisphere of the brain matures first and the last to mature is the left hemisphere of the brain. Each of these areas will be explored in more detail in this chapter.

Carla Hannaford (2005:93–94), a professor of biology, provides the following more detailed account of the development of the cerebral neocortex, citing the approximate ages at which these structures develop:

1 *Reptilian brain (conception to 15 months)*:
   - Development of basic survival needs like safety, food, touch and shelter.
   - Starting with the vestibular system sensory development starts, followed by hearing, tactile, smell, taste and finally seeing – rich sensory activation.
   - Reflexes are integrated via motor development through core muscle activation, neck muscles, arms and legs, leading to rolling over, sitting, crawling and walking – motor exploration.
2 *Limbic system/relationship (15 months to 4.5 years)*:
   - Memory development and social development via understanding of self/others, self/emotions, self/language.
   - Emotional exploration, language exploration/communication, imagination, gross motor proficiency.
3 *Gestalt (right) hemisphere elaboration (4.5 to 7 years old)*:
   - Processing and cognition of the whole picture.
   - Movement, rhythm, image, emotion, intuition.
   - Integrative thought and outer speech.

4   *Logic (left) hemisphere elaboration (7 to 9 years old)*:
- Linear math processing as well as detail and linear processing/ cognition.
- Reading and writing skills development and the refinement of the elements of language.
- Music, art, sports, dance, manual training technique development.

5   *Frontal lobe elaboration (8 years old)*:
- Skills refinement because of fine motor development.
- Control of social behaviour and inner speech.
- Two-dimensional focus via fine motor eye teaming for tracking and foveal focus.

6   *Increased corpus callosum elaboration and myelination (9 to 12 years old)*:
- Whole-brain processing.

7   *Hormonal emphasis (12 to 16 years old)*:
- Social consciousness develops through learning about the body, self, others, community and meaningful living.

8   *Refining cognitive skills (16 to 21 years old)*:
- Future planning and play with new ideas and possibilities because of whole-mind/body processing and social interaction.

9   *Elaboration and refinement of the frontal lobes (21+ years old)*:
- Global/systems thinking and high-level formal reasoning.
- The increase of altruism, love, compassion as emotions are refined.
- Insight.
- Refinement of fine motor skills.

Based on this evolutionary developmental mechanism and attachment theory, Schore (2019) developed his regulation theory. This theory holds that the essential development task of the first 2 years of human infancy is the co-creation of an attachment bond of emotional communication and regulation between the mother and infant. Through her interactions with the infant, the mother unconsciously appraises and regulates the nonverbal expression of the infant, and thereby the development of its central and autonomic nervous systems.

If a secure attachment is created through optimal attachment experiences between the mother and infant, two modes of self-regulation will develop over time. The first is interconnectedness, where interactive regulation of emotions is accessed while being subjectively engaged with other humans in an interconnected context. The second is autonomy, which happens in an autonomous context while subjectively being disengaged from other humans, where auto-regulation of emotions is activated. Emotional wellbeing is defined by modern attachment theory as the non-conscious switching between these two modes, depending on the context.

One of the central tenets of polyvagal theory is that individuals co-regulate each other's nervous systems, and this happens via the ventral vagal system and the right hemisphere of the brain. McGilchrist (2019) points out that due to the right hemisphere being more myelinated than the left, it is more accurate and faster at discriminating and interpreting facial expressions, vocal intonation and body gestures. It is especially good at understanding the subtle cues that come from the eyes. And as we have seen from the previous arguments, we get the signals for safety from each other's facial expression and tone of voice. Schore (2019) emphasises that this co-regulation, which happens in the right hemisphere of the brain through tactile-gestural nonverbal, auditory-prosodic and visual-facial communication, is the psychobiological core of the emotional attachment bond between the mother and the infant. And as is the case in polyvagal theory, the automatic handling of nonverbal affective cues in infancy is an implicit neurobiological non-conscious joint process operating outside the realm of verbal experience. As Schore (2019) puts it, it is the result of the synchronised operation of the mother's right hemisphere interacting with the infant's right hemisphere of the brain.

According to Schore (2019) and Hannaford (2011), the right hemisphere matures before the left hemisphere. It is therefore understandable that this preverbal communication and attachment develops via the right hemisphere. Furthermore, the quality of these relational attachment transactions will shape the development of the right cortical–subcortical systems. This in turn will impact later personality development and functions, as Schore (2019) points out. This is especially true of survival functions that act beneath conscious awareness at ultra-fast timeframes. These early attachment experiences lay the foundations for coping mechanisms which act at levels beneath conscious awareness to maintain basic regulation when confronted with environmental challenges. These coping mechanisms become the internal working models that are accessed to perceive, appraise and regulate social emotional information and to guide action in novel and familiar interpersonal environments. Where these relational attachment transactions have been positive, it will be much easier for the individual to activate the right hemisphere and the ventral vagal system to engage the social engagement system.

On the other hand, drawing on the work of Watt (2003), Schore (2019) observes that frequent disorganised, disoriented, insecure attachment histories are affectively burnt into the infant's early-developing right hemisphere. Such early experiences (including the relational trauma of abuse and neglect) are imprinted into the right cortical–subcortical systems, and during periods of interpersonal emotional stress these disoriented, insecure internal working models are non-consciously accessed and used. Consequently, if children grow up with dominant experiences of separation distress, fear and rage, they will go down a neurologically pathogenic developmental pathway. These pathways often lead to early-forming pathologies and personality disorders. Not having access to the social engagement system, these people will tend to be living in a constant state of fight-or-flight, or in a dissociated dorsal vagal state.

Schore's physiological hierarchy

Porges (2017) mentioned that the human nervous system retains the three neural circuits, which are organised in a phylogenetic hierarchy. In this hierarchy of adaptive responses, the newest circuit (ventral vagal system) is used first. If that circuit fails to provide safety, the older circuits are recruited sequentially, namely the sympathetic system (fight-or-flight) and then the dorsal vagal system (freeze). Schore's (2019) regulation theory adds the next level to that phylogenetic hierarchy. In times of severe stress or regression, Schore (2019) believes that "functional regressions reflect neurobiological structural regressions". What he means is that there is a shift between the cerebral hemispheres, and then within the hemispheres. The first shift is a shift from the later-developing explicit left hemisphere and its verbal, cognitive and analytical functions of the conscious mind. This is accompanied by a shift from mild to moderate surface emotions (anxiety, pleasure, anger) and left brain-to-left brain conscious verbal communication, to the early-developing implicit right hemisphere and its nonverbal, emotional, imagistic functions of the unconscious mind. Functionally, there is a shift to strong, deep emotions (intense love, elation, rage, terror, grief and utter despair) and right brain-to-right brain unconscious nonverbal emotional communication. This is followed by a shift from conscious cognition (the later-forming cortical system) to unconscious bodily based affect (the early-maturing subcortical systems). The final shift is from the central nervous system to the autonomic nervous system.

Hence there is a horizontal and vertical shift within the central nervous system which makes it easier to understand how regulation theory and polyvagal theory are easily integrated. Essentially, they are both describing the same physiological responses to environmental demands. Their only difference is that they place the emphasis of the functional contribution to the process on different anatomical parts. This hemispheric shift is the physiological basis for Hannaford's (2005) hemispheric dominance preference, related to learning.

Interpersonal neurobiology of human development

By integrating these physiological processes, Schore (2019) makes another valuable contribution. He does not see these unconscious behaviours as the result of repressed emotions or experiences, as it is espoused in traditional psychological thinking. Rather, he sees the unconscious as physiological learnt responses in the developing right hemisphere. In fact, he translates the brainstem as the physiological substrate of the deep unconscious, the limbic system as the unconscious, the right hemisphere as the preconscious, and finally the left hemisphere as the higher levels of the conscious mind. The unconscious processing of emotional information is mainly subsumed by the right hemisphere subcortical root, and it is in the right hemisphere that unconscious emotional memories are stored. This is because the emotional right hemisphere is dominant in human infancy. As a result, Schore (2019) sees the right hemisphere as the psychobiological substrate of the human unconscious mind and Freud's dynamic unconscious. Drawing on his own work and the work of Tucker and Moller (2007), Gainotti (2006), Devinsky (2000) and McGilchrist (2019), he mentions that several studies have found that unconscious processing of emotional information is mainly subsumed by a right hemisphere subcortical route.

At the same time, the right hemisphere is involved in maintaining a continuous, coherent and unified sense of self. According to McGilchrist (2019), the right frontal region of the brain is critical in this personal "interior" sense of the self with emotional, personal memories and history. This is because the right hemisphere is more engaged by autobiographical and emotional memories. Which is not surprising, given that the sense of self develops because of the interaction of the right hemisphere with another right hemisphere. From infancy to death, this rapidly acting emotional processing is vital to survival in helping the individual to cope with stresses and challenges. It is thus critical to emotional resilience and wellbeing because it is responsible for the highest-level regulation of behaviour and stress in the brain.

And it is in the right hemisphere of the brain that Schore's (2019) regulation theory and Porges's (2017) polyvagal theory integrate or converge. Schore's (2019) regulation theory holds that the right hemisphere of the brain is continuously shaped by social experiences, especially those that involve emotional relationships, which is aligned with Porges's (2017) social engagement system of the ventral vagal nerve. In both theories, nonverbal communication takes place beneath the level of awareness via facial, voice and gesture cues. As Porges (2011) has shown, the hypothalamic–pituitary–adrenal axis is asymmetrical, and when it comes to the responses associated with emotions, the right side has greater control of physiological responses. His work shows that stimuli produced in the right hemisphere cause greater cardiovascular responses than those produced in the left hemisphere. Referring to Porges's work, Schore (2019) mentions that damage to the right hemisphere has a negative impact on vocal intonation, facial expression and reactivity of the autonomic nervous system.

Together, Schore's (2019) regulation theory and Porges's (2017) polyvagal theory help to transform psychoanalytical theory from a theory of the unconscious mind to what Schore (2019) calls a *"theory of mind/brain/body"*. Physiologically, the autonomic nervous system and hormonal systems are now part of the unconscious right hemisphere of the brain, thereby inextricably linking the unconscious system to the body. And the same applies to the conscious mind. Schore (2019) mentions that if we mean by conscious that part of the mind that is aware of its own awareness, and brings the world into focus, makes it explicit and allows it to be formulated in language, then almost all that activity lies in the left hemisphere.

This physiologically based human developmental understanding leads to an interpersonal neurobiology of human development. It helps us understand how communicating brains align and synchronise their neural activities with other brains through relational mechanisms. Especially where emotional relationships are involved, these social interactions *between* brains shape the emotional circuits *within* brains. This process starts very early where the mother shapes the limbic autonomic circuits in her child's developing right hemisphere. Furthermore, drawing on the work of Orlinsky and Howard (1986), Schore makes the point that the nonverbal, prerational stream of expressions of voices, faces, gestures and smells that binds the infant to the mother continues as an interpersonal, intuitively felt, affective relational communication process throughout life. And all of this happens in the right hemispheres of the interacting individuals.

The important thing here is that it is within the context of a relationship with another brain, another individual, that the self-organisation of the developing brain occurs. This social synchronisation mechanism, which is central to human bonding from infancy as well as all later emotional communication, is therefore interpersonal. It moves us from a one-person psychology paradigm to a dynamic two-person or interpersonal psychology paradigm, where humans co-regulate each other's autonomic and central nervous systems, just like in polyvagal theory. In other words, according to McGilchrist (2019), the development of our inwardness and that of others is an intersubjective shared experience. According to Schore (2019), we now understand that experiences shape the structure and function of the mind and brain. In other words, the function and structure of the brain are shaped through experiential learning in an interpersonal context. Polyvagal theory and regulation theory therefore give us the physiological basis to understand how complex responsive processes are formed and kept in place, and how they can be unconscious and conscious at the same time.

Schore (2019) mentions that a similar paradigm shift is happening within neuroscience. There is a shift from the current intrabrain focus, used in cognitive neuroscience, to developing fields of affective neuroscience (especially social neuroscience) and exploring interbrain interactions. This is because of advances in brain research that allow for simultaneous measurement of two brains interacting with each other in real time. When neuroimaging technology first appeared, research was aimed at the localisation of a specific brain function in a particular brain region. The research focused on intrabrain activity during sensory, motor or cognitive tasks. Research then shifted to the whole brain and functional connectivity analysis. Functional neuroimaging facilitated another paradigm shift. The shift is beyond intrabrain activity to interbrain activity in an interpersonal context, to quantifying the brain interactions between individuals transcending the boundary of the skull. This research aims to measure the different patterns that are activated between two brains as they engage with each other during different affectively charged interpersonal interactions.

Referring to the research of Dumas, Nadel, Soussignan, Martinerie and Garnero (2010), Schore mentions that these researchers found that the right temporoparietal cortex in one partner is synchronised with the right temporoparietal cortex of the other partner. That is because the right temporoparietal junction is known to be activated in social interactions, and is centrally involved in states of empathetic understanding, attention processing and perceptual awareness. The right lateralisation system is involved in making sense of another mind. By simultaneously measuring cerebral activities in pairs of communicating individuals, these researchers found that establishing mutual understanding of novel signals synchronised cerebral dynamics across both individuals' right temporal lobes. According to their findings, nonverbal intersubjective communication, and the processing of novelty and meaning, is generated in the right and not left hemisphere.

Schore (2019) is of the opinion that stress-regulating and stress-inducing transactions between a mother and infant, and between a therapist and client, are good candidates for this kind of research. Relational psychoanalytic models emphasise the intersubjective influences that flow between two affectively communicating minds on a conscious and unconscious level; and the processing of this emotional and social information is transmitted from the right hemisphere of the individual to the right hemisphere of the other individual, as well as through their autonomic nervous systems.

Collectively, the shift in neuroimaging research from an individual within-brain perspective to a social between-brain perspective challenges the idea that the self can and does exist in isolation. The idea that it can is a mere abstraction. Rather, the self evolves through a process of experiential learning and co-regulation via the central and autonomic nervous systems transacting with the environment, of which the social environment is the most important part. This thinking is in agreement with the principles of complex responsive processes. It is the interaction of all these individual nervous systems that leads to the formation and maintenance of complex responsive processes.

The asymmetrical brain

Up until now, we have put most of the emphasis on the right hemisphere of the brain. We have two brain hemispheres for a reason, however, and the more we access both hemispheres the more intelligently and effectively we can function within our particular environment. As Hannaford (2005) mentions, to be proficient at anything in life we need to engage both hemispheres. The psychiatrist Iain McGilchrist (2019) emphasises that his work tries to add to our understanding of how the brain functions, and to improve our understanding of our own minds. He does not, however, offer a causative mechanistic understanding, but rather uses the science of the brain to offer a descriptive phenomenological model of the brain and mind. He agrees with Schore (2019) and Hannaford (2005) that the brain is co-created in social relationships, but he goes even further in seeing our brains as being moulded by, and in turn moulding, the culture in which we live. This notion is in agreement with the theory of complex responsive processes.

The left brain/right brain myth

In his book *The Master and His Emissary*, McGilchrist (2019) states that he does not believe in the left brain/right brain myth, which holds that certain functions occur in the left hemisphere of the brain and others in the right. He is at pains to highlight just how difficult it is to pinpoint functions within the brain, despite the advances made in neuroimaging technologies. Just because an area lights up on an image does not mean that the area is fundamentally responsible for a certain function. Likewise, one cannot assume that areas which do not light up are not involved. For example, one of the problems is that only effortful tasks will show up on an image; in other words, the more a person is an expert at something, the less that function will show up on an image as brain activity. Furthermore, the more complex a task is, the more widely distributed networks come into play, and so it becomes harder to know exactly what one is measuring. Even neuroscience is still not as precise as we would like to believe. Our knowledge is continually evolving.

Despite these difficulties, we now know that both hemispheres can deal with words or images, but they deal with them in different ways. As McGilchrist (2019) shows, any attempt to segregate sets of functions within specific hemispheres has been disregarded. Evidence has been building up that every identifiable human activity is taking place at some level in both hemispheres. The important contribution that McGilchrist (2019) makes is to suggest that it is *how* and not *what* is done that is different in each hemisphere. He has dedicated his life to understanding why every known creature with a neuronal system has a system that is asymmetrical, as has been discussed at length in this chapter so far. The question that intrigued him is why did we evolve an asymmetrical system, when the world and environment we interact with is not asymmetrical? His argument is that the brain exists to make connections, so why is it divided? And why is the corpus callosum, the major connection between these hemispheres, getting smaller and more inhibitory in its function as we evolve, and not larger and more functionally facilitatory? According to him, people are right when they object to the idea that each hemisphere is involved with everything we do. At the same time, they are wrong if they believe there are no differences. He believes that we have been misled in trying to describe *what* each hemisphere does. Rather we should be looking at *how* each hemisphere does it.

The hemispheres are more connected within themselves than they are connected to each other. And as McGilchrist (2019) argues, the biggest division in the brain is between the two hemispheres, which allows them to function relatively independently of each other. For example, even though the visual pathways of each human brain hemisphere are similar, how the world is seen phenomenologically is not the same. Interhemispheric information transfer is therefore still important, because we need both hemispheres to see the whole and at the same time be able to focus on the detail.

Drawing on neurological research, McGilchrist shows how the two hemispheres contribute to the richness in experience; and in explaining how this happens, he is inadvertently explaining Kolb's (1984) experiential learning cycle. It is the right hemisphere that tends to ground experience (Kolb's concrete experience), and it is seen as the physiological substrate of the unconscious. The left hemisphere then makes the implicit explicit (Kolb's reflective observation); it brings the world into focus. It tends to unpack, clarify and create meaning from what has been made explicit, allows it to be formulated in language, and in so doing becomes aware of its own awareness (Kolb's abstract conceptualisation). The conscious mind's activity therefore lies ultimately in the left hemisphere. The right hemisphere then takes what the left hemisphere has made conscious and produced, and reintegrates it with its own understanding (Kolb's active experimentation), thereby producing a new, more enriched whole and closing that loop of the experiential learning cycle. To learn effectively, the two hemispheres of the brain therefore need to cooperate. Even though each hemisphere has its own understanding of the world, the world we know and experience is synthesised from the "knowing" and the work of both hemispheres.

The hemisphere power struggle

McGilchrist's (2019) thesis is that despite the need for cooperation, the hemispheres are in fact involved in some sort of power struggle. This is because humans have two different modes of experience, and with them two fundamentally opposed realities. Yet each of these opposing realities are important in bringing about the recognisable human world. He believes that these differences are rooted in the bi-hemispheric structure of the brain. And which hemisphere's version of the world comes to predominate will determine our phenomenological experience of the world. Both McGilchrist (2019) and Hannaford (2005) argue there is evidence that individuals consistently prefer one hemisphere over the other. For Hannaford (2005), it is especially under times of duress or stress that this becomes more evident.

The important thing to remember is that both hemispheres seem to be involved in some way in almost everything we do as humans, and especially in almost all mental processes and mental states. Information is constantly conveyed between the hemispheres. And this information is transmitted in both directions several times a second. The corpus collosum is the main band of neural tissue that connects the two hemispheres and allows for the transmission of information and communication between them. Interestingly, as McGilchrist (2019) mentions, the bulk of the connection fibres are, however, there to inhibit. So, the main function of the corpus collosum is to stop the two hemispheres from interfering with each other, and to produce functional inhibition. Paradoxically, then, the corpus collosum is involved in both the transfer and inhibition of information between the hemispheres. And as McGilchrist (2019) points out, the severing of the corpus collosum through split-brain surgical procedures produces surprisingly little effect on patients' everyday functioning; they function quite normally.

As the brain evolved more asymmetry and increased in size, interhemispheric connectivity decreased. At the same time, there was an extraordinary expansion of the human frontal lobes, from 17 per cent of the total brain in the lesser apes to 35 per cent in humans. And the biggest difference between the former and latter is in the proportion of white matter, due to myelination. As was mentioned previously, myelination is the development of fatty sheaths covering the nerves and axons, which greatly increases the speed of information transmission. And interestingly, there is more white matter in the right hemisphere than in the left. Once again, one starts to see the integration of polyvagal theory (the myelinated ventral vagal nerve) and regulation theory (the more myelinated right hemisphere) on a physiological level.

With the evolution of the frontal lobes, however, humans gained the ability to stand back from the immediacy of their experience. They now had the ability to reflect on that experience, conceptualise what is going on, come up with plans and take control of the world instead of passively responding thereto. The frontal lobes therefore give humans the capability to reflect on their experience and to think in rational, simplified and objective ways. According to Stacey (2010), we abstract ourselves from this experience and create narratives and philosophies by generalising, simplifying and categorising the experiences as first-order abstractions. With the evolution of the frontal lobes, therefore, humans developed the ability to learn from their experience. According to McGilchrist (2019), this involves both going into the felt, lived world experience, and rising above the immediate experience, which humans do via reflection and conceptualising. Whatever one has learnt through this ascent needs to be brought back and integrated into the lived experience to enrich that experience. Here again, McGilchrist (2019) is referring to experiential learning, without explicitly calling it that. Going through this cycle enables humans to exploit and use their environment, and at the same time it enables humans to be more empathetic towards each other. It gives humans the ability to trust and betray their fellow human beings. And these abilities are what contribute to creating and maintaining complex responsive processes.

Lateralisation of function

One thing humans share with other vertebrates is the lateralisation of functions within the brain. McGilchrist (2019) emphasises that unlike humans, birds and animals do not experience the problems posed by the frontal lobes. They do, however, experience competing needs when it comes to paying attention to the environment they inhabit. A bird, for example, needs to narrowly focus its attention on a seed on the ground, to differentiate it from a small stone or piece of grit. Yet at the same time, while it is foraging for food it needs to pay attention to the bigger environment to be aware of possible predators. To overcome this challenge, parts of the brain are kept distinct so that the two functions do not interfere with each other. The bird uses its right eye (which works with the left hemisphere) to look for seeds on the ground, and the left eye (which works with the right hemisphere) to continuously scan the wider environment. It would therefore appear that an evolutionary advantage of lateralisation is that it enables the carrying out of dual-attention tasks.

McGilchrist (2019) suggests that the right hemisphere appears to be deeply involved with social functioning, which is in agreement with polyvagal theory and regulation theory. In the case of primates, it is involved with the expression of social feelings. In lower animals and birds, this seems to be the case as well where chicks, for example, use their left eyes (right hemisphere) to differentiate familiar members of the species from one another. He goes on to say that in most animal species, the right hemisphere is related to emotional responses, while the left hemisphere inhibits emotional responses. Just like animals, humans need to monitor two incompatible forms of attention at the same time: one being very narrowly focused on our needs, and the other being much more broadly focused on what is going on in the world at large. So, each hemisphere pays attention to the world in different but consistent ways. The left hemisphere has a narrow-focused attention and sees things abstracted from the context or environment; it will then reconstruct the whole from the parts. This is very different from the "Gestalt whole" to which the right hemisphere pays attention. The right hemisphere sees things in their context and as a whole, and as a result has a much wider breadth of attention. And, in agreement with polyvagal theory and regulation theory, McGilchrist (2019) stresses that empathy, understanding emotions and that way of paying attention to the world are functions of the right hemisphere.

A central hypothesis of McGilchrist (2019) is that how we pay attention to the world changes what we are paying attention to. In other words, how we pay attention to the world changes the world. The most important hemispheric difference lies in the type of attention that each hemisphere gives to the world. Not only are we shaped by our environment due to the type of attention we pay to it, but we alter it and become partners in its creation. This idea of co-creation is very similar to the idea of co-regulation as put forward in regulation theory and polyvagal theory. For example, if I see another person as a friend, the type of attention I will give that individual will be different to what I will give to the same individual if I see them as a potential enemy. The type of attention I give that individual will change the experience I have of that individual. Subjectively, the experience has changed, yet objectively nothing has changed. Do I see the planet as our living, evolving home that needs to be cared for, or as a material resource to be exploited for selfish capital gain? Depending on the attention chosen, different actions towards the planet will follow. As McGilchrist (2019) points out, the nature and direction of our attention makes us creators or co-creators of the world we inhabit and of ourselves. So, depending on the attention given to anything, that attention will determine what one finds. And the same applies to the brain, because it turns out that the hemispheres of the brain have different ways of constructing and experiencing the world. Despite the differences, we need both hemispheres to effectively experience and engage with the world.

Experience is unpredictable because it is constantly in motion; it is an endless flow. The challenge, however, is that for us to know anything it must have enduring properties, which is difficult when our experience of reality is a constantly changing flow. This takes us into the heart of the philosophical question of what consciousness is. According to the philosopher Christian de Quincey (2005), the world = things + experiences of those things. Things can be physical objects like matter or energy, or nonphysical objects which are mental content like thoughts and ideas. Experiences are what know the objects:

> Objects are what we know. Subjects (that's us) are what do the knowing.... Consciousness is what knows or feels or is aware ... without consciousness, all this world would be forever unknown and unfelt.... Therefore, consciousness is the ability that matter/energy has to feel, know, and direct itself.
>
> (De Quincey, 2005:79)

Therefore, for us to know and direct our experiences we need to step outside of the constant flow and the immediacy of our experience. According to McGilchrist (2019), to do this, the brain has to attend to the world in two very different ways, and thereby brings two different worlds into being. The first is a deeply lived experience of a unique individual world of complex, embodied, deeply connected, interdependent wholes in continuous flux, constantly forming and reforming. This is the world experienced through the right hemisphere. Here we experience the world pre-reflectively, holistically, before we divide it into bits. In this world the subjective and objective are held in suspension, and the two poles embrace each other in their togetherness. In the other world, our experience changes to a "re-presented" version of what is experienced in the right hemisphere. The left hemisphere brings about bounded, separate, essentially fragmented entities that are static and grouped into classes.

In this regard, McGilchrist's thinking is in agreement with that of the physicist David Bohm (1995). Bohm argued that relativity and quantum theory imply that the world should be looked at as an "undivided wholeness in flowing movement" (Bohm, 1995:11). He went on to talk about the implicate order and the explicate order of reality. Even though he did not explicitly talk about the left and right hemispheres of the brain, it is clear that the implicate order is primarily a right-hemisphere activity, while the explicate order is primarily a left-hemisphere activity.

Bohm tied these two ways of experiencing the world to human development, which is congruent with the development and maturing of the nervous system. Noting that humans are aware of movement from the earliest stages of life, sensing it mainly in the implicate order, he suggests that the implicate order is experienced much more immediately and directly than the explicate order, which requires learning a complex construction. One reason why we do not notice this primacy of the implicate order is that "we have become so habituated to the explicate order, and have emphasised it so much in our thought and language, that we tend strongly to feel that our primary experience is that which is explicate and manifest" (Bohm, 1995:206).

It is the left hemisphere that makes things explicit, and in so doing isolates and fixes things, making them mechanical and lifeless. Here the subjective and objective appear as separate poles. Yet this way of experiencing the world through the left hemisphere enables us to know things, to learn, to direct and make things.

The important thing to remember, even as we explore this difference, is that the brain is a dynamic system, and that anything we experience cannot be tied down to just one bit of the brain. There are no bits in the brain, there are only interconnected and integrated networks. One cannot, however, get away from the obvious differences that exist in the hemispheres. The right hemisphere is heavier, larger, longer and wider than the left. And for McGilchrist (2019), there must be a reason for that. As well as being bigger, the right hemisphere has more white matter (is more myelinated) than the left. According to McGilchrist (2019), this reflects the right's attention to the global picture and to facilitating communication across the regions. It must be open to everything that exists apart from ourselves, trying to avoid preconceptions as far as possible. It does not focus on what it already knows, it is associated with Kolb's (1984) concrete experience, being open to pure experience and the novelty it brings. Referring to several imaging and lesion studies, he concludes that the intensity of attention, which involves sustained attention, alertness and vigilance, is reliant on the right hemisphere. It dominates when it comes to global, flexible and broad attention. He points out that patients with a left-hemisphere lesion who have an intact right hemisphere prefer a global approach.

By contrast, the left hemisphere is the domain of selectivity (which involves divided and focused attention), transfers information within regions and prioritises local communication. The dominant attention mode is therefore narrow and focused. Patients with an intact left hemisphere and who suffer a right-hemisphere lesion tend to arrive at the overall picture by putting all the pieces together. The left hemisphere plays a critical role in processing our experiences. It must recognise whatever we experience through certain qualities that we categorise into similar experiences we have had before. And those experiences are associated with certain feelings and beliefs. The advantage is that it gives us the ability to predict and use what we know. It is associated with Kolb's (1984) reflective observation and abstract conceptualisation. It is very useful in that it allows us to come up with a hypothesis about what is going on and what to do, in response to what has just been experienced. The problem, however, as McGilchrist (2019) makes clear, is that this processing eventually becomes so automatic that we no longer experience the pure experiential world, but rather an abstracted conceptual idea or virtual reality, a represented world that we bring into being ourselves. It is a copy of the real world that exists conceptually in the mind, brought about by the left hemisphere's highly focused and selective attention.

As a result, anything that is new is first presented in the right hemisphere, before it comes into the focus of the left hemisphere. New experiences tend to come from the peripheral field of vision, and regardless of the side from which they come, it is the right hemisphere that directs attention to what is coming from the edges of awareness. McGilchrist (2019) mentions that it is not just new experiences, but the learning of any new information or skill, that engages more attention from the right hemisphere than the left. Even if it is learning to play a musical instrument, or the information is verbal in nature, it is first attended to by the right hemisphere. It is moved to the left hemisphere only once the skills have become familiar through practice. The left hemisphere deals with what is known and prefers what is known. It works with prediction and prioritises what is expected. This makes it very efficient at working with what is known and where things are predictable. Whenever the assumptions must be revised, however, it is not as efficient as the right. The right is far more efficient in flexibility of thought and set shifting, because it is responsible for inhibiting immediate responses to environmental stimuli and one's own immediate response to anything. As a result, it is more effective and efficient at exploring an array of possibilities and solutions to a problem. The left hemisphere tends to latch onto the single solution that seems to fit the situation the best. It sticks to what it knows.

It is no surprise that the three functional contributions that most neuropsychologists would choose of the right hemisphere, according to McGilchrist (2019), are the capacities to empathise, to read the human face and to sustain vigilant attention. This conforms with what is expressed in regulation theory and polyvagal theory. Because much of what happens in the right hemisphere is at an unconscious and implicit level, it is more difficult to express through language. As a result, this is often done through metaphor and narrative. Its view of the world is both/and, integrative, synthetic, inclusive and ambiguous. It sees the need for both hemispheres. The paradox is that this hemisphere is more multifaceted and harder to articulate, yet it already includes the left hemisphere's point of view, which often appears to stand in contradiction to that of the right hemisphere. So, at a "meta" level the right hemisphere can use the left hemisphere's preferred style, but not *vice versa*. This is because the right hemisphere has a greater degree of myelination, which facilitates greater connectivity and the quick transfer of information between the cortex and the centres below the cortex. (Which helps explain why the right hemisphere and ventral vagal system are central to regulation theory and polyvagal theory.) As a result, it is better at integrating different kinds of information from all the different senses and bringing them together in consciousness. This includes integrating information from memory, the eyes, ears and other sensory organs, and in so doing it helps to create the very complex but coherent experience we have of the world. This ability to integrate over time and space, together with the ability to pay attention to a broad field, being open to whatever might be, allows for the recognition of broad and complex patterns. As a result, the right hemisphere perceives and sees the "whole" big picture.

This rapid and complex integration is something of which the left hemisphere is not capable; because of its narrow focus of attention on the detail, it tends to perceive and take a local short-term view. McGilchrist (2019) mentions that a functional contribution of the left hemisphere is to aid the individual in grabbing stuff. Its evolutionary adaptation lies in the service of amassing things and grasping them; it specialises in utility. Secondly, it seems to prize simple answers to everything. Consistency is very important in left hemispherical thinking, hence the claim to explain everything that exists through the same mechanistic models. McGilchrist (2019) believes that this thinking is seen in those people who espouse reductionist science and technological solutions, and implement bureaucratic systems to deal with what are complex human problems. As a result, they often deny one aspect of irreconcilable problems. For example, if you cannot reconcile consciousness and matter, you just deny that one of them exists. Thirdly, the left hemisphere is the speaking hemisphere, and its worldview is easier to articulate. It relies on the literal aspects of language to make meanings explicit. Its view is either/or, fragmentary, exclusive and analytical. More importantly, it is not aware of what it is missing. It views the world in a simple, unambiguous way that is easy to articulate, and hence the truth is thought of as straightforward and single. It is this mechanistic world and atomistic society of the left hemisphere that has become the most dominant worldview in Western culture. This is because at a neural level, the left hemisphere is more closely interconnected within itself, hence the self-referencing nature of its worldview. It deals with the world that it already knows, the very world it created.

Attention hierarchy

The question then is, how do these two very different ways of attending to and experiencing the world relate to each other? McGilchrist (2019) suggests that the relationship is via an attention hierarchy. Any new experience is more likely to be registered and present in the right hemisphere, because that is where experience is grounded. In Kolb's (1984) language, it is our concrete experience. It is our global attention that comes first, and it takes precedence over what we pay attention to, and in so doing it guides whatever the left hemisphere will pay attention to at a detail and local level. So, the right hemisphere grounds our attention, and then it gets processed further in the left hemisphere. In Kolb's (1984) language, it would start the processes of reflective observation and abstract conceptualisation. The right hemisphere, therefore, controls where attention will be oriented towards, because exploratory attention of the right hemisphere has dominance. Once the priority has been established, the left hemisphere helps to grasp what has been prioritised. We tend to think that we build up a picture of something via a serial process of putting the bits together. But as McGilchrist (2019) points out, the building up of a picture from the bits is the way our left hemisphere consciously and verbally puts it together when asked to do so after the fact.

I put forward a similar argument in Lane, Kahn and Chapman (2019), in that whenever a model is written up, it appears to be logical, structured and neat. This applies to Kolb's (1984) experiential learning cycle as well. But learning conversations and learning can be very messy, and it is only after the fact, upon reflection, that we structure it into a neat, serial process. The truth is that we first experience and see reality as a whole or a Gestalt. That is because the right hemisphere is concerned with the whole. Whatever it receives from the senses, regardless of whether this comes from the left or right, it integrates into a single, complete world of experience. The left hemisphere, as McGilchrist (2019) emphasises, will be concerned only with the parts that it uses, that is right spaces and the right side of the body. This is borne out in split-brain patients where the left hemisphere attends only to the right visual field, while the right hemisphere will attend to the entire visual field. The left hemisphere breaks the whole into parts to grasp it physically and mentally for utility.

So, the paradox is that this attention hierarchy is more like a cycle. It starts off in the right hemisphere, which grounds and integrates the experience; attention is then shifted to the left hemisphere where it is manipulated, and finally it is returned to the right hemisphere. Or as McGilchrist (2019) puts it, the right-to-left-to-right progression. Once again, this is the same cycle we see in Kolb's (1984) experiential learning cycle. Everything starts as concrete experience (right hemisphere), and to make sense of the experience we start to reflect on it (reflective observation), and form some hypothesis about what is going on, or what our next action will be (abstract conceptualisation). Both of those aspects seem to be activities of the left hemisphere. Finally, we must act on what was reflected on or conceptualised (active experimentation), which in McGilchrist's terms would be the reintegration into the right hemisphere.

The right sees the whole as a Gestalt; it is not based on the summation of the parts. Due to it seeing everything in context and its integrative power, its understanding is based on recognising complex patterns, not through putting bits of information together, but as the Gestalt "aha" moment. The left breaks the whole into its parts in an attempt to "know" it, through reflection and abstract conceptualisation. Because it is an abstraction it is decontextualised, and can fall into the trap of slavishly following the internal logic of the situation, even if that logic contradicts the lived experience in that moment. Yet its intellectual power, according to McGilchrist (2019), is exactly its ability to decontextualise things through abstraction and then to categorise them. It is superior at identifying simple figures and shapes. It re-presents what presents in the right hemisphere by creating abstract classes of things and storing these as information that does not change across specific instances. By contrast, the right is more global and holistic, and deals with things as they are encountered in the real world and in context. It is especially concerned with the relations between things in the context of the world, and the uniqueness and individuality of each existing being and thing. Its ability to process things holistically enables the right hemisphere to recognise individuals as Gestalt wholes through the integration of things like their faces, voices and gaits. These are all cues that are important in polyvagal theory and regulation theory.

It is important to emphasise McGilchrist's central argument again, that it is not *what* is done in each hemisphere but *how* it is done that is important. Both hemispheres work with units and aggregates, for example, but how they work with them, and the mode of attention that is utilised in each case, is profoundly different. The right will see individuals (units) within an undivided contextual whole (an aggregate). The left will see parts (units) as belonging to a category (an aggregate) that it has abstracted from the context. Hannaford (2011) provides a very simplified summary of what McGilchrist is talking about (see Table 2.1). According to her, the functions are transposed in some individuals; as a result, she prefers to refer to the left hemisphere as the logical hemisphere and the right hemisphere as the Gestalt hemisphere.

As can be seen from Table 2.1, both hemispheres are involved with language, sports, art and music, to name but a few. The truth is, both are involved with everything we do. But it is how they are involved that differs. Because the right hemisphere sees things in their context, it is more interested in the personal, in others as individuals, and in whatever is living. It is the mediator of empathy and social behaviour. It is particularly good at identifying the facial expression of emotions, especially as it relates to individual faces. This is because the right hemisphere is more intimately connected with the limbic system, the ancient subcortical system that is involved with all kinds of emotions. As a result, the right hemisphere is deeply connected to the self as embodied, because of its capacity for emotion and its ability to understand how others feel by reading the cues from their tone of voice, facial expression and body language. These cues and emotional shifts are picked up in the observer's right hemisphere within 300–400 milliseconds. It experiences our body as something that is part of our identity. By contrast, the left sees and experiences the body as something from which we are relatively detached. It is just another thing in the world like all other things. The implication of this, according to Schore (2019), is that we have two self-images. One is consciously maintained, and

Table 2.1 Summary of differences between the brain's hemispheres

Logic left hemisphere	Gestalt right hemisphere
Processes from pieces to the whole.	Processes the whole then deals with pieces.
Parts of language.	Language comprehension.
Syntax, semantics.	Image, emotion, meaning.
Letters, printing, spelling, sentences.	Rhythm, dialect, application, flow.
Numbers.	Estimation, application.
Analysis, logic, linear.	Intuition, estimation.
Techniques.	Flow and movement.
Looks for differences.	Looks for similarities.
Controls feelings.	Oriented towards experiences and feelings.
Language-oriented.	Prefers drawing, manipulation.
Sequential thinking.	Simultaneous thinking.
Future-oriented.	Present-oriented.
Time-conscious.	Less time-conscious.
Structure-oriented.	People-oriented.
Sports (hand-eye/foot placement).	Sports (flow and rhythm).
Art (media, tool use, how to).	Art (image, emotion, flow).
Music (notes, beat, tempo).	Music (passion, rhythm, image).

Source: Adapted from Hannaford (2011:90).

the other is almost wholly unconscious. In most people, the conscious self-image is associated with the left hemisphere. This self-image is, however, also subject to unconscious influences. Indeed, sometimes the conscious self-image is fashioned in reaction to unconscious feelings, traumas and feared inadequacies that the person does not want to possess. Yet despite that, it nevertheless or unconsciously maintains those traumas, inadequacies and feelings. By contrast, the unconscious self-image is maintained within the right hemisphere. It is influenced by the current and the experience of how the two self-images interact.

The left hemisphere is concerned with what it knows. As a result, it likes things that are human-made, because it knows this inside-out and it provides certainty. They are not living things, and they can be represented schematically, geometrically and abstractly. It develops rules for how the world operates because it needs certainty and it needs to be right. The right hemisphere is concerned with experience, living things that are constantly changing and moving. As a result, it is constantly new and beyond our grasp. The right hemisphere has a tolerance for uncertainty, and the ability to hold several ambiguous possibilities together without having to choose one outcome. These differences between how the hemispheres prefer to deal with the world show up in the way that we tend to communicate with each other, as put forward by the physicist David Bohm. Bohm taught us the difference between dialogue (right hemisphere) and debate (left hemisphere). For example, dialogue involves equality and respect between partners; whereas debate is about winning or losing, about trying to prove a point. Dialogue is aimed at finding out new possibilities, and learning through inquiry and disclosure; while debate is about "knowing", and aims to defend one's position by persuading. Dialogue uses questions, and enquires into assumptions; while debate asserts "answers", and justifies or defends assumptions. Dialogue is able to see connections and relationships, to see the whole encompassing the parts, thereby creating shared meaning among many; whereas debate sees only differences and distinctions, breaks problems into parts, and chooses one meaning among many (Zohar, 1997:139).

I had previously been under the impression that one way of communication was preferable to the other. I now understand that we need both, depending on the environment; yet one might be more relevant than the other at a particular point in time. In times of certainty, debate might be the way to go; whereas in times of uncertainty, dialogue might be more appropriate. It gets back to McGilchrist's point, that both are ways of communicating, but how it is done in each hemisphere is very different.

The problem with the left hemisphere (and debate), as McGilchrist (2019) points out, is that it tends to do more of what it is already doing and already knows, as if it were stuck in a hall of mirrors from which it cannot escape. By contrast, the right hemisphere (and dialogue) sees the whole and the broader perspective, and can espouse more than one point of view. It can accommodate both its own and the left hemisphere's perspectives, whereas the latter can accommodate only its own perspective. Each lead us to experience the world in different ways, and yet both are essential.

According to McGilchrist (2019), the first way to experience the world is to be fully present to things with all their interconnections, impermanence and changeability. It is to be part of the whole that is forever flowing and in flux. Subjectively, we experience ourselves as being connected and part of the whole and not isolated from an objective world. Hence the right hemisphere pays attention to the "other", everything that exists apart from ourselves. It is deeply relational in that it is given life by these relationships. It is essentially an encounter with something or someone other to us. It is the kind of knowledge that allows for a sense of the uniqueness of the other. This experience and knowledge is not easily captured in words because it is not certain or fixed. We experience the whole as a Gestalt moment and not by trying to list the parts. It is the knowledge we gain from one being coming together with another person, as a whole. It is subjective and changes from person to person. The way I experience another person can be totally different to how you experience them. We know this world through our concrete experience, we are fully and openly immersed in the experience. In German, this way of knowing is known as *kennen*. To *kennen* something is to never fully know it, because it is forever in flux, in a flow, evolving and changing. This speaks to knowing the world through Kolb's (1984) concrete experience. It is the domain of the right hemisphere.

The second way is to detach ourselves, to step outside the flow of our concrete experience and to re-present that experience and the world through abstract conceptualisation. Here we abstract, fragment and compartmentalise the experience of the whole into static bits, pieces of information that are impersonal, disengaged, certain and fixed. We make the experience and the world explicit, less truthful yet more useful for manipulation, which gives us a sense of power to know it and to operate thereon. It is the knowledge we gain from what we call facts. It is the only knowledge recognised by science because it has certainty, and it is fixed. It does not change from person to person, and the context is irrelevant because its findings are repeatable, which is its strength. In German this way of knowing is known as *wissen*. To *wissen* something is to pin it down so that it is repeatable and becomes routine and familiar. It is a self-contained virtual world that the left hemisphere creates. This speaks to knowing the world through Kolb's (1984) abstract conceptualisation.

Dialectical synthesis

The danger is to believe or see it as an antagonistic relationship, where the one hemisphere negates the other, or at worst that they merely complement each other. McGilchrist (2019) believes that their incompatibility allows for a dialectical synthesis; it allows for something new to arise. So, we are back to the central thesis of McGilchrist's book. Everything new starts off in the right hemisphere, which grounds and integrates the new experience; attention is then shifted to the left hemisphere where it is manipulated and becomes familiar, and finally it is returned to the right hemisphere, what he calls the right-to-left-to-right progression. And just like the experiential learning cycle, this is a never-ending process. Is this the physiological explanation or basis for the dialectical process of thesis, antithesis and synthesis of the German philosopher Hegel (1770–1831)? McGilchrist (2019) sees the gaining of knowledge and our understanding of the world as this dialectical process. We have an experience (registered in the right hemisphere); we reflect on it and then compare it conceptually (in the left hemisphere) to something we already know, by observing the similarities and differences; then we act on it (returning it to the right hemisphere).

McGilchrist (2019) goes so far as to suggest that although both hemispheres contribute to our knowledge of the world, and both need to be synthesised, the right hemisphere has precedence. This is because only the right hemisphere can synthesise into a whole what both hemispheres know. The right hemisphere does not have to synthesise its own experience of the world, because it already experiences it as a whole; it does not break things into parts, so it does not have to integrate. The right hemisphere has only to synthesise and integrate what the left has broken into parts, analysed and turned into something else. It also has precedence in terms of experience because anything new is delivered first to the right hemisphere. And as was mentioned by Schore (2019) and McGilchrist (2019), the processing of preconscious and unconscious information, including social understanding, happens in the right hemisphere because it is in direct contact with the embodied, lived world.

It is only after information has been presented to the right hemisphere that the left gets to re-present it and make it conscious by bringing it into focus, making it explicit and formulating it into language. In so doing, the left hemisphere helps to unpack the experience by using structure and certainty and forcing the implicit to become explicit. Without it, there would be only pure experience. It is therefore a staging post in the processing of experience. But if the process stops there, there would be only abstract concepts, so it must be returned to the world of experience. Simply put, the process starts in the right hemisphere, the left hemisphere makes it explicit and analyses it, and finally the right reaches a synthesis of left and right. The re-presented, virtual world of the left is reintegrated and returned to the embodied lived world of experience as a new synthesis and transformed into something new. Once again, McGilchrist (2019) is explaining Kolb's (1984) experiential learning cycle on a physiological level. McGilchrist (2019), Schore (2019) and Hannaford (2005) all agree that the most important hemispheric difference lies in the type of attention that each hemisphere gives to the world. Not only are we shaped by our environment due to the type of attention we pay thereto, but we alter it and become partners in its creation through the process of experiential learning.

The connection between experiential learning and the neocortex

Kolb and Kolb (2017) mention that James Zull, a professor of biology and a colleague of theirs, was the first to make explicit to them the connection between neocortex regions and experiential learning. For Zull (2011), Kolb's experiential learning theory runs parallel with the biology of how the nervous system works. Zull (2011) suggests that sensing (concrete experience), remembering (reflective observation), theorising (abstract conceptualisation) and acting (active experimentation) engage different regions of the neocortex, and that these are the four pillars of learning.

Concrete experiences, whatever they may be, are presented in the sensory and post-sensory part of the cortex. As we start to reflect on the experiences, this takes place in the temporal integrative cortex. Abstract conceptualisation happens in the frontal integrative cortex, and active experimentation takes place in the premotor and motor cortex. This is obviously a gross oversimplification, as any model of reality is, of many complex processes going on all over the brain. The point Zull is trying to make is that the underlying biological structure of the brain is the foundation for experiential learning. We all have the same foundation; we all have the four main lobes and a left and right hemisphere. As a result, there are certain functions and aspects of the brain that remain the same. He refers to these aspects as being part of certain "constancies", and these are the aspects provided by nature. There are three categories of "constancy":

1   The physical world with its objective structures and processes.
2   The human brain with its structures and connections.
3   The processes in the brain, in terms of how connections are modified, plus the time involved in those modifications that then lead to change (Zull, 2011).

Expanding on this concept, Zull (2011) suggests that the purpose of the brain is to produce behaviour. And by behaviour, he means movements that result from actions of the skeletal muscles. The first problems that any human must solve are movement problems. In fact, movement was one of the first problems our evolving ancestors had to solve as they moved out of water onto land. The main job of the brain is therefore to take sensory data and generate action therefrom. And this action can be under conscious or unconscious control. Whether that sensory data relate to a simple reflex or complex task, for the nervous system to function it needs physical movement. All sensory data are recorded or presented in the back of the cortex, and are then moved to the front of the cortex which is responsible for movement and action.

Left and right hemisphere lateralisation is found in all humans and primates. As well as the recording of sensory input at the back of the cortex, it is moved to the front of the cortex for action, combined with the basic functions of sensory, motor and integration in different regions of the cortex. This structure and function are a given of nature. Zull (2011) believes that this results in certain natural "constancies" of the integrative cortex.

In agreement with Hannaford, Porges, Schore and McGilchrist, he sees the right hemisphere as being responsible for the big picture and the left hemisphere as being responsible for details. The back region of the integrative cortex is responsible for receiving information and for identifying "what" is happening and "where" it is happening. The manipulating of the "what" and "where" information to plan and create future actions happens in the front regions of the integrative cortex. At the same time, the identifying and manipulating of the "what" for both the big picture and detailed views of the world happen in the bottom part of the integrative cortex, whereas the "where" happens in the top part of the integrative cortex. At a very broad and high level, this allowed Zull to identify the following eight broad functions of nature's integrative cortex that are "constancies" in all humans and primates:

1   Identify the parts in the big picture.
2   Manipulate those parts in the big picture.
3   Perceive the relationships in the big picture.
4   Manipulate the relationships in the big picture.
5   Identify the parts of the detail.

6 Manipulate those parts in the detail.
7 Perceive the relationships in the detail.
8 Manipulate the relationships in the detail (Zull, 2011:226).

These general structures and functions of the brain are provided by nature, and they give us the amazing capacity to learn from our experience and how to survive in our environment. Zull (2011) is, however, in agreement with Schore, McGilchrist, Porges and Hannaford that the brain learns and changes itself through experience, which leads to the development of the mind. It is through the sensing, recording and reproducing of experiences that the individual's brain learns to think, decide and act. And the brain, along with the autonomic nervous system, does this in response to its environment. As it develops its responses and learns to survive in that environment, it develops into a mind. He is therefore in agreement with Schore's theory of mind/brain/body. According to Zull (2011), the biological foundations might be the same, but the resulting mind that develops through experience and nurturing is completely unique and unpredictable in every individual. He makes the point that minds cannot be categorised in any reliable way because they are each so unique. Similarly, I subscribe to the same definition of "mind" as Porges (2021:123): "One can view the mind as a process that establishes a network to support the flow of energy and information between the body, brain, and relationships." And the relational nature of the mind enables connections with the environment and other people.

Here Zull is in agreement with Jan Smuts, because his view of the uniqueness of every mind is similar to Smuts's (1973) idea of "personology" and the uniqueness of every individual. Although Smuts (1973) saw the mind as the "most important and conspicuous constituent" of this evolutionary process, the body is an integral part that gives "the intimate flavour of humanity to Personality" (Smuts, 1973:261). The whole is, however, more important than the parts:

> Mind and Body are elements in the whole of personality; and ... this whole is an inner creative, recreative and transformative activity, which accounts for all that happens in the Personality as between its component elements.
> (Smuts, 1973:261–262)

There is therefore a "creative Holism in Personality". Even though my body and mental structure can have some resemblance to my parents and ancestors, my personality is indisputably mine. The personality is not inherited; it is a creative novelty in every human being that makes every person a unique individual. Smuts (1973:262) called this the science of "Biography". I would now argue that this science of "Biography" is the study of how the individual learns from experience and in so doing becomes a unique mind and personality, even though we have the same biological foundations. For example, the physical connections between neurons can result in memory, but using the resulting memories to solve problems is a function of mind according to Zull (2011), and that is a unique process. So how does this uniqueness develop from the biological foundations and experiential learning?

Hannaford's physiology of learning

We have already seen that polyvagal theory and regulation theory provide some of the explanation for the development of this uniqueness from the same biological foundations. Polyvagal theory taught us that the autonomic nervous system continually scans the environment through neuroception for cues of safety and threats, and then triggers the appropriate behaviours unconsciously. What is safe for one individual might be a threat for another, so over time the nervous system has learnt what is safe or a threat for that individual. And from regulation theory we learnt that many of those cues for safety or threat are formed in early attachment with the primary caregiver. In both these theories, we see the elements of nature (same physiological structure) and nurture (learning to respond to the environment) at work.

Hannaford (2005, 2011) reiterates that how we learn is firstly determined by our safety and the quality of our relationships with our caregivers. Our learning starts in the womb. She mentions that if the mother is stressed, the foetus will react with basic reflexive moments in response to that stress, and in so doing the foetus is learning the survival response. On the other hand, if the mother is peaceful and joyful, the foetus will explore ever more complex movements, thereby growing and developing the brain. In her work, Hannaford shows how the sensory-motor systems of the body have an influence on the human brain's ability to adapt and reorganise itself, and thereby contribute to the development of the unique minds in all of us. Given what we have learnt from polyvagal theory and regulation theory, and the structure and function of the brain, she sums it up as follows: "Learning is a highly natural process, invigorated by our interactions with other people through our sensory-motor experiences and sense of connectedness and appreciation" (Hannaford, 2011:13). The essence of her work is that learning involves not only the brain but the whole body; the mind cannot exist without the body.

As Zull (2011) mentioned, the purpose of the brain is to produce behaviour. And by behaviour he means movements that result from actions of the skeletal muscles. That is because the entire brain structure, according to Hannaford (2005), is intimately connected to and developed by the movement mechanisms of the body. Emotional safety and physical movement play a critical role in the creation of nerve cell networks. And these cell networks, which make up the entire nervous system, are fundamental to learning because the nervous system is a dynamic, self-organising system. Because these neural wirings and networks develop in response to our life experiences, the nervous system is never static, and it does not follow a master plan. It is unique to every individual. The more we move and learn, the more the neural pathways connect in highly complex patterns. And this plasticity gives our nervous systems enormous potential to grow and change. In fact, we are all designing and redesigning our own complex nervous systems through our interaction and response with the environment. As we receive sensory stimulation and initiate movements for action, our nerve cells connect with other nerve cells and form networks, which is learning.

Neurons are nerve cells that specialise in transmitting electrical messages throughout the body. Although no two neurons are the same, Hannaford (2005) mentions that there are three main types of neuron: sensory, intermediate and motor. All sensory information is brought to the central nervous system (brain and spinal cord) via sensory neurons. This sensory information comes from the ears, eyes, nose, tongue, skin and proprioceptors. (Proprioceptors are sense organs located throughout the muscles, tendons, joints and the inner ear. Their function is to provide the central nervous system with information concerning balance, muscle position and tension, and joint activity.) The intermediate neurons bring all this information together in the spinal cord and the brain, process it, and initiate action by sending information to the appropriate motor neurons that originate in the brain. The motor neurons then carry the messages to the various glands and muscles to activate the appropriate action.

Bundles of these neurons are what form nerves. The more that each neuron is activated and used, the more myelin is laid down over the neuron. (As mentioned previously, myelin is the fatty deposit that insulates the nerve and increases the speed of nerve impulses.) As we initiate movements in response to the sensory stimuli that we have received, the neurons form extensions called dendrites. These dendritic extensions bring the nerve cells into communication with other nerve cells. And as they do that, they form ever-increasingly complex, interconnected networks of neural pathways. These pathways are in a continuous state of becoming and changing, depending on the amount of stimulation they receive or do not receive. It is through these pathways that our thoughts and reactions travel as electrochemical impulses.

As Hannaford (2005) points out, the neurons with the most connections (an average of 300 000) are located in the cerebellum, which is the primary movement centre of the brain. For her, this points to just how important movement and experience are to learning. In her view, our nervous system is a free-form information network, and depending on which way our experience pushes us we custom-design our own nervous system to meet the demands of the environment. Eventually, we build base patterns of neurons, on which we continue to build all our lives. In other words, these neural pathways develop mostly as a result of stimulation and experience gained from interacting with our environment. We bring in information and build the neural networks from the experiences we have, which in turn allows us to use that information to make sense of our world and to thrive therein. A big part of experience is sensory input that we receive via our sensory organs. This plasticity of the nervous system in response to our experiences allows for thought, creativity, and life-long learning and development.

Nerve nets are developed first in the reptilian brain (or basal ganglia as it is known in humans), because it is the first to develop, and in evolutionary terms is the oldest part of the brain. The basal ganglia consist of the brainstem, cerebellum, pons and medulla oblongata. As was mentioned previously in the discussion of polyvagal theory, both vagal pathways originate in neighbouring parts of the medulla oblongata (the part of the brainstem that connects to the spinal cord). The main task of the medulla oblongata is self-preservation. And it does this by monitoring the outer world through the exteroceptors, our external senses. According to the psychiatrist Harald Blomberg (2015), these include visual, tactile, kinaesthetic or proprioceptive, and vestibular senses. The medulla oblongata then activates the appropriate physical responses and movements to the sensory input by relaying signals to the motor organs. All sensations will first go through the brainstem, then to the limbi and/or neo-cortex for interpretation. When we sleep, for example, we close down the basal ganglia, and we do not receive information from or react to the outer world. In addition, the brainstem directs respiration, heart activity and other life-sustaining processes. As a result, the basal ganglia are responsible for the brain/mind's survival imperative. Along with the vagal nerve, they initiate the fight, flight or freeze response in response to danger or stress. This part of the brain develops prenatally, and according to Hannaford (2005), during the first 15 months after birth we develop 100 trillion nerve cells that link all the senses and muscle movements.

The next to develop is the limbic system, which consists of the thalamus, hypothalamus, basal ganglia, amygdala and hippocampus. It is the area of the brain that lies between the basal ganglia and the cerebral cortex, and it is where most of our emotional processing occurs. All incoming senses except smell are relayed via the thalamus, and at the same time it relays motor impulses from the cerebral cortex through the brainstem to the muscles. The hypothalamus controls our waking and sleeping states, body temperature, food intake and the pituitary gland, as well as being involved in aggression, rage, pain and pleasure. The amygdala is involved in bodily states related to emotions, especially facial expressions and body language, and has links to brain areas involved with cognitive processing. It is responsible for coord-inating bodily reactions that serve as internal warnings, thereby enabling us to assess a situation and respond appropriately with anxiety and fear or happiness. It plays a central role in polyvagal theory and regulation theory by unconsciously adjusting our behaviours; for example, in response to facial cues. Throughout life, new nerve cell growth occurs in the hippocampus. It forms short-term memories by using incoming sensory input from the thal-amus, movement coordination in the basal ganglia, and emotions from the hypothalamus. With nerve net activation in the hippocampus, these short-term memories can become long-term memories throughout the body and brain.

The hippocampus is the seat of our episodic memories, which are memories of events we have experienced personally. It is therefore responsible for our experience of individuality.

Impulses between the cerebellum and the frontal lobe are connected and organised by the basal ganglia to help control body movements, especially fine motor control of facial and eye muscles which communicate our emotional states. And it is these fine motor control movements that are critical in both polyvagal theory and regulation theory. The basal ganglia play an important role in coordinating thoughts involved in planning the order and timing of future behaviours. Combined, these systems that make up the limbic system play a crucial role as an emotional filter of all our experiences of the world, in that they help us to determine the meaning, value and survival potential of each of these experiences. And they do this in the light of all of our past experiences. Our emotions help us to interpret our experiences and shape our view of the world and how we respond thereto. As we have seen, it can engage the social engagement system or trigger the fight, flight or freeze response.

As Hannaford (2005) stresses, objectively, every experience is simply an event; but 80 per cent of what we perceive is shaped by how we pay attention thereto. Here she is in agreement with McGilchrist's (2019) central hypothesis that how we pay attention to the world changes what we are paying attention to. In other words, how we pay attention to the world changes the world. Both agree that we change our reality by choosing what we pay attention to and focus on. Our emotions colour the perceived event and determine how we respond to it, and the limbic system plays a critical role in that learning process. In fact, Hannaford (2005) emphasises that to learn and remember something, the wiring of the limbic system shows that there must be sensory input, movement and a personal emotional connection. As with sensory development, the neural network of the limbic system must be developed, and this is done through exploring and expressing emotions, as was discussed in regard to polyvagal theory and regulation theory. It is with the development of the limbic system that we see things in context for the first time. It enables us to understand our place in society and our relationship to everything else.

Every sensory experience we have therefore starts in the brainstem or reptilian brain. It then moves through the limbic system (thalamus) which monitors the sensations and incorporates emotions. Finally, it is consciously realised in the last part of the brain to evolve and develop, the most plastic part, the neocortex. The neocortex is the thin layer that covers the cerebrum. The latter is the largest part of the human brain. The neocortex contains 10 to 20 billion nerve cells and approximately 85 per cent of the total neurons of the brain, even though it makes up only one-fourth of the brain's total volume. The grey matter of the neocortex, which is unmyelinated cell bodies of neurons, gives it its plasticity, which enables it to have an unlimited ability to form new dendrites and reorganise dendritic patterns in response to new experiences.

The white matter, myelinated axons, carry sensory information to the neo-cortex very fast, and then carry its motor commands to the body.

At birth, the neocortex constitutes only 25 per cent of its adult weight, and it then starts to grow by increasing dendrites and glial cells in response to taking in sensory experiences and creating mental models of the world. It is the trans-action among the sensory, emotional and motor areas of the brain that allows us to create meaning from our sensory experiences. We organise our experi-ence by developing the base patterns, which in turn involves the four different lobes contained in each hemisphere of the cerebrum:

- The *occipital lobe* is the primary visual area. It receives sensory input from the eyes, and interprets movement, shape and colour. It relates pre-sent to past visual experiences.
- The *temporal lobe* is the primary auditory area, and interprets the characteristics of rhythm, sound, and pitch. It is the vestibulo area receiving sensations from the semi-circular canals of the inner ear, and dealing with balance and vibrational and gravitational sense.
- The *parietal lobe* is the general sensory area. It is responsible for proprio-ception, touch, pressure, heat, cold and pain. It is the somesthetic associ-ation area that integrates and interprets sensations.
- The *frontal lobe* is the primary motor area that controls muscles all over the body. It includes the frontal eye field area which controls the volun-tary scanning movements of the eye, and Broca's area, where thoughts are translated into speech.

These four lobes receive information and stimuli via the brainstem and limbic system and from the opposite side of the body, because the brain has a crossover pattern where each side of the body communicates with the opposite brain hemisphere. This information is then collected from the four lobes in each hemisphere and integrated in the gnostic area, organised and reorganised with sensory motor memories. As a result, we can understand new experiences based on considering our past experiences. In other words, in agreement with Zull (2011), Hannaford (2005) sees the physiological basis for experiential learning being the same in all humans. It is what nature has given us. Both hemispheres contain the four lobes and all the functions until specialisation, which is unique to every individual, starts to occur. It is the connections and neural networks that we make from birth onwards, and build up through nur-ture, that make us all unique:

> Indeed, these connections are ourselves, constantly moderating our experi-ence of the world, constantly changing as experience is integrated with connections we have already made. And they are expressed and embodied in the knowledge, competencies and skills that make every human being unique and irreplaceable.

> (Hannaford, 2011:79–80)

It must, however, be remembered that we develop base patterns of neurons on which we continue to build all our lives. In other words, these neural pathways develop mainly as a result of stimulation and experience gained from transacting with our environment. And as Hannaford (2005) points out, our first interaction with the environment is in the womb. Since survival is our most primary need, at around 9 weeks *in utero* as the Moro reflex for survival develops, we develop our first base pattern of neurons for survival. Hannaford (2011) believes it is at this time that we develop a lateral dominance, by developing a lead hand, foot, ear and eye to react quickly in a survival or stressful situation. For example, a new-born baby will turn their dominant ear out to listen for danger, whether they are lying on their stomach or back. If it perceives danger, the Moro reflex will be activated, and the arms and legs will fly open and shut and the baby will cry to either bring help or scare the intruder away.

These lateral dominance functions are established very early, and become the familiar way that we approach any new learning situation. Even though we do learn to grow beyond these lateral profiles as we learn new adaptive strategies and skills, these basal connections and profiles can and will influence our behaviour throughout our lives. This is especially so when we are confronted with novel situations and when we are under stress. Hannaford (2005) mentions that under stress it is not uncommon for individuals to exhibit a preference for left (analytical) or right (Gestalt) processing. Using a preferred hemisphere is a more efficient pattern to react quickly in a survival or stressful situation than using both hemispheres. Although it is an efficient reactive pattern, it is only when we use both hemispheres of the brain that we are proficient at anything and function more intelligently. Two examples of this would be creativity and use of language. Creativity is not exclusively a function of the right hemisphere; it requires flow, image and emotion from the right hemisphere, plus logic and technique from the left hemisphere. In the same way, efficient use of language requires emotion, image and dialect from the right hemisphere, and words, proper sentence structures and verbalisation from the left hemisphere. Like everything we do in life, these two examples are whole-brain processes. The same can be said for experiential learning; for it to be optimal and effective, we need whole-brain processing.

Integration of physiology development and Kolb's experiential learning cycle

A fundamental hypothesis of this book is that by integrating knowledge of the physiology and development of the central and autonomic nervous systems with experiential learning theory, we get a better understanding of how experiential learning develops, and how we develop and become the unique personalities that we are. An extension of that hypothesis is that different physiological states will have a direct impact on the quality and effectiveness of experiential learning. Table 2.2 provides an approximation of how and when experiential

Table 2.2 Landmarks of cerebral neocortex development and experiential learning

Hannaford's landmarks of cerebral neocortex development	*Kolb's experiential learning cycle*
Reptilian brain (conception to 15 months old)	*The exploration/mimicry cycle*
Basic survival needs; sensory development; motor development.	Starts off as simple reflex-stimulus and response process. Later starts to move into exploration and mimicry. The stage of sensory motor development. Involves cycling through sensory and post-sensory, and premotor and motor areas of cortex.
Limbic system/relationship (15 months to 4.5 years old)	*The exploration/mimicry cycle*
Understanding of self/others, self/emotions, self/language. Emotional exploration; language exploration/communication; imagination; gross motor proficiency; memory development; social development.	More complex exploration and mimicry. Starts to copy sensory information and repeating it in actions like talking. It is still the embodied mind where perception and responses are outside of conscious awareness, and tied to the specific context.
Gestalt (right) hemisphere elaboration (4.5 to 7 years old)	*The exploration/mimicry cycle*
Whole-picture processing/cognition. Image, movement, rhythm, emotion, intuition. Outer speech, integrative thought.	Gestalt hemisphere elaboration is usually outside of conscious awareness. It is a function of the right hemisphere.
Logic (left) hemisphere elaboration (7 to 9 years old)	*The instructional/recall learning cycle*
Detail and linear processing/cognition. Refinement of language. Reading and writing skills. Technique development: music, art, sports, dance, manual training.	Emphasises cycling between frontal integrative cortex and temporal integrative cortex. With it comes development of reflection and working with abstract information – strengths of left hemisphere.
Frontal lobe elaboration (8 years old)	*The instructional/recall learning cycle*
Fine motor development. Inner speech (control of social behaviour). Fine motor eye teaming for tracking and two-dimensional focus.	As the instruction/recall cycle develops it does not replace or negate the exploration/mimicry cycle.
Increased corpus callosum elaboration and myelination (9 to 12 years old)	*Emergence of the full experiential learning cycle*
Whole-brain processing.	Involves reflection, forming of abstract plans and ideas, and acting on them.

Table 2.2 Cont.

Hannaford's landmarks of cerebral neocortex development	Kolb's experiential learning cycle
Hormonal emphasis (12 to 16 years old)	The experiential learning cycle
Learning about body, self, others, community and meaningful living through social consciousness.	Involves reflection, forming of abstract plans and ideas, and acting on them.
Refining cognitive skills (16 to 21 years old)	The experiential learning cycle
Whole mind/body processing, social interaction, future planning and play with new ideas and possibilities.	Involves reflection, forming of abstract plans and ideas, and acting on them.
Elaboration and refinement of the frontal lobes (21+ years old)	The experiential learning cycle
Global/systems thinking. High-level formal reasoning. Refinement of emotions. Insight. Refinement of fine motor skills.	Involves reflection, forming of abstract plans and ideas, and acting on them.

Source: Adapted from Hannaford (2005) and Kolb and Kolb (2017).

learning develops, in terms of the underlying physiology that has to develop to enable the experiential learning cycle.

The first cycle that develops is what Kolb and Kolb (2017) refer to as the "exploration/mimicry learning cycle". This learning cycle first shows up in the developing child as a simple reflex of stimulus and response which involves no intervening cognitive activity. It is the predominant learning cycle from conception until about the age of 7. It is the true embodied mind that receives ongoing perceptions and responds to the immediate context in which it is embedded. And most of this happens outside of conscious awareness, which as we have seen happens in the right hemisphere. This cycle happens as it continuously cycles through the motor and sensory cortex working with concrete experience and actions.

The next cycle to develop is what Kolb and Kolb (2017) refer to as the "instruction/recall learning cycle", which prefers to work with abstract conceptualisation and reflective observation, and tends to focus on learning second-hand knowledge. It does this by cycling through the frontal integrative cortex and the temporal integrative cortex. It works with information in the form of language, images and abstract symbols that are usually received via visual and auditory senses. This usually happens around the age of 7 to 9, when the logic (left) hemisphere elaborates. It is the learning cycle that is strongly shaped by culture and by traditional formal educational practices.

Between the ages of 9 and 12, there is an increase in corpus callosum elaboration and myelination, and with that there is the development of whole-brain processing. It is most probably during the latter part of this period that the full experiential learning cycle starts to come into play for the first time. From here onwards, it seems to be the dominant cycle that we use under normal conditions. Kolb and Kolb (2017) mention that even with the mature capacity to use the full experiential learning cycle, we all retain the exploration/mimicry cycle. Once again, this is no surprise, as evolutionary development does not disregard what came before, but rather incorporates it and adds thereto. Like the hierarchical development of the autonomic nervous system and the brain, there is a hierarchical developmental process involved with the experiential learning cycle, which is natural as the experiential learning cycle is a function of the enabling physiology.

The brain–heart connection and experiential learning

According to Hannaford (2005), the quality of our learning, that is whether it is natural and easy or difficult and forgetful, is determined by the heart. In this regard, she is echoing what we have learnt from polyvagal theory and regulation theory about the connection between the heart and the brain via the vagus nerve. Childre and Martin (2000) refer to the discipline of neurocardiology, which combines the study of the heart and the nervous system, to show that the heart communicates with the body and the brain in three ways: biochemically (through hormones and neurotransmitters), biophysically (through pressure waves) and neurologically (through nerve impulses). And it is through these communication systems that the heart has an influence on the brain and the rest of the body. They mention that from a neuroscience perspective the heart qualifies as a brain in its own right, as it is an intricate network of neurotransmitters, neurons, support cells and proteins. And because of that, it is able to act independently of the brain. With every heartbeat, information on blood pressure, hormones and heart rate is sensed and processed by this heart–brain in the heart. It is then translated into neurological impulses and relayed to the brain via the vagus nerve and sympathetic afferent nerves in the spine to the medulla oblongata.

The medulla oblongata is that part of the brainstem that connects to the spinal cord, and is the origin of both the ventral and dorsal vagal system, as we discovered in regard to polyvagal theory. Childre and Martin (2000) mention that these neural messages from the heart affect neural activity in the cortex (higher thought and reasoning) as well as the amygdala (emotional centre). And in so doing, according to Hannaford (2005), emotions, senses and information are combined for learning to happen. Biochemically, the brain is affected by powerful hormones produced by the heart, including norepinephrine secreted by the intrinsic cardiac adrenergic cells, and atrio-natriuretic factor. The former can assist or decrease learning because its effect on the brain is to increase alertness and focus attention, but also to increase restlessness and anxiety; the latter affects the region of the brain that regulates emotions. Brain processes and learning can, therefore, be facilitated or hindered by the precise nature of the heart's input via the vagal nerve. In other words, our physiological state has a direct impact on the quality of our learning.

The impact of the ventral vagal state on experiential learning

When we are in the ventral vagal state (or the social engagement system is operational) we are in a safe, relaxed, secure and receptive state. In this state, the heart will register a coherent HRV pattern, and send a neural message to the amygdala to stay in this safe state. At the same time, the heart sends a message to the thalamus as well, which activates it to easily take in sensory information from the environment, and the prefrontal cortex can fully under-stand the sensory information coming in. As a result of this coherent state, the prefrontal cortex can learn this incoming information and remember it. This coherent state facilitates and leads to the production of new nerve cells in the hippocampus, and there is optimal hormonal functioning throughout the body due to the release of atrio-natriuretic factor and norepinephrine. In this state, learning is easy and happens naturally, and the two hemispheres of the brain are working together as an integrated whole. My hypothesis is that for experi-ential learning to happen easily and naturally, we need to be in a ventral vagal state. Although she does not explicitly say the same, Hannaford comes very close to explaining the experiential learning process in this state:

> According to researchers, in order to correctly perceive, learn from and remember our experiences, there must be coherent activity of clusters of neurons, especially in the prefrontal cortex in order to render unified scenes and meaning from all the diverse sensations in our environment.
>
> (Hannaford, 2011:88)

For Kolb (1984), the essence of experiential learning is to create meaning from our experiences. And, according to McGilchrist (2019), this happens because of the dialectical process where the new sensory information is picked up first in the right hemisphere, the left hemisphere makes it explicit and analyses it, and finally the right reaches a synthesis of left and right. The re-presented, vir-tual world of the left is reintegrated and returned to the embodied, lived world of experience as a new synthesis and transformed into something new, all of which is optimal in a ventral vagal state. Furthermore, in the ventral vagal state, Zull's (2011) eight broad functions of the integrative cortex will happen easily and naturally as well, and be integrated as a whole as per the dialectical pro-cess. And according to Kolb and Kolb (2017), episodic memory is associated with the full learning cycle. This is memory for autobiographical experiences that are grounded in the context of time and space. Furthermore, because it includes the emotions associated with those experiences, it remembers experiences in their fully lived quality, and it is associated with integrating sensing, reflection, abstraction and actions. The reason is that the integration of these episodic memories happens in the hippocampus (working optimally in this state), which draws on stored auditory, visual, olfactory and other information throughout the neocortex of the brain. The ventral vagal state therefore facilitates the optimal state for experiential learning to happen naturally. Porges agrees that this state is a prerequisite for us to have access to our higher brain structures: "Safe states are a prerequisite not only for social behaviour but also for accessing the higher brain structures that enable humans to be creative and generative" (Porges, 2017:47).

The impact of the sympathetic state on experiential learning

But what happens when we slip out of the ventral vagal state as a result of being stressed, feeling frustrated, threatened or fearful? The heart will instantaneously respond to these feelings and generate an incoherent and chaotic HRV pattern. The neural message that is sent by the heart to the amygdala will trigger and move the autonomic nervous system into the sympathetic state, getting the body ready for fight-or-flight. At the same time, a neural message from the heart to the thalamus causes it to let in only sensory information directly related to the environmental threat. Any sensory information not directly related to survival is shut out. As a result of that, the message going to the prefrontal cortex is incoherent, so we do not learn or remember. There is fuzzy thinking, poor memory and a lack of creativity, because the cells in the hippocampus lose their dendritic connections.

It would seem that in this state, lateral dominance becomes a factor. Just like we all have a dominant hand, foot, eye and ear, Hannaford (2011) believes that we favour one hemisphere of the brain over the other. This preference for one hemisphere over the other shows up in Kolb's (1984) preferred learning styles as well. And it is during times of stress that we tend to show a preference for the dominant hemisphere. This is a pattern that I can identify with experientially, after having spent thousands of hours coaching individuals and teams.

I have noticed that left hemisphere-dominant people, who seem to prefer working with what Kolb and Kolb (2017) refer to as the "instruction/recall learning cycle", tend to become very rational and analytical about a confined piece of logic, and they seem to lose the bigger picture when they are under stress. This is because the "instruction/recall" cycle of learning, which prefers to work with abstract conceptualisation and reflective observation, tends to focus on learning second-hand knowledge. And it does this by cycling through the frontal integrative cortex and the temporal integrative cortex. It works with information in the form of language, images and abstract symbols that is usually received via visual and auditory senses. This sensory information is decoded in the back integrative cortex which creates images and meaning.

The "instruction/recall" learning cycle uses semantic memory and knowledge, which is symbolic knowledge of the world. The important thing is that it is internalised and consciously known knowledge that is detached from the concrete experience and context from which it occurred. It is retained conceptual representations that are organised in terms of meaning. This would include the meaning of rules, words, numbers and social constructs. It helps to create models of the world that can be transformed through analysis and reflection. And the reason it can do that is because it has the capability to represent states of the world that are not present all the time. This is memory and knowledge that is generalised, in that it is independent of context and personal experience. It is interesting that the Kolbs see this "instruction/recall" learning cycle as being the same as Daniel Kahneman's (2011) "remembered/thinking self", which is the self that has been constructed through memories based on concrete experiences. The "instruction/recall" learning cycle is used to create meaning from those concrete experiences through cognitive interpretations.

The problem, however, is that this cycle produces generalisations that only partially grasp the essence of the experience, which we have seen is one of the limitations of experiencing the world in the left hemisphere. It is therefore a biased representation of the self that is directly experienced. And as we have seen, these are all aspects of experience in which the left hemisphere excels. In Zull's (2011) terms, their world and reality seems to shrink to identifying and manipulating the parts of the detail, and perceiving and manipulating the relationships in the detail; and the bigger picture gets lost. The problem is that this linear and sequential analysis and logic is applied to what they already know, and they can become trapped in their own conceptually created world. In this state, debate seems to be the only communication option available to them.

For as McGilchrist (2019) reminds us, the left hemisphere cannot deliver or take in anything new from the outside, because it can only unpack and manipulate the details of what the right hemisphere has given it. Furthermore, the left hemisphere is less myelinated and more connected within itself and within the regions of the hemisphere than the right hemisphere. Hence it has a self-referencing nature in that it works with what it already knows, the world it has created for itself. As a result, the dialectical process breaks down, and they can become trapped in their own hall of mirrors.

Right hemisphere-dominant people, who tend to prefer what Kolb and Kolb (2017) refer to as the "exploration/mimicry learning cycle", seem to have a different problem. This learning cycle first shows up in the developing child as a simple reflex of stimulus and response which involves no intervening cognitive activity. It is the true embodied mind that receives ongoing perceptions and responds to the immediate context in which it is embedded. And most of this happens outside of conscious awareness, which as we have seen happens in the right hemisphere. This cycle happens as it continuously cycles through the motor and sensory cortex working with concrete experience and actions.

This is the domain of procedural memory, which retains learned connections between stimulus and response and does not involve the cognitive activity of working memory. Procedural knowledge operates only in the present time–space context. It is unconscious knowing that operates in the very present "now". The "exploration/mimicry" learning cycle, that senses and acts without cognitive interpretation intervening in the process, ties back to Daniel Kahneman's (2011) "fast-thinking experiencing self". This self is based on direct concrete experience. In Zull's (2011) terms, the problem is that people who prefer the "exploration/mimicry" learning cycle get stuck in identifying and manipulating the parts in the big picture, perceiving and manipulating the relationships in the big picture. For as McGilchrist (2019) reminds us, the right hemisphere has a higher degree of myelination, and as a result it has a greater degree of connectivity and transfers information very fast between the cortex and the centres below the cortex. Meaning that it is better at integrating perceptual processes and information from various senses.

The problem is that this is all done implicitly because all preconscious information and the attentional system that detects stimuli outside of conscious focus, including most social understanding, happens in the "unconscious" right hemisphere. As a result, they find it difficult to make their logic and reasoning explicit; they battle to communicate and express what they are experiencing, and to control their emotions. Schore (2019:274) sums it up as follows:

> For example in a resting state, right hemisphericity can be associated with a quiet alert state. But it can also be associated with a history of more frequent negative affect, lower self-esteem, and difficulties in affect regulation.

They can "see" the big picture and have an intuitive feel of what needs to be done, but they find it very difficult to make that explicit and communicate it. How do you communicate the interconnected whole that you are experiencing? It is very difficult. This is because the right hemisphere sees the whole before the whole gets broken into parts in an attempt to "know" it. So once again the dialectical process breaks down.

In both these scenarios, experiential learning will not be happening naturally and easily, because for that to happen, we need both hemispheres to be working together as an integrated whole. We need the right hemisphere to deliver the new from the outside to the left hemisphere where it can unfold the implicit, make it explicit and unpack it. This unpacked, unfolded and analysed detail then needs to be returned and reintegrated with the bigger picture and the whole of the right hemisphere. The art is to learn to get back to a ventral vagal state as quickly as possible to facilitate optimal experiential learning by going through the entire experiential learning cycle. And the quickest way to do that is to experience love and appreciation, do deep abdominal breathing and to move. All of these strategies are discussed in later chapters.

The impact of the dorsal vagal state on experiential learning

Finally, what happens if we slip into a dorsal vagal state? This was the first part of the nervous system to evolve; it is the unmyelinated portion originating in the brainstem known as the dorsal motor nucleus of the vagus, which evolved with the reptilian brain. It is responsible for immobilisation, feigning death and behavioural shutdown. The other important thing to mention here is that we tend to think in a binary, either-or way, of seeing things as black or white. It is only in an extreme case that the dorsal vagal state will cause a complete behavioural and psychological shutdown and complete immobilisation. In less extreme cases, as Dana (2018) reminds us, individuals are disconnected from themselves, from others, and from their internal and external resources. There is a feeling of being lost and unable to find their way back into connection. In other words, the dorsal vagal state, like the other two states, consists of a spectrum of behaviours and is not an either-or state; it is state of gradation. And the reason for that, as Schore (2019) has pointed out, is because "functional regressions reflect neurobiological structural regressions".

To illustrate this point, it is worth referring to a case study that Bessel van der Kolk (2014), a psychiatrist who works extensively with post-traumatic stress disorder (PTSD), refers to in his book *The Body Keeps the Score*. The case study involves a husband and wife who both survived an 87-car pile-up that happened to be the worst road disaster in Canadian history. This is a good example of the shift from conscious cognition (the later-forming cortical system) to unconscious, bodily based affect (the early-maturing subcortical systems). And lastly, from the central nervous system to the autonomic nervous system.

As Van der Kolk (2014) points out, when trauma survivors are asked to discuss their experiences their responses will vary and are not uniform. One individual's heart will start racing and their blood pressure will increase, while another might just start developing a migraine headache. Another individual might simply shut down emotionally and not feel any changes. The responses to a traumatic event are unique to every individual. And Van der Kolk shows this by referring to the fMRI image scans of the flashbacks of both the husband and wife to the same traumatic event. The husband's scan showed that the amygdala was very active. The amygdala is involved in bodily states related to emotions, especially facial expressions and body language, and it has links to brain areas involved with cognitive processing. It is responsible for coordinating bodily reactions that serve as internal warnings, thereby enabling us to assess a situation and respond appropriately with anxiety and fear or happiness. In this case, it did not distinguish between the past or the present, and it triggered the stress response involving the hormonal and nervous systems as if the accident were happening in the present. Hence the husband's sweating, racing heart rate and extremely high blood pressure as he came out of the scanner, symptoms of the stress he experienced in reliving the trauma of the accident. This is facilitated by the left and right dorsolateral prefrontal cortex being deactivated. When that area is deactivated, people have no sense of the past, present or future, and become trapped in the moment, because they have lost their sense of time.

In the case of the husband, the thalamus was deactivated as well. All incoming senses except smell are relayed via the thalamus, and at the same time it relays motor impulses from the cerebral cortex through the brainstem to the muscles. Throughout life, new nerve cell growth occurs in the hippocampus. It forms short-term memories by using incoming sensory input from the thalamus, movement coordination in the basal ganglia and emotions from the hypothalamus. With nerve net activation in the hippocampus, these short-term memories can become long-term memories throughout the body and brain, which becomes our autobiographical memory. According to Van der Kolk (2014), as a result of the thalamus being deactivated, trauma is not remembered as a coherent story with a beginning, middle and end. Rather, it is remembered as isolated sensory imprints. Trauma survivors remember physical sensations, images and sounds along with intense emotions, helplessness and terror. Because of its connection to the cerebral cortex, the thalamus normally plays an important part in concentration, paying attention and learning, all of which is compromised by trauma. This is understandable, because if there is no coherent, integrated story to reflect on, how do you reflect on it and come up with an alternative conceptual framework to experiment with? It is very difficult when you are working with disparate, fragmented pieces. As a result, this is a suboptimal state for experiential learning to take place.

In contrast, the wife's fMRI scan showed that very few areas of the brain were activated. Van der Kolk (2014) refers to this as depersonalisation, one of the symptoms of dissociation caused by trauma. It is a manifestation of the biological freeze reaction of the dorsal vagal state. In this case, the wife completely dissociated her fear and felt absolutely nothing. It is very difficult in this state to remember, think, feel and make sense of what is going on, because most of the brain is deactivated. Porges describes what happens with dissociation as follows:

> Basically, the old vagal circuit enables a biobehavioural shutdown … When mammals shut down, there is a massive reduction in oxygenated blood going to the brain … The ability to make decisions and even the ability to evaluate the situation may be compromised. These features are consistent with dissociation.
>
> (Porges, 2017:161)

In this state, it is very difficult to learn. The reason, according to Schore (2019), is because the registration of the traumatic state is on a sensory motor level; it is preverbal, so no language is available for the presentation of the memory. There is a shift of dominance from the later-developing conscious left mind to the early-developing right unconscious mind, which is the clinical problem of regression. And given that strong and even overwhelming emotional memories are stored in the right unconscious mind, the traumatic memory is not remembered, but relived and re-enacted. Van der Kolk (2014), Dana (2018) and Hannaford (2005) all agree that the only way to help somebody in this state is to help them change their physiological state and their relationship to their bodily sensations. The important thing is to help them reactivate those brain structures that were deactivated during trauma. And we now know that this is impossible if they remain in a dorsal vagal state. They need to move back up through the sympathetic state into a ventral vagal state. And it would seem that physical movement is one of the best strategies to achieve that. Ratey and Hagerman (2008:84) sum up the problem and the solution very eloquently: "Just keep in mind that the more stress you have, the more your body needs to move to keep your brain running smoothly."

Summary

This chapter explored the development of the central and autonomic systems and the roles they play in learning, more specifically experiential learning. As a result, I put forward the working hypothesis that in a ventral vagal state experiential learning will happen naturally, and that it is the optimal state for learning to happen. In other words, the individual has access to the entire experiential learning cycle. In a sympathetic state, individuals will default to either the exploration/mimicry learning cycle or the instructional/recall learning cycle. Which cycle they will default to will be determined by their dominance profile. In a dorsal vagal state, they will default to an extreme version of the exploration/mimicry learning cycle, which is a suboptimal learning state. More importantly, however, it is through these various learning states that we co-regulate each other's nervous systems and develop as human beings. "Thus, learning becomes the vehicle of human development via interactions between individuals with their biological potentialities and the society with its symbols, tools, and other cultural artefacts" (Kolb, 1984:133).

Chapter 3

Movement and experiential learning

Introduction

The main hypothesis put forward in this book is that we develop as human beings within the context in which we find ourselves, including the social context, and we do so by learning from experience. And by experiential learning, I do not mean mere cognitive learning. As we have seen from Hannaford's (2005) work, our nerve networks grow out of unique transactions and sensory experiences in our environment. It is through our senses that learning first starts to happen. It starts with our initial sensory experiences, which lay down intricate nerve networks and patterns that serve as the foundations for higher-level brain development and our free-form information system. And the intricacies of these patterns are shaped by all the activities we experience, and by our environmental circumstances. It is these internal and external sensory experiences that continuously modify, change and create more complex images of ourselves and the world, resulting in new and continuous learning. This is because each new novel experience contributes to us updating our free-form information system and causing it to become more elegant.

Movement, learning and development

The development of the nerve networks, the central and autonomic nervous systems, and ultimately learning, all depend on movement. Moshé Feldenkrais, the nuclear physicist who developed the Feldenkrais Method, a movement-based learning method, is probably one of the earliest pioneers to recognise the total integration of movement, learning, the environment and human development. He suggested that a person is made up of three entities: nervous system (the core of the person); body (the envelope for the core); and environment (consisting of space, gravitation and society). The nervous system relates to the body through the nerves and senses, and to the outside world through nerve endings and senses. Yet the nervous system has no direct perception of the outside world – the distinction between the person or "self" and the outside world must be learned. The nervous system learns to recognise which

DOI: 10.4324/9781003356424-4

information signals come from the body (or the self) and which come from the outside world:

> This is the beginning of consciousness; by learning to recognise how our bodies are oriented, we come to know ourselves. Subjective and objective realities are thus organically dependent on the motor elements (the nerves, the muscles, and skeleton), which are oriented by and react to the gravitational field.
>
> (Feldenkrais, 2010:32–33)

The nervous system and the body therefore develop in response to the environment. This complex process is achieved through learning because the nervous structures look for order. Feldenkrais (2019) believes that a complex nervous assembly needs constancy and consistency of environment. Hence the nervous system will look for order and find it, or it will make order where it does not exist. And because living organisms move incessantly, the nervous system has to arrange its own mobility and arrange the mobile changing world to make sense of what is going on. Here we see the physiological basis for the creation of meaning that is so central to experiential learning and logotherapy.

Given how central movement is to the development of the nervous system and to learning, it is not surprising that Feldenkrais (1977) saw the correction of movement as the "best means of self-improvement". In other words, he saw movement as being critical to human development, but at the same time as a tool or methodology for human development. He saw human life as a continuous process, and movement as a means to improve the quality of that process. Feldenkrais (1977), in agreement with Hannaford (2005) and Zull (2011), mentions that we inherit the structures and tissues of the nervous system. But their function and structural development is developed through individual experiences and experiential learning. Waking and sleeping are the two common distinguished states for humans. Learning happens in the waking state, which according to Feldenkrais has four components: sensations, feeling, thought and movement. Each of these components can be used to improve the quality of life because they all influence each other:

- *Sensation*: This includes the five senses of taste, touch, sight, hearing and smell, and kinaesthetic sense. The latter would include rhythm, orientation in space, and pain.
- *Feeling*: This includes conscious and unconscious emotions such as super-sensitivity, self-respect and inferiority.
- *Thinking*: This includes all the functions of the intellect.
- *Movement*: This includes changes in the state and configuration of the body and its parts, both temporal and spatial (Feldenkrais, 1977).

So why does Feldenkrais opt for movement as the best option for self-improvement and human development?

1 The nervous system is mainly occupied with movement. This is because we cannot sense, feel or think without all the actions initiated by the brain and nervous system to maintain an upright body against the pull of gravity, and to know where and what position we are in.

2 The quality of movement is easier to distinguish. We know more about movement than about thinking and emotions like love and anger, for example. It is easier to learn and to recognise the quality of a movement than the quality of these other factors.

3 We have a richer experience of movement. We have more of a capacity for movement than for feeling and thought, because we all have experiences of movement. Many of us suppress feeling and thinking out of social fears.

4 Movement is important to self-value and self-image. The ability to move, and our physical build, are possibly more important to our self-image than anything else. Difficulties in moving undermine and distort personal self-regard.

5 All muscular activity is movement. Hearing, talking and seeing, for example, all require muscular action, hence all actions in the human body originate in muscular activity. Even states of mind are linked with the motion of the actions. Complete relaxation of the muscles will lead to slow and feeble actions, whereas excessive tension will lead to jerky and angular movements.

6 The state of the nervous system is reflected in movement. We have already learnt that certain muscular actions are associated with the ventral vagal, sympathetic and dorsal vagal states; this is reflected in facial expressions and the tone of the voice. It is the nervous system that mobilises the outward and visible changes we see and hear; impulses from the nervous system activate the muscles to function in a certain way. And as Porges (2017) reminds us, without us even being aware of it at the cognitive level, as soon as the nervous system has determined that it could be unsafe, our body has already started a sequence of neural processes which trigger defensive behaviours such as fight, flight or freeze on a neurophysiological level. As Dana (2018) puts it, the physiological state shapes the response and neuroception shapes the physiological state.

7 Movement is the basis of awareness. We become aware of what has happened through neuroception in the autonomic and central nervous system only when it reaches our muscles – in other words, when the muscles in our heart, lungs and face organise themselves into patterns known as love, fear or anxiety. We become aware of what is happening in the nervous system when we become aware of the change in our attitude, stance, stability and tension in the muscles. It is mainly through the muscles that we become aware of what is going on inside us.

8 Breathing is movement. Our breathing reflects every physical effort, disturbance and emotion. Numerous systems have been developed by humans to induce calming through breathing techniques. To breathe

correctly, we need to have an appropriate placing of the skeleton with respect to gravity.

9   Hinges of habit. For Feldenkrais, the key neurological issue is as follows:

> Owing to the close proximity to the motor cortex of the brain structures dealing with thought and feeling, and the tendency of processes in brain tissue to diffuse and spread to neighbouring tissues, a drastic change in the motor cortex will have parallel effects on thinking and feeling.
>
> (Feldenkrais, 1977:38)

> This is important, because habitual patterns are imprinted on the nervous system. The nervous system reacts to exterior stimulation with habitual, ready-made patterns. A change in the motor basis of any of these patterns will break that pattern's cohesion, making it easier to produce changes in thinking and feeling. We have already seen how the nervous system unconsciously works out whether or not there is an environmental threat and triggers the appropriate behavioural response. This is because the lower brain systems are automatic, and produce actions that are much faster than the part of the brain that generates thought. Ultimately, we want to learn to act or react in response to the given external situation not according to habit, but with the appropriate response.
>
> (Feldenkrais, 1977:33–39)

For Feldenkrais, there is a direction to human development. And that direction is towards an increased capacity to direct these older processes and actions that we inherited from our evolutionary past, to inhibit them, speed them up or increase their variety through our capacity for awareness. And by awareness, he means the capacity to concentrate and the capacity to analyse. Fortunately for us, the nerve paths in the third brain system are more elaborate and longer than those in the reptilian and limbic systems. As a result, there is a delay between what is engendered in the neocortex and its execution by the body. For Feldenkrais (1977), the possibility of creating an image of an action and delaying the execution thereof is the basis of intellectual judgement and imagination. More importantly, Feldenkrais (1977) sees this delay between the creation of a thought for a particular action and the actual execution of the action as the physical basis for awareness. This delay between stimulus and response, and the ability to choose our response, are fundamentally important in logotherapy as well. It is this ability to delay our actions between the intention and the execution that enables humans to become aware, and as a result learn to know themselves.

For Feldenkrais (1977), it is awareness that gives humans the capacity for things like abstract thought, imagination, judgement, differentiation and generalisation. The more we become aware of our muscular movements, the more we can differentiate in which neurological state we are in, and in so doing we can improve the quality of our lives. Awareness and self-improvement help us to develop even more as humans. And for him development is "the harmonious coordination between structure, function, and achievement" (Feldenkrais, 1977:51). It is the complete freedom from either self-compulsion (being completely at the mercy of the sympathetic and dorsal vagal systems) or compulsion from others (we can regulate our ventral vagal system). In this process, Feldenkrais (1977), like McGilchrist (2019), warns of the danger of the left hemisphere, the emissary, becoming the master. Harmonious development calls for the total integration of the human being:

> Creative, spontaneous thought must maintain a link with the early brain structures. Abstract thought that is not nourished from time to time from deeper sources within us becomes a fabric of words alone, empty of all human content.
>
> (Feldenkrais, 1977:52)

We develop through learning, which needs attention, awareness, time and discrimination. And to discriminate we need to sense, to sense differences; but if we cannot feel, we cannot sense differences. And if that happens, we cannot distinguish between our actions. For Feldenkrais (1977), without the ability to differentiate we cannot learn nor increase our ability to learn. Just think about it: if you do not know what physiological state you are in (ventral vagal, sympathetic or dorsal vagal state), you are the mercy of your nervous system and your emotions, and you cannot choose the appropriate action.

Feldenkrais (2019) has shown us that there is an emotional state associated with every pattern of impulses that reaches the nervous system from the muscles and viscera. There is therefore a personal-conditioned pattern of muscular contractions corresponding to every emotional state. He points out, for example, that there is inhibition of the extensor muscles in all emotionally disturbed people. Movement thus shows the state of the nervous system and its degree of development. Through movement we learn to feel our bodies, which helps us to sense differences and whether our chosen actions are appropriate to the environmental stimulus. More importantly, through movement we can change the state of our nervous system and our emotions, because muscular contractions can be controlled voluntarily, which gives us a feeling of control and power over our emotions and sensations.

Movement and the development of the nervous and sensory systems

The first of the sensory systems to develop and to begin myelination 5 months after conception is the vestibular system, whose main component is found in the inner ear. It controls our sense of movement and balance, and hence our ability to act against gravity. It maintains static equilibrium, which refers to the orientation of the head and the rest of the body relative to gravity when you are standing still. It is also responsible for dynamic equilibrium, which refers to the position of the head and the body in response to sudden movements. The mechanisms of the inner ear gather information about the head's position relative to the ground. Every time we move our heads, the mechanisms in the inner ear are activated and send sensory nerve impulses to the brain via the vestibular nerve. Because these impulses pass through nerve tracts to the cerebellum, corrective instructions are issued, particularly to the core and neck muscles, to contract or relax. We therefore learn about gravity through the vestibular system, which is considered the entryway into the brain, and this system connects to every muscle in the body, either directly or indirectly. The reason is that our muscles must adjust instantly so that we do not lose our equilibrium or balance. Hence movements like walking are useful throughout life because they help to maintain balance and equilibrium, while at the same time keeping the brain active and growing new nerve cells and connections.

According to Hannaford (2005), it is upon this sense of gravity that the other senses like touch, hearing, taste and smell build to give us our first images of the world. Sight is accommodated only at a later stage when we integrate these increasingly complex sensory images. Furthermore, the vestibular nuclei, which are neurons in the medulla oblongata and pons, carry impulses from the semi-circular canals in the inner ear and from the cerebellum to the reticular activating system. The reticular activating system is a dense nerve net in the brainstem, and it carries impulses to the neocortex to "wake it up" so that it can take in stimuli and respond to the environment. According to Hannaford (2005), this connection between the vestibular system and the neocortex is so important that when we do not move and activate the vestibular system, we do not take in information from the environment. Hence every movement we make stimulates the vestibular system, allowing it to take in information from the environment, which in turn stimulates the brain for new learning.

Proper functioning of the vestibular system therefore contributes to the functioning of the coordination of vision with movement, balance, locomotion and discrimination of speech and language. These are all skills on which we rely throughout our lives to function effectively in the world. Hannaford (2005) mentions that stress and a lack of vestibular system development cause erratic or low functioning in the reticular activating system, which in turn leads to hypo- or hyper-vigilance and difficulties in maintaining concentration, focus and attention. These are all factors that are seen in individuals with attention deficit hyperactive disorder (ADHD). These individuals tend to lose their balance easily as well. To stay alert, and to activate the reticular activating system, they must constantly move, wiggle and turn their heads. In the absence of movement, their brains experience reduced activation.

The development of the proprioceptive system (sense organs that are located throughout the muscles, tendons, joints and the inner ear), which gives the body its sense of itself in space, is intimately tied to the vestibular system. It uses our muscle sense to explore our environment. This system is constantly aligning every part of the body so that we can move in a secure, balanced way. Balance is constantly maintained when the feedback system between muscles and proprioceptors is developed well through continuous use. Hannaford (2005) mentions that stress can interfere with this system, in that the functioning of the balance system is thrown out, which leads to us losing our physical sense in space and our balance.

In a non-stressed state, the system gives the necessary feedback to maintain optimal contraction and relaxation of the muscles for balance to be maintained, and for the shoulder and neck muscles to readjust to keep the eyes level. For, as Hannaford (2005) mentions, 95 per cent of vision takes place in the brain from the association with proprioception, touch and hearing. Less than 5 per cent occurs in the eyes. Even though the images come in through the eyes and are funnelled through the thalamus to the occipital lobe, which processes the primary vision, all the cerebral lobes must contribute information for full vision to take place. The incoming image is associated with information from the sensory and motor cortices and learned sensory and movement functions. We tend to believe that vision happens simply because we have eyes, but as Hannaford (2005) makes clear, vision is learnt. The brain assembles our visual world from learned information from other senses like proprioception and touch.

To make the point, Hannaford (2005) refers to an experiment in which scientists wore glasses fitted with mirrors which turned their view of the world upside-down. At the same time, the glasses turned the world back-to-front. Initially, the participants found it difficult to move and were bumping into things all the time. The healthy vestibular system quickly worked out that the world had changed, and together with touch and proprioception provided feedback for the eyes to adjust. As a result, the participants in the experiment soon saw the world just fine and could walk around with no problems. That was until they stopped wearing the glasses and again started to bump into things, until they had once more gone through the entire relearning process. Feldenkrais (2019) refers to a similar experiment in the United States, involving two people, one sitting in a wheelchair and the other pushing it. Both wore the inverted glasses. The one pushing the wheelchair soon learnt to see normally, while the one sitting in the wheelchair kept seeing everything upside-down.

The eyes are therefore designed to move and accommodate for light so that they can give us as much sensory information as possible about the environment. As a result, they must be actively moving for learning to occur. The incoming image information is integrated with other sensory information like proprioception and touch to build up a system of visual perception. For vision to develop fully, the eyes need to experience the world as a whole, with its three-dimensional focus. They did not evolve to sit for long hours in front of television sets, computers and books, which keep our eyes focused on two dimensions. One of the symptoms of an underdeveloped vestibular system, for example, shows up in the muscles that control movements of the eyes. There is a tendency to undershoot or overshoot their position for optimal effectiveness when the individual reads. Vision is therefore an integrative function that happens in the neocortex as a result of various sensation inputs like sight, touch, hearing and proprioception. It is these sensations and experiences that constitute learning and consciousness, for it is from them that we develop the neurological base patterns on which thoughts and concepts develop.

The development of the brain, nervous system and senses is dependent on movement. Movement is essential to life and to learning. Hannaford (2005) emphasises that even when we are still, our bodies are filled with movement. Even when you are sitting still and meditating, there is the contraction and expansion of your lungs, there are nerve impulses, the beating of your heart and blood moving through your body. All new experiences and information are anchored and integrated into our neural networks through movement. That is because every movement is a sensory motor event linked to the understanding of our environment. For example, our eyes, nose, ears and tongue are aligned to environmental inputs through the movement of our head. More subtle movements of our eyes allow us to adjust our focus to see far or near. More importantly, every time we move in an organised manner our brains are activated and full integration happens, and as a result learning can happen naturally. Hannaford (2005) suggested that as much as 95 per cent of lifelong learning occurs through sensory-motor experience of the environment, while formal training may account for only 5 per cent of learning:

> Movement is an indispensable part of learning and thinking. Each movement becomes a vital link to learning and thought processing ... Thinking is a response to our physical world. In studying the brain, we can understand it only in the context of a physical reality, an action reality.
> (Hannaford, 2005:120)

The purpose of the brain is to produce action

Zull (2011) suggests that the purpose of the brain is to produce behaviour; and by behaviour he means movements that result from actions of the skeletal muscles. In the same vein, Hannaford (2005) suggests that learning is about building skills; and it is through the movement of muscles that all skills are built. It does not matter whether these are athletic skills, or musical skills, or intellectual skills used in classrooms or the professions. The key argument in her book is that human development and learning are dependent on movement. There is a direct connection between the frontal lobe areas of the brain, which are important in coordinating thought, and the motor control areas of the brain.

It was long thought that the cerebellum controlled only gross motor movement. We now know that it plays a critical role in learning. With an average of 250,000 to 300,000 synaptic connections per nerve cell, the cerebellum has more neurons than any other part of the brain. The cerebellum appears to be the main sensory system, and when it receives input from the vestibular system it examines, evaluates and integrates the sensory information. It then relates it to motor functions by relaying the information to the rest of the brain via the hippocampus, substantia niger, basal ganglia in the limbic system and the motor cortex of the frontal lobe. Furthermore, the cerebellum correlates postural and kinaesthetic information about the position of the body in the gravitational field, together with the vestibular nuclei. The cerebellum possesses very fast conducting pathways between itself and the neocortex. So much so, that it adds 5 to 10 per cent to the speed with which the cortex can put together information and reason. Moving while learning will therefore increase the learning!

How we move, how the muscles adjust for maximal benefit during resting and active periods, and the timing and dynamics of movement for coordination, are all learnt movements, which are the responsibility of the cerebellum. One of its main functions is therefore to make our movements smooth, rhythmic and coordinated. To keep our visual field fixed on the retina of the eye as we move, the cerebellum must continuously adjust movements of the head. It provides memory retention for motor learning, like learning to roll over, sit up, crawl and walk, through its connection to the hippocampus. Furthermore, the cerebellum and basal ganglia, via the thalamus, activate the part of the prefrontal cortex that has to do with spatial working memory and reasoning. The cerebellum therefore plays a critical role in higher cognitive functions like attention, judgement, planning and the control of impulses. There are important nerve connections from the cerebellum and the centres of speech in the left hemisphere, namely the areas of Wernicke and Broca. According to Hannaford (2005), computer imaging shows that the cerebellum is almost inactive while watching TV, yet it is the most active part of the brain during learning. Ratey and Hagerman (2008) go so far as to say that exercise involving complex movements also involves a full set of cognitive functions. This is due to the connection between the prefrontal cortex and the cerebellum, which along with movement, coordinates attention, thoughts, emotions and social skills.

The psychiatrist Harald Blomberg (2015) mentions that the cerebellum is underdeveloped at birth and experiences substantial growth after 6 months. This growth, and the development of nerve nets and nerve cells in the cerebellum and its connections to the frontal lobes, is the result of rhythmic baby movements. These rhythmic movements are therefore critical in linking up the frontal cortex, and with it the development of the power of speech and attention. This is due to the sensory stimulation caused by the rhythmic movements, which stimulates the development of nerve nets in the brainstem, cerebellum, basal ganglia and neocortex. As a result, attention and concentration improve, and at the same time hyperactivity and impulsivity decrease. It is therefore understandable that a dysfunction of the cerebellum could affect the functioning of many other parts of the brain, especially the cortex. As a result, it could affect control of impulses, attention, judgement, planning and abstract thinking. It may also affect speed of information processing, working memory, eye movements, reading comprehension, speech development and learning.

Movement and early development

The first thing all humans need to learn is how to move in and respond to their environment. And as we have previously mentioned, it starts in the reptilian brain. In the first year of life, this involves a major feat in coordination and strength as the child goes from inert lying, to rolling over, sitting up, crawling and then walking. With the practice of each movement, elaborate nerve networks are established. Early movements are reflexive (i.e. involving the reflexes), which are vital for survival. Blomberg (2015) points out that these automatic, stereotyped movements of the reflexes are controlled from the brainstem. The first reflex to develop *in utero* at 9 weeks is the Moro reflex, which is followed by more elaborate reflexes. These reflexes allow the newborn and infant to grasp (the palmar grasp reflex), lift its head (the tonic neck reflex) and eventually roll over, sit up, crawl and stand.

The important thing to remember is that these reflexes do not disappear, they eventually integrate with the higher nerve centres in the vestibular, limbic and sensory-motor systems of the cerebrum. Blomberg (2015) mentions that these reflexes must be integrated for the child to develop proper motor abilities. Once again, it is rhythmic movements that stimulate the basal ganglia to mature and integrate the primitive reflexes. Signals from the proprioceptive, tactile, vestibular and visual senses are received by the basal ganglia, which respond by sending signals downward to the brainstem and spinal cord. These signals in turn will inhibit or modify the primitive reflexes. In other words, the stereotyped and sweeping movement patterns of the primitive reflexes are transformed into the more precise and well-balanced movement patterns of the postural reflexes. The primitive reflexes are therefore inhibited and transformed by the basal ganglia and integrated into the movement pattern of the baby to become lifelong postural reflexes.

This is all brought about by the spontaneous rhythmic movements that a baby makes before they learn to walk. Once integrated, these primitive reflexes remain in the brainstem and should remain inactive. If the inhibiting effect of the basal ganglia is disrupted by something like Parkinson's disease, old age or trauma injuries like whiplash, the primitive reflexes can reappear. This is evidenced in the inability to balance and keep stable, sit down and rise up, and walk normally. Integration of the primitive reflexes will therefore facilitate the ability of the child to regulate its level of activity. Where these reflexes do not integrate with the higher functions, the child will tend to be hyper-vigilant, reactive and reflexive. These are the kinds of behaviour witnessed in autism, aggression, phobias and ADHD. More importantly, it is movement that keeps these primitive reflexes integrated with higher movement patterns.

The vestibular system, which is tied to the core muscles of the abdomen and back, plays a critical role in that it activates the muscles that first work to lift the head. As the neck muscles strengthen, the child is able to lift the head and start to see the world with two eyes and to hear the world with two ears. As it follows a sound with its ears and uses the core muscles to move the whole body, the baby learns to roll over. And over time, by lifting the shoulders as well as the head in response to sensory stimuli, the shoulder girdle area is strengthened. With use, the nerve nets to the core muscles elaborate and myelinate. This enables the child to hold itself up, to sit against gravity and eventually to crawl.

Because it is a cross-lateral movement, crawling activates the development of the corpus collosum, the main band of neural tissue that connects the two hemispheres of the brain and allows for the transmission of information and communication between them. As a result, both sides of the body start working together, including the arms, legs, eyes (binocular vision) and ears (binaural hearing). At the same time, the shoulders and pelvis work together as well. The senses more fully access the environment because of this equal stimulation, and both sides of the body can move in a more integrated way for more efficient action. As a result of this stimulation of the vestibular system, the kinaesthetic senses and tactile stimulation, new nerve nets develop and myelination occurs in the brain. What is known is that more efficient crawlers stabilise more quickly when standing, can walk for greater distances and fall less often while learning to walk. It is also well known that children who miss the vitally important crawling stage may exhibit learning difficulties later in life, which once again highlights just how important movement is to learning.

For as Blomberg (2015) points out, without this stimulation from movement, the maturing of the brain is delayed or impaired. Lack of movement obstructs the development of the brain. The good news, however, is that regular rhythmic exercises and reflex integration exercises can stimulate the development of new nerve connections in the brain. Movement improves the function of the prefrontal cortex by stimulating the reticular activation system, the limbic system, the basal ganglia, and most importantly, the cerebellum. In doing that, it develops the nerve nets of these areas so that the prefrontal cortex gets enough stimulation for its proper functioning. We can integrate information about external events with our inner emotions, drives, experiences and memories when the nerve connections between the limbic system and the prefrontal cortex are sufficiently developed. This enables us to react in appropriate ways, and to adapt to the changes of the world around us and to our own inner needs. The flipside of the coin, according to Blomberg (2015), is that if the nerve nets between the prefrontal cortex and the limbic system are not sufficiently developed due to motor handicaps, this can result in low muscle tone or disease. Or if the prefrontal cortex is not sufficiently stimulated from the basal ganglia or the cerebellum, there is a risk of switching off the prefrontal cortex and becoming overwhelmed by our emotions.

The importance of movement throughout life

Movement and the continuous stimulation of the vestibular system is important throughout life, not just in early development. Joan Vernikos (2016) spent five decades working for NASA studying the impact of zero gravity on astronauts and how to keep them healthy. She soon concluded that many health problems on earth are related to the fact that we do not make sufficient use of gravity and move enough. She defines movement as a change in position, which can be internal, external or emotional. Learning how to move during the first few years of life by changing position involves learning how to live in gravity. Like Hannaford, therefore, Vernikos sees learning and movement as inseparable. We have evolved to live with gravity and it is our lifeline. She points out that gravity is sensed primarily through the vestibular system and proprioception. Those senses give us the necessary sense of acceleration and direction to enable us to relate to the environment as we move. The vestibular system in the inner ear, located near the centre of the brain, controls balance and coordination, and needs to be constantly stimulated by movement in gravity.

According to Vernikos (2016), the vestibular system is so important that if it is damaged or goes silent, the rest of the body will waste away and prepare metabolically to shut down. Because of the reduced-gravity environment in space where there is no up or down, astronauts returning from space show problems with maintaining their balance and coordinating their movements. In fact, Vernikos (2016) mentions that every system in the human body deteriorates as a result of living without gravity. This was all learnt from astronauts returning to earth. Part of the problem of doing research with astronauts while they are in space is that you need a control group as well as the experimental group. In this case, you need some astronauts to exercise in space while others do not. This created an ethical problem, in that it was already known to be important for all astronauts to exercise to counteract the physiological changes observed from microgravity exposure. As an alternative, Vernikos developed the bed-rest studies, which involved volunteers on earth continuously lying in beds for days.

Due to those experiments and studies, Vernikos (2016) became interested in whether the changes we experience as we age are due to chronological age or due to lifestyle. She soon discovered that due to gravity we can actively influence how we age. In essence, her research showed that the physiological changes taking place in highly fit astronauts in space in a near-zero-gravity environment are similar to those of the elderly. In other words, a near-zero-gravity environment produces ageing changes and speeds up the ageing process. What surprised her even more was that the result was the same for healthy men and woman on earth who continuously sat or lay in bed. An example of the effects of gravity deprivation is the fight-or-flight response. In a life-threatening situation, one of the options available is to flee from the threat. This physical response is dependent on the ability of the nerves and muscles to rapidly react to the threat. It is, however, only through continuous, repetitive, gravity-using movement that reaction times are reduced and this state of preparedness is achieved; it cannot happen in a gravity-deprived environment. Some of the other ageing effects that came up in these studies were arterial stiffness, decreased brain blood flow or decreased cerebral oxygenation, brain shrinkage and vision problems. These are just the obvious ones that have a direct impact on learning; Vernikos's research uncovered a total of 41 ageing effects. The changes that we recognise as ageing are similar and accelerated in space, and when we do not adequately make use of gravity on earth. The good news, however, is that all the adverse effects experienced by astronauts were reversed when they recommenced gravity-using movements once they returned to earth.

Vernikos's (2016) concern is that humans in modern society are moving far too little, and spending far too much time sitting. This is compounded by the fact that our modern chairs require far less effort to sit down and get up, and we sit for prolonged periods of time. Less affluent societies sit as well but they tend to do far more floor-sitting. She goes so far as to say that the amount of floor-sitting, kneeling and squatting that a society does can almost predict the physical mobility of that society. A large proportion of people in modern societies sit down to do their work. When you work is the time that you want the brain to be operating at its optimal level. Yet prolonged sitting leads to sluggish circulation in your legs and lower body, which ultimately deprives the brain of blood flow, oxygen and glucose.

The way to counter this is to stand up and move about as much as possible throughout the day. The change in posture triggers the vestibular and brain balance systems, which causes the redistribution of blood throughout the body. As a result, blood pressure sensors in the heart and neck are stimulated to maintain blood supply to the brain as you stand. What surprised Vernikos most was that her research revealed that standing up maintained blood pressure, stamina and blood volume more effectively than walking. It was, however, how many times one stood up that brought about these benefits, and not for how long one stood up. Interestingly, even exercise once a day cannot counteract the effects of sitting for the rest of the day. Vernikos (2016) mentions that even though astronauts exercise in space to improve endurance and strength, it does not prevent all the other changes. And sitting too much, according to her, has the same effect, because while you sit the sense of direction and acceleration is removed and there is no change in posture and position. As a result of this lack of change in posture, there are no signals triggered by the vestibular system and it goes silent, leading to some sensory deprivation. In this case, the individual is deprived of the ability to sense gravity and direction. As Hannaford (2005) has pointed out, this is because the lack of stimulation to the vestibular system leads to the deactivation of the reticular activating system, which is responsible for carrying impulses to the neocortex to "wake it up" so that it can take in stimuli and respond to the environment.

There is no doubt that moving less impacts the entire body and the nervous system. The grey matter of the neocortex of the brain, which is unmyelinated cell bodies of neurons, gives it its plasticity, which enables it to have an unlimited ability to form new dendrites and reorganise dendritic patterns in response to new experiences. It is involved in motor control and coordination. According to Vernikos (2016), there is less grey matter in sedentary people, and this has an impact on coordination and balance. Performance, locomotion, learning, memory, movement and coordination are all associated with grey matter. The white matter, myelinated axons, carry sensory information to the neocortex very fast and then carry its motor commands to the body. Vernikos (2016) points out that as we age, brain function is disrupted due to the decrease in nerve fibre activity. Physical activity is critical for structural integrity of white matter, as Hannaford (2005) has made clear.

Vernikos (2016) emphasises that white matter is also affected by the amount of time spent sitting. She refers to similar research carried out by the China Astronaut Research and Training Centre, which provided neuro-anatomical evidence of brain dysfunction resulting from prolonged sitting and lack of movement. This research found that grey matter volume decreased in the temporal lobes, the right hippocampus and the bilateral frontal cortex lobes, accompanied by some fractional changes in white matter tracts. More interesting were research findings from the University of Illinois involving adults aged 60 to 80 who were monitored using accelerometers. Detrimental effects were suffered on the white matter of their hippocampus by those who sat the most hours. The hippocampus is the seat of our episodic memories (memories of events we have experienced personally) and is the brain region most important to memory and learning. It is responsible for our experience of individuality. More importantly, even if they exercised at the end of the day for half an hour, it did not prevent the negative effects on the brain that came from prolonged sitting. The message is simple – structured exercise is good to build strength and endurance. It does not, however, counteract the consequences of sitting too much for the rest of the day and not changing posture frequently.

What about people who are forced to sit in wheelchairs all the time due to lower-body paralysis? Vernikos (2016) is of the opinion that even these individuals can benefit from harnessing gravity. Obviously, this will depend on how each individual is able to use their bodies. The reason why they can still harness gravity is because the sensors that control this blood pressure response are above the point of spinal cord damage, and as a result the body still perceives and reacts to postural change. Changing posture from lying down to sitting up frequently continues to be beneficial even for these individuals. And many of them benefit from exercising their upper bodies and achieving amazing athletic feats.

Given the physiological impact that a lack of movement and prolonging sitting has on the brain, it is not surprising that Vernikos (2016) refers to a number of studies from around the world showing a higher risk of depression and psychological distress associated with a lack of movement and prolonged sitting. As she points out, this actually involves a vicious cycle because one of the consequences of depression is increased sitting. This is not at all surprising given that the depressed person has moved into what Porges (2017) referred to as the dorsal vagal state. In this state, there is a freezing of gross motor activity combined with a limited repertoire of behaviours. Because the body and mind have moved into conservation mode, the individual can be too tired to think or act. Lack of energy, isolation, memory problems and dissociation could be some of the daily living problems associated with this state and the resulting depression.

Type of movement matters

Given that movement is so important to our development and ongoing health, what kind of movement or exercise should we be doing to facilitate learning? Both Phil Maffetone (2000), a chiropractor turned successful triathlon coach, and Vernikos (2016) draw a distinction between health and fitness, terms which are often used interchangeably by the general public:

- *Health* is a state in which all the body's parts are in balance. This includes the glands, hormones, organs, nerves, bones and muscles. Or it can mean the absence of disease. It is about how you feel and function.
- *Fitness* is the ability to be physically active and is defined by what one is fit to do. It normally involves exertion.

Health and fitness are therefore two different things. Maffetone (2000) emphasises that being fit does not necessarily make you healthy, any more than being healthy makes you a fit athlete. Building on this, Vernikos (2016) sees movement and exercise as two different things and they are not interchangeable:

- *Movement* is the foundation of health. To move effectively, we rely primarily on gravity. Although standing up does not burn many calories, it does raise blood pressure and heart rate. At the same time, it requires physical, cognitive and emotional interaction because it usually involves a purpose. For example, just think of any household task or manual work that must be performed. Because it is low-intensity, it is aerobic, meaning that it uses fat for fuel. Fat is an excellent long-term energy source. Movement can be long in duration and many blood vessels are involved.
- *Exercise* is essential for fitness. It increases oxygen consumption to burn calories, using sugar as its main fuel source. Sugar is a very short-term energy source. It is therefore anaerobic. And exercising in an anaerobic state can be maintained only for short durations.

Exercise therefore makes you fit to do something and usually involves occasional heavy exertion. The problem is that many people have come to believe that if they exercise occasionally, or a few days a week, then they are healthy. Furthermore, in doing that, they believe that they can be inactive for the rest of the time. To be healthy, we need to move about all day. Vernikos's (2016) research shows that we need both: the foundation of life is moving and exercise should build on that foundation. Maffetone (2000) agrees and believes that there should be a balance between the two. We should become as healthy as we can through movement and as fit as we can through exercise. According to him, one of the imbalances that we are seeing in industrialised societies is people who are fit but unhealthy. The reason is that in the last few decades, humans have drastically reduced their natural level of physical activity (movement). And in a sense, exercise became an artificial activity to maintain a certain level of physical activity. Exercise is therefore seen as an activity done apart and separate from our normal daily chores, to make up for the deficiencies in movement created by living in modern industrialised societies. Given that not many of us will voluntarily go back to a pre-industrialised way of life, exercise will continue to be an artificial activity to maintain a certain level of physical activity for most of us. Add to that the fact that more and more people are doing their work sitting down because of digitisation. We must therefore make peace with the fact that sitting is an integral part of our modern lifestyles. The key question is, how can we incorporate movement and exercise into our lives in such a way that we continue to learn and develop as human beings for as long as possible in this modern industrialised world?

Based on decades of research for NASA, Vernikos (2016) suggests that a good place to start is to change posture as often as possible. And by that she means alternating between sitting and standing up, to continuously stimulate the vestibular system. Her bed-rest studies in 1992 produced results that surprised her. The results showed that standing up once every hour for 16 hours was more effective than walking 16 times a day every hour for the same amount of time. Why 16 hours? Because during the remaining 8 hours in the day, the subjects were asleep. Based on these findings, she hypothesises that exercise can counteract the effects of sitting. *It is not the exercise itself that does it, however, but the additional postural changes that go along with exercise.*

More importantly, standing up frequently works with or without exercise. This is because when you sit for a while, your heart does not have to pump as hard and as the blood pools to your feet, your ankles might swell. As a result, less blood reaches your brain. When you stand up, things get worse before they get better: the blood drains from your brain and rushes to your feet even more. The heart and circulation instantly react to correct this drain of blood from the brain. To resupply the brain cells with oxygen, cardiac output and stroke volume is increased, thereby expanding blood volume to pump blood up to your brain. It therefore helps your brain cells function better to stand up frequently. At the same time, it must be emphasised that prolonged static standing should also be avoided. Static standing and working for hours in front of a computer at a standing desk simply defeats the purpose because gravity will pull the blood back to your feet the longer you stand still. Therefore, to maintain increased blood flow to the brain, you need to keep moving up and down.

According to Vernikos (2016), interrupting sitting by standing up often and walking around is the secret to health. She is not the only one to suggest this. Shane O'Mara (2020), Professor of Experimental Brain Research at Trinity College Dublin, refers to research done at the University of Tel Aviv showing that the mere act of regularly standing up changes the state of the brain and mobilises neurocognitive resources that would otherwise be quiescent. The mere act of standing up constitutes a call to action and cognition.

In fact, Vernikos (2016) goes so far as to say it is even better to alternate your posture as frequently and with as much variety as possible. In other words, stand, sit, bend to pick something up, bend sideways and kneel to garden or pray, all of which will keep the vestibular system stimulated. This is no surprise because that is exactly how all of us developed our nerve networks and our nervous system when we were children. We did not exercise; instead, we lifted our heads, rolled over, sat up, crawled, stood up and eventually walked. As children, we simply played, ran, walked, climbed and rolled down hills, and we did it with ease. All these activities involved changing our head position often, which stimulated the vestibular system and cross-lateral movements which integrated the left and right hemispheres of the brain.

The question then is, if it is so simple, why are we all not doing it? Why do we have to read books or watch documentaries that remind us about the importance of movement? Hannaford believes that there are two reasons contributing to this lack of simple movement in our lives:

> (1) the strongly held misconception in our society that mind and body are separate, that movement has nothing to do with intellect, and (2), that physical activities which are simple, take very little time, and depend on no technologically associated assistance, can't be very useful.
>
> (Hannaford, 2005:125)

Yet the work and research of Porges, Schore, McGilchrist, Hannaford, Blomberg, Kolb and Vernikos show us that we all learn and develop through experiential learning and movement. The two cannot be separated, they are one and the same process:

> Every learning situation deals basically with the same steps: sensory input, integration, assimilation, and action. Simple integrative cross-lateral movements which focus on sensory activation and balance,

facilitate each step of the process by waking up the body/mind system, and bringing it to learning readiness.

(Hannaford, 2005:125)

Note that Hannaford is talking about the experiential learning process: input, integration, assimilation and action.

Walking

Another form of integrative cross-lateral movement that activates the balance and sensory systems is walking. Bipedalism, the ability to walk upright on two feet, is what separates humans from all the other primates. Early in life, we transition from a stable, crawling stance to an upright walking stance within a matter of months. The normal activities of daily life are severely limited when we are incapable of controlling our own locomotion because of injuries that paralyse us. Bipedalism is a very efficient form of locomotion, in that it is more economical in terms of calorie burn than moving on all four limbs. As a result, bipedal walking generally and automatically minimises energy expenditure while maximising the terrain covered. O'Mara (2020) points out that this makes humans exceptional walkers, possibly the best walkers of all species, which explains why we were able to disperse across the entire planet. And we did this by walking in small, social migratory groups. If such a group walked only 5 kilometres per day for 300 days, they would cover 1,500 kilometres within that timeframe. Over a few years, the distance covered would become substantial. O'Mara (2020) therefore sees walking as being social at its core.

And like everything else in life, we learn to walk through experience. It is through experience that we develop the neural circuits that allow us to walk throughout our lives. And this is done by taking thousands of steps a day and risking dozens of falls. Once we have learned to walk, we walk upright, with heads up, allowing us to scan the far horizon, at the same time leaving our hands and minds free. To walk upright with coherent motion and direction, while continuously adjusting to changes in surfaces and traction to keep ourselves perpendicular to the walking surface, we need balance. In Vernikos's (2016) opinion, walking is the most comprehensive coordination and all-round balance movement. This apparently simple action requires our brain and nervous system to be coordinated, and for systems like balance, sight and sensations to be communicating in harmony. In fact, as Earls (2020) points out, the entire body is used for walking. The legs and pelvis are assisted by the trunk and the arms. One of the requirements of walking is that the eyes are kept relatively level; as a result, the whole body works together to lessen the amount of distortion that reaches the head, for the eyes to remain steady, and to prevent any trauma to the brain because of heel strike. The arms are used in particular to counterbalance the forces going to the head in each of the planes of movement, and each arm works with the movement of the leg on the opposite side to achieve this.

It is important for the head to maintain a relatively flat position parallel to the ground, even if there are changes in the environment or terrain. This is due to the head acting as an "inertial guidance platform" for stabilised movement, according to O'Mara (2020). If you draw a line from the corner of your eyes to the ear canal, there is an imaginary line that, no matter how active you are, the brain will always try to keep approximately parallel with the ground. Without the brain stabilising the head in space during movement, walking would be impossible. Like all animals with a spinal cord, the mechanism that stabilises the position of the head is based in the inner ear, namely the vestibular system.

But as O'Mara (2020) points out, the vestibular system can be temporarily disrupted. This can be done by spinning in circles – or by consuming too much alcohol. How does the system correct itself? It does this by making use of proprioceptors throughout the body, which provide the necessary proprioceptive signals, from the relative position of joints involved in movement like the hips, knees and ankles. For example, by placing a foot flat on the floor, a lying-down-drunk person can relieve their spinning feeling. Contact with the ground is an external input provided by proprioceptors that stabilises the vestibular system and stops your head spinning. While walking, the vestibular system and proprioceptors throughout the body are constantly sensing changes in relative position and tension, and sending that information to the appropriate muscles via the nervous system.

These two systems seem to have given humans an evolutionary advantage. The Neanderthals who shared our world for 300,000 years had larger brains, and larger and more muscular bodies than us humans. So why did we outlast them? One of the theories put forward by Earls (2020) is that it could be due to the vestibular system. The inner ear has its origins in the lateral line organs of fish, which were used to perceive vibrations from the surrounding environment. These piscine sensory organs evolved into the human ear. This gave us not only the ability to hear but also the ability to sense movement and orientation. This is because the semi-circular canals of the inner ear can perceive all three of these dimensions. Coordination, balance, running and throwing would have been more difficult for Neanderthals than *Homo sapiens*, because Neanderthals' skulls show that their semi-circular canals were smaller and less developed than those of *Homo sapiens*.

This superior inner ear system gave us balance and coordination, enabling us to chase prey to exhaustion and death, the ability to accurately shoot arrows and throw spears, and enhanced navigation skills. The latter is especially important in helping the hunter find his way back home from a long hunt. Evidence indicates that Neanderthals rarely travelled far from their main encampments. O'Mara (2020) points out that navigation involves the ability to perform a simple task known as "point-of-origin finding". This is dependent on our sense of stability and direction provided by the vestibular system. Our sense of space is not only visual in nature; even blind people can also find their way around. He refers to a number of studies showing that learning to walk and navigate in extended three-dimensional space does not require normal vision.

Our cognitive map, which is our sense of space, is largely constructed without our awareness. This is because our spatial sense is built up from our experience of walking about in the world. Contrary to what we think, it is largely built up without the senses that we use to interact with the world. We are therefore capable of learning about our world just by walking in it, even without seeing. This is because the cognitive map (our sense of space) is inscribed in the hippocampus. Throughout life, new nerve cell growth occurs in the hippocampus. It forms short-term memories by using incoming sensory input from the thalamus, movement coordination in the basal ganglia and emotions from the hypothalamus. With nerve net activation in the hippocampus, these short-term memories can become long-term memories throughout the body and brain. Our spatial sense, which is inscribed in the hippocampus, is activated most effectively at walking speed, which gives rise to a reliable and repeated electrical rhythm in the brain known as the theta rhythm. And as O'Mara (2020) mentions, when humans (like all other mammals) walk about in the environment, there is theta expressed in hippocampal formation. It is a signal that the brain is engaged in movement and active exploration within the environment.

The brain's memory, mapping and navigational systems are therefore intertwined. To walk somewhere, we are dependent on the brain's navigation system. Yet the mere act of walking provides vast amounts of information for the navigation and mapping systems of the brain. It is a mutually reinforcing and enriching loop. Add to that a better-developed proprioception system, which gives us the perception of where the body is in space, and you have the ability for the brain to carry out other tasks and jobs because it no longer has to pay too much conscious attention to the surrounding environment. In other words, it adds to our efficiency because it gives us the ability to walk without paying conscious attention to walking.

O'Mara (2020) sees walking as being a holistic activity that aids every aspect of our being and it uses the brain in multiple ways. Not only does it exercise the muscles, but the act of regular walking leads to plastic changes in the structure of the brain through the production of brain-derived neurotrophic factor (BDNF). It is therefore not surprising that walking is associated with improved moods, creativity and a general improvement in the quality of our thinking. More importantly, according to O'Mara (2020), walking changes activity in the brain in subtle yet powerful ways. Simply put, the brain receives inputs from the outside world (the sensory side of the nervous system), and the central component of the nervous system then processes these inputs. The processed results can affect behaviour through some form of output via the motor neurons and muscles. By measuring these various activities during walking, it emerges that walking measurably changes brain activity for the better. Sight, hearing and reaction times all improve during active movement.

Another benefactor is the cardiovascular system; regular walking protects the heart against factors that promote heart disease. There is a tendency to think of the brain and heart as two different systems, yet we know that there is strong and direct connection between the two via the vagus nerve. The heart not only receives information from the brain but also sends information (including emotional information) to the brain via the vagus nerve, independently of the sympathetic nervous system and the spinal cord. This functional relationship between the brainstem and the heart is known as cardiac vagal tone. Furthermore, Childre and Martin (2000) refer to the new discipline of neurocardiology, which combines the study of the heart and the nervous system, to show that the heart communicates with the body and the brain in three ways: biochemically (through hormones and neurotransmitters), biophysically (through pressure waves) and neurologically (through nerve impulses). And it is through these communication systems that the heart has an influence on the brain and the rest of the body.

A healthy heart developed through regular walking therefore has a positive impact on the brain and *vice versa*. One of the ways this occurs is via a hormone known as atrial natriuretic peptide (ANP), produced in the muscle tissue of the heart, which moderates the body's stress response by reducing activity in the hypothalamic–pituitary–adrenal axis:

> What's so interesting about ANP is that it increases as the heart rate increases during exercise, thus illustrating another pathway by which physical activity relieves both the feeling of stress and the body's response to it.
>
> (Ratey and Hagerman, 2008:79)

Ratey and Hagerman (2008) refer to research done by neuro-psychiatrists in Berlin in 2006, where 10 healthy adults agreed to be injected with CCK-4 (a panic-inducing substance), and then walked on a treadmill for 30 minutes at a moderate pace. The results showed that ANP concentrations increased, while feelings of panic and anxiety decreased at the same time. Ratey and Hagerman (2008) also point out that in an article (Fricchione, 2004) in the *New England Journal of Medicine* (*NEJM*) reviewing treatments of generalised anxiety disorders, exercise was not mentioned at all; the emphasis was on anti-anxiety drugs, although therapy and relaxation also received a nod. Two cardiologists interested in anxiety as a risk factor for heart disease were particularly surprised at the omission. They responded to the *NEJM* article by pointing out that "Exercise training has been shown to lead to reductions of more than 50 per cent in the prevalence of the symptoms of anxiety. This supports exercise training as an additional method to reduce chronic anxiety" (Lavie and Milani, 2004:2239, quoted in Ratey and Hagerman, 2008:101). These comments provide further evidence about the connection between the heart and the brain.

Unlike running, walking always involves one foot being on the ground. As a result, walking involves collaboration between bottom-up proprioception input from the feet and legs, and top-down control from the brain. There is, however, a third level of collaboration involved, according to O'Mara (2020). It is a mid-level rhythmical control system within the spinal cord, and it functions as a "central pattern generator" (CPG), a circuit in the nervous system that produces regular rhythmic motor patterns and controls our natural walking pattern. Because the CPG is in the spine, it shows that the brain does not control all the fine details of all the activities of the body. In effect, this means that the CPG generates the ongoing pattern of walking in the individual without much supervision by the brain.

This frees the brain to concentrate on other tasks. One of those tasks, as we have learnt from polyvagal theory, is to scan the environment for threats. The nervous system is continuously evaluating the risks in the environment through neuroception. The nervous system quickly works out whether the situation in the environment, and the people in the environment, are safe, dangerous or life-threatening. According to Porges (2017), neuroception happens without our conscious awareness because it takes place in the primitive parts of the brain and it gets its cues of safety or threat from body movements, face movements and vocalisation. Humans can naturally and rapidly assimilate potential sources of threat while walking. When these social cues are identified, according to O'Mara (2020), there is a rapid top-down intrusion by brain systems concerned with social interaction, which interrupts the ongoing work of the CPGs. In other words, the CPGs are quickly and rapidly interrupted by a command signal from the brain.

Because the brain and nervous system have picked up information about the intended movement of the other person, inferred from where they are gazing, the individual can quickly correct their walking trajectory to avoid any threat. This information offered by others, and registered by the nervous system through neuroception, is incorporated into our non-static cognitive map. Possible threats and places of refuge are logged dynamically without us being aware of this. In other words, our cognitive maps afford us a flexible way of interacting with the world while we are moving through it. Walking helps us to build up these cognitive maps through experience by walking in the environment. And as we have now seen, neuroception is an integral part of the cognitive map and walking improves that process as well. Neuroception is dependent on sight, hearing and reaction times, all of which improve during walking. The mere act of walking around in the environment can therefore be seen as an act of unconscious experiential learning for the body and the mind.

Aerobic and anaerobic exercise

Throughout life, new nerve cell growth occurs in the hippocampus, which is critical to memory and our cognitive maps of the environment. One of the contributing factors to new nerve cell growth is BDNF, a key molecule which might be thought of as a kind of molecular fertiliser produced within the brain, according to O'Mara (2020). BDNF supports structural remodelling and growth of synapses, which boosts learning and memory very effectively. Ratey and Hagerman (2008:45) mention that "BDNF gives the synapses the tools they need to take in information, process it, associate it, remember it, and put it in context." BDNF also provides the brain with a remarkable degree of resilience, including resistance to damage arising from infection, trauma or ageing. A simple and straightforward way to raise BDNF levels in the brain, and particularly in the hippocampal formation, is aerobic exercise. Hence Ratey and Hagerman (2008) see a direct connection between exercise and improved learning, and they mention three reasons why that is so. Firstly, it prepares and encourages nerve cells to bind together, which is the cellular basis for gathering new information. Secondly, it spurs the development of new nerve cells in the hippocampus. Thirdly, it optimises the mind for improved attention, alertness and motivation. More importantly, aerobic exercise also contributes to the creation of new brain cells in the mature adult and keeps the brain in good working condition.

So what do we mean by aerobic exercise? All human skeletal muscles contain a mix of aerobic and anaerobic fibres. Aerobic fibres make up the vast majority and contain more blood vessels than anaerobic fibres. Aerobic fibres use fat as their predominant source of energy and have the ability to burn sugar as well. Anaerobic fibres, on the other hand, cannot use fat and use sugar (glycogen) as the main energy source. This sugar is usually stored in the muscles and liver with the other source being blood sugar. It is a relatively scarce resource and can supply energy for only a short period of time. Aerobic exercise is therefore the ability to move or exercise in such a way that the body obtains most of its energy through burning fat; whereas anaerobic exercise uses sugar as the predominant source of energy. Which energy source predominates during exercise is determined by the duration and intensity of the exercise. Walking, running, cycling and swimming can all be aerobic; but if the intensity is too high, they become anaerobic, which can be a major stressor on the body, and push it into the sympathetic nervous state.

So how can we determine whether we are in an aerobic or anaerobic state? The easiest way to determine this is by measuring your heart rate, either by counting your pulse or using a heart rate monitor. The latter has become very popular and depends on certain formulae to determine what zone you are in. The most well-known formula is 220 minus age, with the difference between the two being multiplied by a percentage between 65 and 85. So for a 50-year-old individual the formula would be:

220 – 50 = 170 beats per minute,

which is the maximum heart rate to exercise at.

To calculate the aerobic zone for this individual, it would be between:

170 * 65% = 110 beats per minute, and
170 * 85% = 145 beats per minute.

The question is which is the right number for the individual? It is normally an individual choice. And given our "no pain, no gain" culture, there is a pretty good chance that the individual will go for the higher number. But what if the individual is on regular medication, has a heart condition or has allergies? This formula does not take that into consideration. To overcome that problem, and through years of training triathletes, Maffetone (2000:61–62) developed an alternative formula to determine an optimal heart rate for aerobic training. His formula is:

180 – age = maximum heart rate.

Then modify that number by selecting one of the categories that suits your fitness and health profile:

- Subtract an additional 10 if you are recovering from a major illness or are on regular medication. This includes things like heart disease, a hospital stay or an operation.
- Subtract an additional 5 if you have not exercised before, exercised irregularly, have been exercising with an injury, get more than two cases of flu or colds per year, or have asthma or allergies.
- Use the (180 – age) number if you have not got any of the above-mentioned problems and have been exercising at least four times per week for up to 2 years.
- Add an additional 5 if you are a competitive athlete who has been training for more than 2 years without any of the above-mentioned problems, and you have made progress in competitions without injuries.

The net figure will be your maximum aerobic heart rate. As soon as you go over that heart rate, you will be in the anaerobic zone. So let us assume the same 50-year-old, who has a heart condition and is on blood pressure medication: 180 – 50 = 130. Then subtract 10 for the heart condition: 130 – 10 = 120. The maximum aerobic heart rate for this individual is therefore 120 beats per minute. This maximum aerobic heart rate of 120 is substantially less than the 145 beats per minute calculated with the 220 – age formula.

Stu Mittleman (2011) is known as one of the world's best ultra-long-distance runners and has been coached by Phil Maffetone. He has refined the Maffetone formula even further. Yet he cautions that any formula is a best guess based on observed tendencies of the general population. He suggests that if you do not have access to a heart rate monitor, an individual can get the cues from their body by becoming aware of how they are feeling, what things sound and look like. The aerobic zone will be burning mostly fat as fuel and it is not over-stressing the body. The first thing that will be noticed is that the visual field is expansive. In other words, the individual will be able to see things across a wide expanse of vision, both directly ahead of them and peripherally. In this state, the world is seen in exquisite detail. At the same time, the individual will have access to their inner world. It is possible to reflect or even daydream while observing the world around you. O'Mara (2020) refers to this as "mind-wandering", a form of active idleness that allows for the collision of ideas. It facilitates divergent thinking, which involves generating a variety of solutions to a problem. More importantly, walking in this zone allows the individual to zoom in on a thought and then zoom out again, placing the detail in the context of other things. In other words, in this zone the mind can easily switch between focusing on the detail (left hemisphere) and the big-picture events (right hemisphere).

O'Mara (2020) refers to these two modes of operating as the active and default mode. The active mode focuses attention and processing on the details (left hemisphere). The default mode (right hemisphere) involves mind-wandering, creating and making connections to the whole, allowing us to integrate past, present and future. Mind-wandering helps us to interrogate our social lives and to create our large-scale personal story. This is because the hippocampus and all the structures connected with it are involved in memory and navigating the environment while we are walking. Thinking is also much clearer because the individual has access to both hemispheres as a result of not being stressed. Because the left hemisphere of the brain controls the right side of the body and *vice versa*, both hemispheres of the brain have to work together when you do a cross-lateral movement like walking.

So it is not surprising that the active and default networks can be engaged simultaneously while walking, enabling us to focus on the detail while simultaneously focusing on the whole. This is an essential requirement for creative thinking. And as O'Mara (2020) points out, walking in the aerobic zone, the speed at which we do not have to continually monitor the environment to prevent us from stumbling and falling, or pay attention that we are not breaking into a run, exerts the best possible effect on creative thinking and cognition. He refers to a piece of research done among Norwegian academics who regularly walked. They found that their thinking was best when the body was not overly taxed, but stimulated and engaged. Another contributing factor could be that the pattern generators in the spine are doing most of the work in the aerobic zone and freeing the mind to do this kind of thinking. Sounds are heard very clearly and all the surrounding sounds can be picked up. Kinaesthetically, the individual feels relaxed and a sense of being one with the world, at one with nature. Breathing is relaxed and low in the belly. There is no hyperventilation or the forced expulsion of air. And in this zone, even when you have finished exercising you will feel energised and that you could continue for longer.

And on a social basis, it is easy to have conversations among the group you are with because walking has a social function as well. Our ancestors walked out of Africa in groups, so we evolved to walk together. Walking in this zone, it is very easy for us to interact with other people. From polyvagal theory and regulation theory, we learnt that we are acutely sensitive to the social signals provided by others. So much so that we co-regulate each other's nervous systems on an unconscious level through facial gestures, speech, body movements and posture. This happens even when we are walking with one or two other humans, and in this context O'Mara (2020) refers to it as interpersonal synchronisation. Humans walking together will unconsciously and naturally start to mimic each other's gait. This leads to the synchronisation of breathing and the heart rate of each individual must perform similar functions at similar times. And at the same time, the brain is looking for cues to what the other person might do next, while still monitoring and controlling what you are doing. In the aerobic zone, walking therefore serves as a profound source of social interaction and connection. Walking in the aerobic zone therefore facilitates the social engagement system and being in the ventral vagal state.

The anaerobic zone, in contrast, burns sugar as the energy source. According to Mittleman (2011), in this zone the first thing you will notice is that your vision changes in depth and dimensionality and becomes more two-dimensional. Peripheral expansiveness fades into tunnel vision, as if you are running through a tunnel. There is a tendency to stare at a spot in front of you. Because you must concentrate on what you are doing in order to keep moving and not fall, internal images are more difficult to access, and the mind cannot wander. Sounds are no longer clear and distinct but instead start to blur together. And auditory information is very close to you. Kinaesthetically, there is a sense of urgency or alarm. One no longer feels at one with nature and the environment; rather, you feel distinct and separate therefrom. You feel alone, on your own trying to survive. Breathing is no longer deep and in the belly. Rather, it is shallow, in the chest and much more rapid. Once again, because you are so focused on what you are doing, it is very difficult to carry on a conversation.

The anaerobic zone engages the mobilisation system (fight-or-flight behaviours), which is dependent on the functioning of the nerves of the sympathetic nervous system. Physiologically, the breath has become short and shallow, and the heart rate speeds up substantially. As a result, there is a natural reduction of vagal tone to the heart and the vagal brake is released, meaning that there is a down-regulation influence of the myelinated vagal nerve. This, according to Porges (2017), means that the range of emotions that can be expressed is greatly reduced. It is very difficult to regulate facial expressions and prosodic vocalisations while you are running. Dana (2018) mentions that in this state the individual will feel the rush of adrenalin and consequently cannot hear friendly voices. There is the added complexity of misreading cues;

for example, a neutral face can appear angry and be experienced as being dangerous.

Furthermore, we know that if this becomes a chronic state, inability to focus or follow through, panic attacks and relational issues can become problems in daily living. The individual will experience a negative impact on cognition, known as cortical inhibition, and as a result is inclined to experience less ability to think clearly, less efficiency in decision-making, less ability to communicate effectively and reduced physical coordination. Simply put, this is because "One thing scientists know for sure is that you can't learn difficult material while you're exercising at high intensity because blood is shunted away from the prefrontal cortex, and this hampers your executive function" (Ratey and Hagerman, 2008:53).

It must be remembered that this is a vital state to help us cope with immediate threats and serves a crucial purpose to keep us alive. It evolved to last for only a very short time until the threat is over. In the same way, in short doses it can help improve our cardiovascular system, and our health and wellbeing. But if we continuously train in this zone without enough rest and proper recovery, it will become chronic and detrimental to our health. That is why Maffetone (2000) refers to the second stage of overtraining as sympathetic overtraining because of the stress it places on the sympathetic nervous system. Symptoms include a higher resting heart rate (especially in the morning), hyperexcitability, general restlessness and a decline in performance.

If nothing is done to address the situation, the individual will eventually move into phase three of overtraining known as parasympathetic overtraining. This is the result of putting stress on the dorsal vagal system of the parasympathetic branch of the nervous system. Symptoms include exhaustion, a relatively decreased resting heart rate, less desire to exercise and compete, and depression. Overtraining therefore follows the same hierarchical pattern that we find in polyvagal theory: if the ventral vagal state is not active, the sympathetic and then dorsal vagal systems are activated. The point to remember is that movement, including walking, at the right intensity helps to facilitate the development of the nervous and muscular systems, which in turn leads to more effective learning and thinking.

Furthermore, we now know that movement at the right intensity is a very effective way to help individuals move up the various states of the autonomic nervous system. In other words, if an individual finds themselves in a dorsal vagal state, we know that talking therapy will not always be very effective in helping them move out of that state. And the reason, as we have seen from cases in severe trauma, is that there are parts of the brain that go offline and the person moves into a physically and/or psychologically frozen state. Trying to get trauma survivors to reflect on the reasons why they are in that state and to come up with a cognitive understanding is psychologically very difficult.

Trauma and movement

Peter A. Levine (1997) is known for his work with trauma. Like Porges and Schore, he believes that the physiological mechanism governing our response to trauma resides in the primitive, instinctual parts of our brains and nervous systems. It is not in the mature cortex and is therefore not under conscious control. Hence, we cannot think our way out of it, and this is one of the reasons that talking therapy is not very effective with severe trauma. The key to healing traumatic symptoms in humans, according to him, is in our physiology. He has extensively studied how animals deal with trauma. If you carefully observe an impala who has just escaped from a lion, for example, even when they return to a more secure situation their muscles will twitch for some time. And the reason for this is that the nervous system is releasing all the built-up energy from the fight-or-flight reaction. Once the process is complete, the impala's entire nervous system returns to a normal state. It is the movement of the flight and the twitching of the muscles afterwards that releases the built-up nervous energy. Levine explains that "These little tremblings of muscular tissue are the organism's way of regulating extremely different states of nervous system activation" (Levine, 1997:97).

When this nervous energy cannot be released effectively through a physiological process, it can cause problems. Levine points out that traumatic symptoms are not caused by the triggering event, but result from the residue of nervous energy that has not been discharged:

> this residue remains trapped in the nervous system where it can wreak havoc on our bodies and spirits. The long-term, alarming, debilitating, and often bizarre symptoms of PTSD develop when we cannot complete the process of moving in, through and out of the "immobility" or "freezing" state.
>
> (Levine, 1997:19)

He goes on to suggest that many war veterans and rape survivors experience this scenario:

> They may spend months or even years talking about their experiences, reliving them, expressing their anger, fear, and sorrow, but without passing through the primitive "immobility responses" and releasing the residual energy, they will often remain stuck in the traumatic maze and continue to experience distress.
>
> (Levine, 1997:22)

We now know that movement can help the individual move out of the dorsal vagal state and into the sympathetic state. The sympathetic nervous system's primary function is to get us to move through fight-or-flight, to get us away from or defend us against any danger. As soon as the movement has achieved its purpose, there is a return to the ventral vagal state. But how is that achieved through movement?

Hartmann (2006) and Levine (1997) both try to answer the question of how humankind historically dealt with trauma before the advent of psychotherapy, which came into being only during the 1880s. Trauma has always been an integral part of human history. Hartmann and Levine discovered that movement was central to the healing and recovery process. Levine (1997) turned to more "primitive" cultures to find the answer to the question. The healing process usually involved community support that creates the environment in which this healing takes place. This is done through drumming, dancing, chanting and getting into a trance state. The process could continue for days and may involve the use of plant substances and other pharmacological catalysts. Even where the ceremonies varied across cultures and tribes, shaking and trembling as the event nears its conclusion is almost always experienced by the beneficiary of the healing. This phenomenon is the same as the one that occurs in all animals when they release bound-up energy. Movement in the form of dancing, chanting and drumming helps to facilitate the healing process. Bodily responses that emerge in the healing process typically include involuntary trembling, shaking and crying as the energy stored in the nervous system dissipates.

Hartmann (2006) puts forward the interesting hypothesis that during the 1880s and early 1890s, talk therapy was not Freud's favourite or even most common form of treatment. Freud's treatment methodology of choice at that time was a bilateral eye-motion technique known as hypnosis. His technique involved waving his hand or his fingers from side to side in front of the patient's face as they followed the movements with their eyes, while suggesting that the person relax and then consider their problem or issue. He also used "tapping", a technique to induce a trance, wherein Freud alternately tapped two fingertips on the person's forehead, cheeks or collarbone, continually from left to right. In effect, Freud was using a bilateral movement technique involving rhythmic stimulation of alternate sides of the body, causing nerve impulses to move from the left hemisphere to the right hemisphere and back, in a particular frequency.

> This cross-patterning produces an organic integration of left-hemisphere "thinking" functions with right-hemisphere and brain-stem "feeling" functions. This integration is a necessary precursor to emotional and intellectual healing from trauma.
>
> (Hartmann, 2006:4)

According to Hartmann (2006), Freud had a tremendous amount of success using this technique, but unfortunately chose to abandon hypnosis because of two bestselling fictional books at the time. The books were stories about how therapists were using hypnosis to take sexual advantage of woman – and unfortunately, the characters in the books described as doing this happened to be Jewish. Consequently, Freud abandoned hypnosis in 1895 due to increasing public paranoia, and (according to Hartmann), turned to prescribing cocaine to clients with neurosis and started to use "talk-therapy" because it was cathartic. Hartmann goes so far as to suggest that:

> Freud's body of work that emerged post-1895 has not well withstood the test of time. Although Freudian analysis is still practised around the world, there are no clean scientific studies that support the efficacy of Freudian psychotherapy or many of the offshoots it has spawned.
>
> (Hartmann, 2006:28)

So why did Freud have success with hypnosis and bilateral movement techniques prior to 1895? Hartmann noted the theory of some researchers that bilateral therapies function by keeping the hippocampus, amygdala, other parts of the limbic brain and the brainstem engaged by actively recalling the traumatising memory, while activating the left and right brain hemispheres in turn. This integrates the functioning of the hippocampus with both brain hemispheres:

> Because the hippocampus is engaged, the processing that would typically happen during sleep happens instead while the person is wide awake, provoking an "emptying" of the hippocampus and the filing and storing of the information it had contained in an appropriate "this-is-the past" part of the brain.
>
> (Hartmann, 2006:13)

As a result, after undergoing bilateral therapy, people wake up the next day aware that what had been disturbing them is now in the past (Hartmann, 2006). This suggestion is in agreement with Van der Kolk (2014), Dana (2018) and Hannaford (2005), who all concur that the only way to help somebody in a dorsal vagal state is to help them change that physiological state and their relationship to their bodily sensations by helping them reactivate those brain structures that were deactivated during trauma. Bilateral movements integrate the entire nervous system and the brain, and thereby activate all the brain structures, bringing about the neurological integration of intellectual and emotional processes involving the hippocampus, corpus callosum and the two hemispheres of the brain.

Based on his research and his work as a trauma therapist, Hartmann (2006) developed his therapeutic methodology based on walking. It involves walking in a relaxed manner, in the natural cross-crawl fashion, with opposite arm and leg swinging forward with each stride, with arms swinging naturally, and lightly holding the problem or issue in front of you. The bilateral, rhythmic motion involved in walking engages the left and right hemispheres of the brain alternatively – the same aspects of the brain that the alternate-side eye movement, alternate-side tapping and alternate-ear sound stimulation therapies work to engage. He goes on to state that

> Numerous studies have associated walking with a reduction of depression, anxiety, and sadness ... Although most assume this is because walking increases blood flow – and, thus, the flow of oxygen and nutrients to the brain – it may also be because of the fact that walking is a bilateral motion.
>
> (Hartmann, 2006:90)

And he is not alone. Ratey and Hagerman (2008:119, 121, 122, 126, 128, 139, 160) refer to numerous studies showing that aerobic exercise has a positive impact on the entire range of depressive symptoms, whether in the form of a disorder or a mild episode. This is because exercise stimulates the brainstem and gives people more energy, passion, vigour and motivation. Exercise also shifts people's concept of themselves by adjusting chemicals such as serotonin, dopamine and norepinephrine. And further,

> unlike many anti-depressants, exercise doesn't selectively influence anything – it adjusts the chemistry of the entire brain to restore normal signalling. It frees up the prefrontal cortex so we can remember the good things and break out of the pessimistic patterns of depression.
>
> (Ratey and Hagerman, 2008:135)

Bilateral, aerobic movements are therefore very effective in helping us move up and through the various physiological states.

Trauma and learning

So why all the concern about trauma and depression when it comes to learning? Because, as Ratey and Hagerman (2008:129) remind us, "The shutdown in depression is a shutdown of learning at the cellular level." It is the extreme example of somebody in a dorsal vagal state. It should be noted that all the states are graded, from mild to severe. Many of us will not end up in the severe states but we all feel the blues, feel down and withdraw to a darker, lonely place at certain times in our lives; this places us in a mild dorsal vagal state. The principal is the same: once learning shuts down at a cellular level, given our hierarchical development, learning is not going to be happening at the higher cognitive levels as well. The only option we have is to move out of the dorsal vagal state and back up through the sympathetic nervous state, where we will usually default to our preferred dominant hemisphere state and the learning cycle associated with that hemisphere. Then hopefully we move into the ventral vagal state that enables us to have access to the complete experiential learning cycle.

Feldenkrais reminds us that this is the aim of human development: it involves an increased capacity to direct these older processes and actions that we inherited from our evolutionary past, to inhibit them, or speed them up or to increase their variety through our capacity for learning. Yet this very capacity to learn is impossible without bilateral and cross-lateral movements of the human body. It seems to be the ultimate paradox of human development that we have to learn to move from experience in order to survive and thrive in this world, and yet that very learning is impossible without movement. Experiential learning, human development and movement are one integral process, they are one and the same thing. Hence the reference to the Integrated Experiential Learning Process. When movement stops, learning stops and ultimately life stops. And nothing makes that as clear as when our most fundamental movement stops, namely breathing.

Movement is therefore the foundation of health, which is a state in which all the body's parts (including the bones, muscles, nerves, organs, glands and hormones) are in balance. Or it can mean the absence of disease. It is through movement that the nervous system develops and forms the base patterns (habits) that we build on all our lives. Initially, it is a process of experiential learning that is prerational and precognitive, based on the exploration/mimicry learning cycle. Eventually, as we develop and mature, it becomes a cognitive rational process based on the instructional/recall learning cycle, finally maturing into the full experiential learning cycle. And as we mature, we learn through experience how to increase our capacity to direct these older processes and actions that we inherited from our evolutionary past, to inhibit them, speed them up or increase their variety through our capacity for awareness. In other words, through experiential learning we become aware of our physiological states and how to manage them more effectively.

Conclusion

This chapter has focused on the importance of movement and the role it plays in the development of the nervous system, experiential learning and human development. The point I have tried to make is that there is a difference between movement and fitness. Fitness is the ability to be physically active and is defined by what one is fit to do. It normally involves exertion; it increases oxygen consumption to burn calories, using sugar as its main fuel source, is therefore anaerobic and can be maintained for only short durations. I am not denying the importance of fitness; it is essential to people who make a living from professional sport and to amateur athletes. In an ideal world we would all be fit and healthy. The truth is that it is possible to be fit and unhealthy. For as we have seen, it is possible to overtax the nervous system and drive it into a sustained sympathetic or parasympathetic state, which is unhealthy and will have a direct impact on the effectiveness of experiential learning and our own development. For optimal human development, we need to learn to move more in an aerobic zone, especially in a modern world where we tend to move less and less. And the COVID-19 pandemic has made that situation worse.

As a qualified personal fitness trainer and an executive coach, I have found myself over the years moving the emphasis to getting my clients to move more and concentrate less on fitness. My experience taught me that my clients work in very complex and stressful jobs. Many of them were already highly stressed, which directly impacted the quality of their learning and decision-making abilities. And in my experience, they either did no exercise, or when they did work out they tended to overexert themselves and overdo it – and instead of managing their stress effectively, the exercise regime compounded their stress problem. And the reason for that is that they had often adapted programmes, heart rate zones and thinking developed for professional athletes. Professional athletes have ample recovery time between their competitive seasons. Executives do not have a recovery period; they are on an exponential treadmill that demands more of them every year. That, combined with my growing understanding of the physiology underpinning our nervous system and experiential learning, has led me to move more towards working with aerobic-based movements.

The principle is simple. Move more and try change your position as much as possible to continuously challenge the vestibular system. Do as much cross-lateral and bilateral movement work as you can, to get the left and right hemispheres of the brain to work together in an integrated way. To move effectively we primarily rely on gravity. Although standing up does not burn many calories, it does raise blood pressure and heart rate. At the same time, it requires physical, cognitive and emotional interaction because it usually involves a purpose. For example, just think of any household task or manual work that must be performed. Because it is low-intensity it is aerobic, meaning that it uses fat for fuel. Fat is an excellent long-term energy source. Movement can be long in duration and many blood vessels are involved. Yoga, Pilates, tai chi, Original Strength, rope flow training and walking are all very good examples of movement work that achieves these principles. Because walking is such a natural cross-lateral and bilateral exercise, I do it as much as possible. In fact, whenever possible, I try to coach my clients while walking. I have found that the quality of the thinking and the coaching sessions improve substantially while we are walking as opposed to sitting down. Given what we have explored in this chapter, I now know that there is a physiological reason and basis for that improvement.

In parting, it is worth noting the connection between physiological states and resilience as well. Open any self-help book nowadays and you will read about the need to be resilient, or to become more resilient, to deal with change. The Oxford Learner's Dictionaries define resilience as "the ability of people or things to recover quickly after something unpleasant, such as a shock, injury, etc.", or alternatively as "the ability of a substance to return to its original shape after it has been bent, stretched or pressed" (Oxford University Press, 2022).

The Cambridge Dictionary defines it as "the ability to be happy, successful, etc. again after something difficult or bad has happened" (Cambridge University Press, 2022b). Resilience therefore has to do with the nervous system's ability to bounce back to a certain state. Developing resilience therefore requires self-awareness about what physiological state we are in at any point in time, and the impact that this state has on our ability to learn affectively.

Summary

This chapter has highlighted the fact that far from being a cognitive model, experiential learning is actually an integrated physiological process. Experiential learning first develops as a result of nerve nets forming as we learn to move in our environment. Those nerve nets form patterns as a result of movement and eventually become the nerve networks used to perform cognitive tasks and to learn. Hannaford's work has highlighted the understanding that as soon as we stop moving, we stop taking in information from the environment and by default we stop learning. How we move and the types of movement we make have a direct impact on our physiological states. The art is to learn how and what type of movement is able to move us out of the sympathetic and dorsal vagal states back into a ventral vagal state, which is the optimal performance and learning state for us as human beings. Human development happens through movement and learning from our experiences as we transact with the environment, including the critically important social environment.

Chapter 4

Human development models

Introduction

Up until now we have looked at how experiential learning and movement contribute towards human development. Any journey that we undertake in life is always made easier with the help of a map or GPS system. The map gives us some idea of where we are heading and some of the critical stages and places along the way. It also warns us of obstacles and dangerous territory that we may encounter on the way. When it comes to human development, it also helps to have a map, in this case theories of human development, that can help us along the journey.

But like all maps, it is a representation of the territory and is not the territory itself. Theories are just that, they are an abstracted representation of lived experience. And so we need to remember Bohm's warning that "our theories are not 'descriptions of reality as it is' but, rather, ever-changing forms of insight" (Bohm, 1995:17). It is with that warning in mind that the theories on human development in this chapter will be presented. Not as absolute correct descriptions of reality but rather as "ever-changing forms of insight" into human development. Acknowledging that it is our fate as humans to be immersed in everyday reality and at the same time to extract ourselves from that reality, reflect thereon and create a hypothesis and theory about what is going on.

In this chapter, I explore three meta-theories on human development that have influenced, and led to the development of, the Integrated Experiential Learning Process. The first is the integral theory of Ken Wilber. From the outset, I want to make it clear that I believe Wilber's theory is *a* theory and not *the* theory. I have found it to be a very useful conceptual framework in which to think and do my work. The second meta-theory that is explored very briefly in this chapter is the Diamond Approach developed by A.H. Almaas. I do little justice to the depth and excellence of his work. But in the context of this book, it is necessary to only briefly make the reader aware of his writings, which I would highly recommend to any person exploring a more integrative approach to life. The last meta-theory explored in this chapter is the experiential learning theory of David Kolb.

DOI: 10.4324/9781003356424-5

I am very aware that I am wrestling with a paradox knowing that we experience reality as a continuous, integrated flow of perceptions which we register in the right hemispheres of our brain. Yet we have the left hemisphere of the brain that needs to conceptualise and make sense of that experience by creating concepts and theories. Hence my hope is that you will see the theories presented below as a synthesis of various disciplines and scientific writings, as a way of looking at our experiences to make sense of them, and not as a causative, mechanistic understanding.

Wilber's Integral Model

Ken Wilber is the author of 21 books and, according to Visser (2003), he is the most widely translated American author of academic works. To try and do justice to his work through a brief introduction is virtually impossible. This section is not an attempt to summarise his work; instead, only parts of his writings that are relevant to this section will be explored. In so doing, large sections of his work will not be dealt with.

The genius of Wilber (1995) is his ability to synthesise an enormous amount of information. He is well known for his work in integrating Western psychology and Eastern spirituality. His four-quadrant Integral Model (Figure 4.1) is a synthesis of various disciples and includes the works of Smuts (1973) and Schumacher (1978) among many others.

	Interior	Exterior
Individual	**Individual experience and consciousness** • Thoughts/ambitions • Feelings • Mood • Sensory input • Images	**Body and behaviour** • Neuro-muscular system • Genetics • Body sensations • Behaviour • Actions
Communal or collective	**Group membership** • Language • Social world • Rituals/history • Customs • Culture – organisation/family	**Social system** • Natural and human-made systems • Technology • Processes and structures • Physical laws • Objects

Figure 4.1 Wilber's four-quadrant Integral Model.
Source: Adapted from Wilber (1996:71).

Wilber's (1995) four quadrants correspond to Schumacher's (1978) four fields of knowledge. According to Wilber (1995), any integrated model or theory must take cognisance of all four quadrants. The individual is always part of a collective or communal body of people. One of Wilber's central postulates is that everything exists within a context. And as we have seen in the previous chapter, it is that context and environment that the nervous system has developed within and continuously learns from experientially. It is very difficult to work with an individual if there is absolutely no understanding of the collective consciousness out of which the individual arises, because nothing can be understood independently of that context.

For both the individual and the communal, there is an exterior and an interior domain. In Wilber's (1995) model, the upper-right quadrant deals with the individual's exterior domain. It is that aspect of the individual which can be identified with the senses, such as the body and its behaviour. It can be seen and measured and consists of things like the neuro–muscular system, genetics, behaviour and actions. For example, if an individual is depressed, a trained technician can perform a computed tomography (CT) scan on them and notice that their neural systems are working in a certain way that has been medically identified as a pattern associated with depression. To treat the depression, a psychiatrist can prescribe Prozac® to manage the condition, a legitimate medical solution to the problem. There is no way, however, that modern medicine can identify why the person is depressed by making use of the right-hand quadrants. To identify the "why", the psychiatrist must move into the upper-left quadrant and enter a dialogue with the patient to explore the latter's interior world.

Another example would be the husband and wife who survived the motor car accident in Canada, referred to by Van der Kolk (2014), discussed in Chapter 2. Their fMRI scans could show which parts of their brains disengaged during the re-enactment of the traumatic event. But the scans could not explain why their brains reacted so differently to the same trauma. The reason for that was discovered only by having a dialogue with each of them to understand how they had built up their survival patterns over time. This is the world of inner experience and consciousness in the upper-left quadrant, much vaguer and fuzzier than the upper-right quadrant. It is the domain of thoughts, ambitions, feelings, moods and images. Yet it is a world that both Smuts (1973) and Schumacher (1978) saw as being critical to the higher advancement of mankind.

The lower-right quadrant is the exterior manifestation of the collective. It is the domain of social systems and would include things like natural and human-made systems, technology, processes and structures, physical laws and objects. It is the collective systems that can be identified with the human senses. In Wilber's (1995) model this is the domain of systems thinking. Unlike many who believe that systems thinking is holistic and the solution to reductionism, Wilber (1995) suggests that it is not. In fact, he refers to systems thinking as "subtle reductionism", in that the general tendency of systems thinkers is to deny the inner domain of the system (Wilber, 1995:423). Classical systems thinking focuses its attention on that which can be seen or measured. It can tell you how a system behaves or what its behaviour is but it does not explore why the system behaves as it does.

That is the domain of the lower-left quadrant. It is the domain of group membership, of things such as language, customs, rituals, history and culture. Individuals are very much influenced by this domain, for example, by the culture in which they grew up. The influence of this domain is very powerful, more so than most individuals would like to admit.

Through applying some thought to the four-quadrant model, it soon becomes apparent that no one discipline or profession can lay claim to having the ultimate truth (see Figure 4.2). Every profession or discipline contains a partial truth. The value of Wilber's (1995) model is that it provides a framework to identify where that partial truth applies. Behavioural psychology, for example, contains partial truths and it is restricted to the upper-right quadrant. It cannot be used to treat a patient with an existential crisis. That is the domain of logotherapy, for example, which resides in the upper-left quadrant. In Wilber's model, the right-hand quadrants are the world of empirical science. Wilber (1995) refers to this as "flatland" because everything in these quadrants can be identified with the

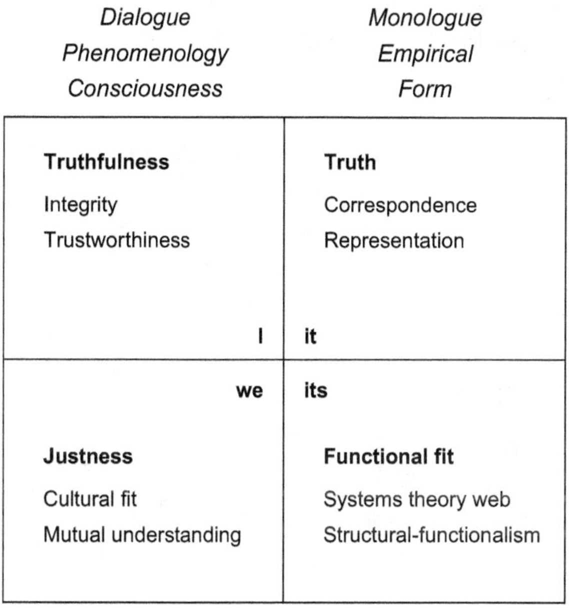

Dialogue *Phenomenology* *Consciousness*	*Monologue* *Empirical* *Form*
Truthfulness Integrity Trustworthiness **I**	**Truth** Correspondence Representation **it**
we **Justness** Cultural fit Mutual understanding	**its** **Functional fit** Systems theory web Structural-functionalism

Figure 4.2 Measures of truth.
Source: Adapted from Wilber (1996:107).

physical senses and can be measured and manipulated. The language that is used to refer to these quadrants is "it" because "it" consists of the behavioural (objective) and the social (interobjective).

The beauty of Wilber's (1995) model is that it gives legitimacy to the world of empirical science, whether that is reductionism or quantum mechanics. Every discipline contains a partial truth and the measure of "objective truth" is different for every quadrant. In the upper-right quadrant, objective truth is sought through the empirical establishment of perceivable facts. In contrast, the upper-left quadrant is the domain of the inner world of the individual; here the measure is truthfulness, which is the accurate perception by an individual of their inner state. What is the objective truth when you are dealing with different cultures? There is no objective truth. Therefore, in the lower-left quadrant the measure of truth is the justness of the mutual understanding among different individuals. The lower-right quadrant is about how the individual fits into the larger system, so the measure is the functional fit.

The left-hand quadrants deal with consciousness and hence empirical science is of no value; in these quadrants, qualitative and phenomenological research is more appropriate and valid. The terms used in these quadrants are "I and We" because the focus is the intentional (subjective) and cultural (intersubjective). Wilber (1995) points out that the right-hand quadrants have traditionally been very strong in Western thinking, whereas Eastern thinking has been very strong in the upper-left quadrant.

Wilber's (1995) model is, however, not limited to Schumacher's (1978) four fields of knowledge. The model incorporates the evolutionary levels of

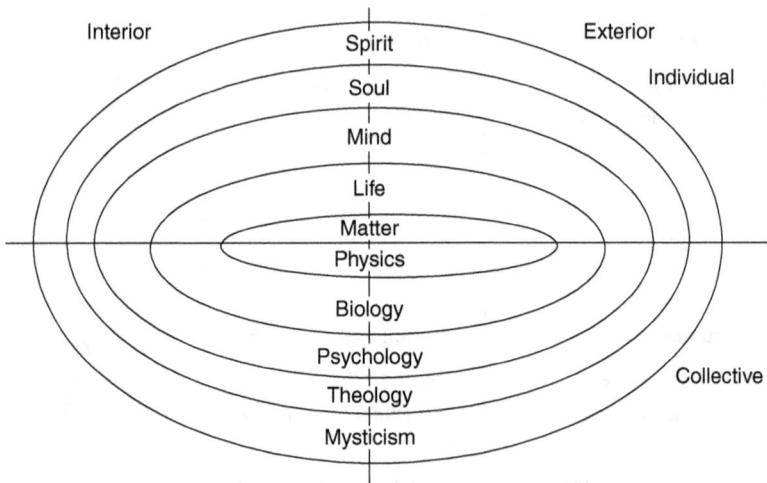

Figure 4.3 Evolution of consciousness.
Source: Adapted from Wilber (2000a:6).

consciousness, as represented in Figure 4.3. Like Smuts (1973) and Schumacher (1978), he believes that life has evolved from matter to life, from life to mind, from mind to soul and from soul to spirit.

Wilber's principles

The following principles form the basis of Wilber's Integral Model and his evolutionary or developmental thinking (Wilber, 1995:35–78).

Reality is composed of holons

Reality is composed of holons (whole/parts) and not things or processes. A "holon" is defined as "that which, being a whole in one context, is simultaneously a part of another" (Wilber, 1995:18). By this he means that reality is composed of wholes that are simultaneously parts of other wholes. Even processes exist as holons within other processes. Therefore, there are no wholes and there are no parts, they only exist as whole/parts. Because holons exist within holons within holons, there is no ultimate "whole". As a result, everything is open to question because everything is a context within a context, to infinity.

Capacities of holons

Self-preservation, self-adaptation, self-transcendence and self-dissolution are four fundamental capacities displayed by holons:

- *Self-preservation.* All holons have a capacity to preserve their own wholeness or autonomy. Although all holons exist within a context, it is not the relationship that defines a holon but its own individual form, structure or pattern. A holon is defined by the relatively coherent and autonomous patterns that it displays.
- *Self-adaptation.* Not only does a holon function as a self-preserving whole; being part of another holon or context, it must adapt to the other holons. Because it is a part, it needs to adapt and fit into its existing environment. As a whole it preserves itself; as a part it must fit in. Hence any holon has a tendency for both agency and communion. Its agency is its ability to express its wholeness to preserve its autonomy; its communion is its ability as a part to be in relationship with something larger.
- *Self-transcendence (self-transformation).* When different wholes come together to form a new and different whole, transformation has taken place. Transformation results in something new and novel; a new whole emerges. This is achieved through "symmetry breaks" in the evolutionary process. Self-transcendence is the ability of a system to go beyond itself and to introduce something new and novel. Evolution is not only a continuous process; important discontinuities can take place as well.

- *Self-dissolution.* Not only can a holon build up, it can also break down. This is due to the constant tension between a holon's agency and communion: the more a holon preserves its wholeness (agency), the less it serves its communion (being a part). There is thus a conflict between the holon's rights (agency) and its responsibilities (communion). This conflict between agency and communion can introduce pathology into the holon. Vertical tension occurs between self-transcendence (the tendency to build up) and self-dissolution (the tendency to break down). In self-transcendence, for example, particles build up into atoms, atoms build up into molecules, molecules build up into cells, etc. In self-dissolution, the process is reversed: cells break down into molecules, molecules break down into atoms and atoms break down into particles. Hence every holon is simultaneously a subholon (part of another holon) and a superholon (itself containing other holons). The capacity of holons is therefore very similar to the principles of complex responsive processes.

Holons emerge

Due to the fact that holons have the capacity to self-transcend, new holons emerge. Central to this principle is the idea that the emerging holon is not completely determined by that which went before it because it contains creativity and novelty. We never know for certain how the holon will emerge or into what it will emerge. The higher we move up the evolutionary scale, the greater the novelty. Physics is a more mature science than psychology, for example, which is not surprising given that humans contain much more novelty than rocks. Humans possess more creativity than rocks, and as a result the human psyche is more vague and more difficult to study than the elements of rocks. Humans are more unpredictable than rocks.

Holons emerge holarchically

Holons emerge holarchically, that is, they form a developmental hierarchy. Each holon emerges from the previous holon with an increased level of complexity. The higher holon will incorporate everything of the junior holon and then add its own new complexity or pattern. Holons build on each other, so each holon incorporates and transcends its predecessor. For example, every organism will incorporate cells but not *vice versa*. Cells will contain molecules but not *vice versa*.

And as we have seen, these principles are fundamental to Porges's (2017) polyvagal theory, which suggests that the nervous system evolved and developed hierarchically and that each of these stages are preserved in the higher stages, meaning that all developmental stages are present and preserved in humans. Schore (2019) and Hannaford (2005) suggest that, just as there is an evolutionary hierarchy in polyvagal theory, there is an evolutionary hierarchy of development in the brain.

Holons include but transcend their predecessors

Each emergent holon transcends but includes its predecessor(s). Each emerging new holon includes the preceding holons and then adds its own defining patterns. In each case, it preserves the previous holons but it negates their partiality. It preserves all the basic structures and functions and drops all the exclusive structures and functions, which are replaced by a "deeper agency that reaches a wider communion". In other words, all the lower is taken up into the higher. At the same time, however, not all the higher is in the lower. The holon includes but transcends its predecessor.

Wilber (1995) therefore believes that the transition from one stage of human development to the next involves differentiation and integration. Differentiation is when the self becomes aware that its own identity is distinct from the identity it attached to a certain stage of development. Having achieved that, the self can proceed to the next stage where it can add to the previous stages to create a new whole. This latter development Wilber (1995) refers to as "integration". The lower sets the possibilities of the higher; the higher sets the probabilities of the lower. Even though a holon transcends its predecessors, it does not violate the laws of the patterns of the lower levels. It is not determined by the lower holon because it cannot be reduced to the lower level. It cannot, however, ignore the lower level. For example, my body is constrained by the laws of gravity and time and space but my mind is not. My mind can explore different times and places; it is not limited to the body. If I fall over the edge of a cliff, however, my mind goes with my body.

Depth and span

The number of levels which a hierarchy comprises determines whether it is "shallow" or "deep"; and the number of holons on any given level is called its "span". Very simply this means that the more levels a holon contains, the greater its depth, and the more holons that exist on a given level, the greater its span. Hence humanity has greater depth than plants and rocks. Rocks, however, have more span than humans and plants. Each successive level of evolution produces greater depth and less span. The higher a holon is up the evolutionary level, the more precarious its existence. This is because its existence depends on a whole series of other holons that it incorporates. Because the lower holons are components of the higher, the higher-level holons cannot be greater in number than the components. It simply means that more depth equals less span. In addition, greater depth means a greater degree of consciousness. Here Wilber is in agreement with Schumacher (1978), who pointed out that higher levels of development always implies "more inner", while lower implies more "external and more outer". There are therefore two dimensions at play, a vertical dimension (deep versus shallow) and a horizontal dimension (wide versus narrow). Changes on the horizontal dimension Wilber (1995) refers to as translation, while changes to the vertical dimension are referred to as transformation.

Evolution and transformation

Wilber (1995) points out that evolution is first and foremost a series of transformations, each producing more depth and less span than its predecessors:

- Destroy any type of holon and you will destroy all the holons above it, but not the holons below it. There are a number of critics who deny the existence of a higher or lower order of reality; to them this is making judgements. But as Wilber (1995) points out, it is possible to determine the evolutionary sequence of things. The following question will locate the level of the sequence: "What other types of holon would be destroyed if we destroyed this type of holon?" (Wilber, 1995:61). So, for example, if all the molecules in the universe were destroyed, then all living cells would be destroyed. Atoms, however, would still exist. Only the higher-order holons would be destroyed, not the lower-order holons, the reason being that the higher-order holons depend upon the lower holons as constituent parts. If all plants were destroyed, life as we know it would cease to exist but matter would still exist. From this, Wilber (1995) deduces the following: the less depth a holon has, the more fundamental it is because it is a component of so many other holons. The greater the depth of a holon, the less fundamental it is because fewer other holons depend on it for their existence.
- Holarchies co-evolve. No holon is isolated, so all holons evolve together. Everything is a system within a system, a field within a field.
- The micro-holon is in relational exchange with the macro-holon at all levels of its depth. For Wilber (1995) this is a very important principle. It means that each layer of depth continues to exist in a network of relationships with other holons on the same level. This is best explained by making use of three levels of existence: matter, life and mind. In the physiosphere (matter), the physical body exists in relation with other physical bodies. It is dependent for its survival on gravitation, light, water and weather. So, for example, the human race reproduces itself physically by maintaining the body through food production and consumption. In the biosphere (life), humanity reproduces itself biologically through emotional-sexual relations. This is usually in families within a social environment. And at the same time, the survival of the social environment depends on the eco-system. In the noosphere (mind), humans reproduce themselves mentally

through "exchanges with cultural and symbolic environments". Societies reproduce themselves culturally through exchanging symbols that are embedded in various traditions and norms of that society.

- There is a direction to evolution. The direction is towards increased differentiation, organisation, variety and complexity. The evolutionary process develops from less complex to more complex systems and from lower to higher levels of organisation. This means that there are increasing levels of autonomy within the context of larger systems. The autonomy is relative because there are no wholes, only whole/parts (holons). Autonomy refers to the holon's enduring patterns, its self-preservation within a given context.

Stratified systems theory and complexity of information

The concept of evolutionary transformation from less complex to more complex systems is fundamental to Jaques and Clement's (1997) stratified systems theory as it is applied to managerial leadership. Even though people live in the same objective world, or in the same organisation, they can actually be living in totally different worlds. Given their level of development, and their ability to manage higher levels of complexity, they actually live in different realities. Jaques and Clement believe that the objective world is "infinite and unknowable". Their argument is that what anyone can know is limited by what they can make sense of at that moment in time. This depends on the vast array of data available to the individual and how they make sense thereof. Jaques and Clement believe that the world anyone occupies is made up of data which that individual has managed to transform into information that works for them. Every individual therefore determines the size of the world in which they live, through the amount of data which they can turn into meaningful information.

As a result, Jaques and Clement have identified four orders of complexity of information. And like all holons, they build on the first order of complexity, integrate it and then transcend it to a higher order of complexity. The four orders of complexity are as follows:

- *First-order complexity: Concrete things (Concrete Order)*: It is the world of things that can be pointed to: there is a tree, there is a person, that is a car, she has blue eyes, etc. The variables are not tangled together, they are clear and unambiguous. People operating at this level can deal only with a small number of variables. It is usually the world of children and young adults – the juniors in organisations.
- *Second-order complexity (Symbolic Order)*: First level of abstraction involving verbal variables. This is where verbal information is used in concepts. We no longer have to point to things; we can use the concepts in normal discourse. Here the variables can be broken down into numerous concrete things and actions, while at the same time being interwoven to

form complex patterns. It allows individuals to discuss their work, follow rules, discuss orders with customers, etc.

- *Third-order complexity (Abstract Conceptual Order)*: Second level of abstraction involving concepts. Here more complex concepts can be used to operate in the conceptual world of the organisation. It is the world of the CEO. Here the variables are large in number, interwoven in complex systems and continually changing. It is difficult in this world to go directly from concepts to concrete reality. Here the individual must be able to translate and pull together a concept like the balance sheet, with all its accounting assumptions, into concrete items like assets, liabilities, expenditure and revenue.
- *Fourth-order complexity (Universal Order)*: Third level of abstraction involving universals. This is a world where the level of complexity transcends those that are normally associated with corporate life. Here the concepts develop into universal ideas that address ideologies and philosophy. This level works with the problems of whole societies. It is the world of Einstein, Socrates, Plato, etc. From this it is very apparent that even though a second-order person lived right next door to Einstein, they would be living in two different worlds. In terms of Wilber's (1995) thinking, Einstein and his second-order neighbour would inhabit the same physiosphere (matter) and biosphere (life). But in terms of the noosphere (mind), they might as well inhabit different planets. Life would have different meanings for each of them (Jaques and Clement, 1997:54–57).

Wilber's developmental process in the individual

Jaques and Clement's (1997) stratified systems theory unfortunately stops development at the upper levels of the noosphere. The tendency in the West has been to stop at the ultimate levels of mind. Wilber (1995), like Smuts (1973) and Schumacher (1978) before him, extends this thinking into the theosphere (divine domain), as can be seen in Figure 4.3. Wilber (1995) therefore sees evolution as a series of developmental stages from matter to life, to mind, to soul and ultimately spirit. Visser (2003) points out that Wilber identified 17 stages of human development that can be subdivided into three main phases: the prepersonal, the personal and transpersonal, as set out in Table 4.1.

Before exploring the model, however, it is important to define the term "consciousness" which is used extensively by Wilber. One of the criticisms I now have of my previous book is that I wrote about consciousness assuming that everyone had the same idea of what that means, and so I never clearly defined what it means. The philosopher Christian de Quincey (2005) starts with a simple equation to define consciousness. The world (the physical universe) consists of things plus experience of things. What does he mean by that? The physical things are made up of matter, energy flows, vibrations and vortices. It is things like trees, stones, lightning, thunder and buildings. At the same

Table 4.1 Wilber's 17 stages of individual development

Phase of development	Stage of development	Domain of development
Transpersonal	17. Ultimate 16. High-causal 15. Low-causal	Spirit
	14. High-subtle 13. Low-subtle	Soul
Personal	12. Centaur 11. Biosocial 10. Mature ego 9. Late ego 8. Middle ego 7. Early ego	Mind
Prepersonal	6. Membership 5. Image body 4. Pranic body 3. Axial body 2. Uroboros 1. Pleroma	Body

Source: Adapted from Visser (2003:82).

time, there are nonphysical things like mental concepts and ideas. Experiences are what know these physical and nonphysical things. De Quincey (2005) mentions that although consciousness is often synonymous with experience, experience is often preverbal, happens before cognition and conceptualisation, and is closer to feeling than to thinking.

He is of the opinion that consciousness and experience can be used interchangeably, if by "consciousness" we mean "primordial subjectivity/interiority". In that case, "Both refer to the capacity for feeling, for being a subject, for ontological interiority, the raw ingredients of all psychic, imaginative, emotional, mental, cognitive, and linguistic phenomena" (De Quincey, 2005:87). And so, he characterises consciousness as that which enables us

> to feel, think, know, intend, attend, perceive, choose, and create … It is the source of all meaning, value, and purpose in our lives and in the world. It is "interior", it is what enables us to feel and know who we are inside – distinct from our external, physical bodies.
>
> (De Quincey, 2005:82)

And this definition is in line with what I believe Wilber means when he talks about consciousness. Furthermore, there are philosophical, psychological and spiritual meanings to consciousness that are all relevant to this discussion. Once again turning to De Quincey (2005) to help define these terms, he defines the philosophical meaning to mean any aspect of reality that is the opposite of "non-consciousness". And by that he means the total absence of any mentality, subjectivity, feeling or experience. As an example, a rock is "non-conscious" because all of those aspects are absent. According to him, therefore, in philosophical terms the light is either on or off. In contrast, when it comes to the psychological meaning, the light switch is always on but consciousness in this case is a function of the dimmer switch. That is, consciousness is always on; it is just a matter of how much it is turned brighter or dimmer. In other words, consciousness in the individual can vary from being slightly self-aware to be being enlightened. Spiritual consciousness refers to a more developed or self-aware state that transcends normal everyday psychological consciousness, and according to De Quincey (2005) involves an increased discernment when it comes to ethical issues. All three of these definitions are relevant to Wilber's model.

It is important at this point to mention that Wilber believes in the existence of a "self" in the individual which is critical in the developmental process. The argument that there is no self because the self cannot be seen or perceived does not hold ground for Wilber. It is the self that integrates, coordinates and organises the "stream of consciousness", and in so doing forms the basis of the individual's sense of identity. It is the self which climbs the "ladder of development". The ladder of development is a metaphor to illustrate the difference between what Wilber calls the basic structures of consciousness and the transitional or replacement stages of development. Visser (2003), using the metaphor of a ladder, identifies the self with the climber and the rungs of the ladder with the basic structures of consciousness: a higher view from each new rung with the transitional or replacement stages. So with every basic structure of consciousness is associated a certain worldview. As the self develops, the basic structures of consciousness remain in place and present, while the transitional stages will disappear. So the body (basic structure of consciousness) remains present throughout individual development, but the typhon (where the self is identified and limited to the body) is a transitional stage that is eventually replaced.

Wilber identified more stages than most scientific development models. In his later work, he reduced these levels to ten basic structures of consciousness and specified the ages at which these structures tend to emerge. Wilber's ten structures of consciousness as defined by Visser (2003), and the ages at which they tend to develop, together with Hannaford's (2005) suggestion of the cerebral neocortex developmental stage that has to be in place for those structures of consciousness to develop can be listed as follows:

1   *Physical structure*: The physical organism emerging prenatally. (Required cerebral neocortex developmental stage: reptilian brain; conception to 15 months old.)
2   *Sensori–perceptual*: Sensation and perception emerging between birth and 3 months. (Reptilian brain; conception to 15 months old.)

3 *Emotional-sexual*: Life force emerging at 1 to 6 months. (Reptilian brain; conception to 15 months old.)

4 *Phantasmic*: Thinking in simple images emerging at 6 to 12 months. (Reptilian brain; conception to 15 months old.)

5 *Rep-thinking*: Thinking in symbols and concepts emerging at 15 months to 2 years. (Reptilian brain; conception to 15 months. Limbic system/relationship: 15 months to 4.5 years old.)

6 *Rule/role-thinking*: Concrete thought emerging from 6 to 8 years. (Limbic system/relationship; 15 months to 4.5 years old. Gestalt (right) hemisphere elaboration; 4.5 to 7 years old. Logic (left) hemisphere elaboration; 7 to 9 years old. Frontal lobe elaboration; 8 years old.)

7 *Formal-reflexive*: Abstract thought emerging from 11 to 15 years old. (Increased corpus callosum elaboration and myelination; 9 to 12 years old. Refining cognitive skills; 16 to 21 years old.)

8 *Vision-logic*: Visionary thought emerging at about 21 years old. (Elaboration and refinement of the frontal lobes; 21 years old and above.)

9 *Subtle*: Experience of archetypes emerging at about 28 years old. (Elaboration and refinement of the frontal lobes; 21 years old and above.)

10 *Causal*: Experience of emptiness emerging at about 35 years old. (Elaboration and refinement of the frontal lobes; 21 years old and above) (Visser, 2003:123; Hannaford, 2005:93–94).

Needless to say, Wilber based his developmental model on Western developmental psychology and the esoteric traditions of Christianity, Judaism, Islam and Eastern spirituality. Given the complexity and wide range of Wilber's developmental work, it is outside the scope of this study to go into the developmental stages in great depth. All that is required is a general overview of the developmental processes; hence the referral to Visser's (2003) summary of Wilber's work.

The prepersonal

According to Visser (2003), Wilber sees the first stages of development as being dominated by the emotions and the body. Here consciousness is merged with physical-emotional reality. Consciousness is asleep. There is no sense of time, self, space or the environment. It is prepersonal because the personality has not developed yet. Unlike many transpersonal theorists, Wilber does not see this as a state of transpersonal bliss. Washburn (1995), for example, is of the opinion that this is a blissful state that is lost as the person develops an ego, and then the self returns to the pre-ego state in the transpersonal stages. In this view, the ego is seen as something bad, it is the enemy of the "spiritual". In his earlier work, Wilber agreed with this view. In his later work, he stressed that it was an error in thinking and referred to it as the Pre/Trans Fallacy.

Because Wilber's (1995) model is a hierarchical developmental model, his argument is that an infant cannot be more spiritual than an adult. In reality, the infant is less spiritual than the adult because it is merged with concrete reality, in that infants are totally ignorant of the mental world and the realms beyond that. Consequently, Wilber (1995) does not see the transition from infant to adult as a fall from paradise, but rather as a difficult emergence from a state of unconsciousness. It is a developmental way forward, not a return to a previous state. In Wilber's (1995) thinking, the ego is not an enemy of the spiritual but a steppingstone to the spiritual. The implications of this are enormous. How often does one hear consultants, coaches and psychologists speak about the fact that the real problem in organisations is people whose egos are too big? The solution, according to them, is to "get rid" of those people's egos, in effect asking those individuals to repress their egos and their development. In Wilber's (1995) thinking, the problem is not that people's egos are too big but that they are in fact too small. The solution is not to "get rid" of the egos but to grow them as big and as fast as possible. It is only when a healthy, developed ego reaches its limitations that it can transcend to the next stage of development.

Starting with the body, the child goes on to develop an ego/personality and once those are well established it moves on to the transpersonal realms of consciousness. As the child develops, it increasingly identifies with its body as the boundary between the self and the outside world. The concept of the self is defined by the boundaries of the body. So the self is very much a body-bound self. At some point in its development, the child will enter the "membership self" stage. Here the child becomes aware that it is part of a larger social system or environment. It is at this stage that the child starts to talk and communicate with important others in its environment, and at this point that the culture into which the child has been born starts to exert an influence. The child cannot think logically. Aided by language, the child now starts to develop concepts of time and can refer to past, present and future. The child also begins to be able to control bodily impulses. As the child starts to explore the world of language, it emerges out of the physiosphere and starts to become a personality.

The personal

The transition from the prepersonal to the personal stage is one of moving from a physical way of functioning to a more mental way of functioning. The child now has an image of itself and is capable of reflecting on that self-image. Whereas the child previously identified itself with the body, identification is now with a mental self. It is at this stage that the id, the ego and the superego come into existence. An important development here is the ability of the mental self to transcend the physical, while at the same time possessing the ability to suppress the physical. Visser (2003) points out that in Wilber's opinion, this phenomenon is at the core of an important imbalance in the psyche of the modern Western individual. As a mental self (ego), the modern Western individual has virtually lost all contact with the body and its functions, hence the Western ideal to dominate the body and nature. This ties in with McGilchrist's (2019) hypothesis that the Western world has been hijacked by the conscious, rational left hemisphere. The emissary has become the master.

Towards the end of the mental stages, the ego matures and the self develops the ability to differentiate itself from the ego. For the first time, the self can separate itself from the body and the ego. It is now in a position to integrate the body and the ego. Wilber (1995) refers to this as the Centaur Stage, the mythological figure that is half human and half animal. The body and the ego are integrated to form a higher union and this stage is characterised by the emergence of the existential crisis. Here the individual becomes concerned with meaning, self-realisation and self-autonomy. The phenomenological concept of intention becomes very important, in that it prompts the individual to ascribe meaning to their lives in the context of a personal vision. Life does not necessarily have meaning but the individual can ascribe various meanings thereto. The individual starts to realise that they are not a victim of circumstance but have the freedom to choose a response to various stimuli, which brings with it a sense of personal freedom. Although Wilber places the existential phase with the personal, it is the gateway to the transpersonal. In Western psychology, it is generally believed that this is the pinnacle of human development; the integrated, autonomous and rational individual is the end-point of human development. Even Jaques and Clement's (1997) stratified systems theory is limited to this band of human development. Their four orders of complexity of information clearly limit the concept of the self to Wilber's personal levels of development.

The transpersonal

Drawing on the works of a number of mystics, Wilber (1995) believes that the self continues to develop into the spiritual realms. In the first stages of the subtle level, the self begins to transcend the personal; it goes beyond the identity of language, thoughts and the ego. The self realises that it is more than just the body and the mind. Eventually the self will enter the higher stages where God and the self are one. It is at these levels of development that the self experiences the dissolution of the subject-object duality. All religious traditions speak of this phenomenological experience. At the ultimate stage of development there is no subject-object duality; all that is left is consciousness.

In the East this concept is certainly not strange. In the West, this kind of thinking has become more tolerated due to globalisation. It is viewed as an Eastern, and in particular a Buddhist, way of seeing the world. Yet even in the West, and in South Africa where we have very strong Islamic, Judaic, Hindu and Christian religious influences, this kind of thinking is not strange or unique. In Islam one has only to refer to the works of Rumi; in Judaism to

Martin Buber; in Hinduism to Sri Aurobindo; in Christianity to St. Teresa of Ávila, St. John of the Cross, Meister Eckhart, and Fathers Thomas Keating, Bede Griffith, Thomas Merton, Anthony De Mello and Evelyn Underhill, to realise that this is the everyday experience of ordinary human beings. It is an expanded experience of human development. Roberts (1993) gives a detailed phenomenological account of her experience of arriving at a state of no-self in her book *The Experience of No-Self*. In the conclusion, she writes that the journey to the state of no-self can take on two views. The first is that it is a supernatural event that constitutes a relentless journey into God. The second is that it is the final process of our natural lifespan, where self-consciousness is finally relinquished and we become mature human beings. Either way, the individual is prepared for a new existence. It is a developmental process in which the identity of the self continually expands until it ends in Unity Consciousness. At each level of development, however, different pathologies can develop.

So, for example, in the early stages of development the self is identified with the persona, and the shadow is seen as not being part of the self. This is the first level of integration, and supportive therapy or simple counselling can be used to help merge the persona with the shadow. If this integration is successful, the identity of the self is expanded to the ego. The self is now identified with the ego but the body is not seen as part of the self. At this level, psychoanalysis, transactional analysis or ego psychology, for example, can be effective in dealing with the integration struggle or any pathology that arises at that level of development. The centaur comes into being when the ego and the body have successfully been integrated. The self as identity ends with the person's skin; the skin is the boundary of the self. Everything beyond that is again seen as non-self or not part of the self. If this integration process continues and is successful, the individual will eventually reach a state of Unity Consciousness. It is the state of existence that the mystics speak about, the final realisation that everything is one. Here the object-subject duality falls away permanently. Mental suffering ceases to exist.

Visser believes that Wilber's genius has been his ability to map out these developmental levels, and to identify the pathologies that can be encountered at the various levels and the various psychological and spiritual therapies that can treat the pathologies, as follows:

1 *Sensory*: Psychosis – relaxing therapy.
2 *Phantasmic*: Narcissism/borderline – structuring therapy.
3 *Rep-thinking*: Neuroses – insight therapy.
4 *Rule/role thinking*: Script-pathology – script-analysis.
5 *Formal-reflexive*: Identity crises – introspection.
6 *Vision-logic*: Existential crises – existential therapy.
7 *Psychic*: Psychic pathology – nature mysticism.
8 *Subtle*: Subtle pathology – theist mysticism.
9 *Causal*: Causal pathology – formless mysticism.
10 *Ultimate*: Ultimate pathology – non-dual mysticism (Visser, 2003:144).

In doing so, Wilber has shown how Western and Eastern psychological approaches can complement and build on each other. He argues that all psychological and spiritual therapies are relevant – one is not better than the other; they each have their place. The question is not which school of therapy is the best, but rather which therapy is relevant for that specific level of development or level of pathology. Hence it is no good trying to treat a patient with an existential crisis using cognitive behavioural therapy; in this case, logotherapy would be more appropriate. In the same way, traditional Western psychology is irrelevant at the spiritual levels. Wilber's (2001) argument is supported eloquently by Roberts, noting as an example:

> the admission of a gentleman who said he was terrified at the thought of losing the self. What he had obviously failed to realise was that the terror and dread he felt *is* self, and that without a self there can be no such feelings.
>
> (Roberts, 1993:180)

Visser (2003) points out that Wilber's plea is for the conventional psychological schools to learn from the contemplative schools, especially with regard to the higher levels of development. But at the same time, he pleads for the contemplative schools to drop their apparent self-sufficiency and open themselves up to vital and important lessons that can be learned from psychology and psychiatry. These schools are more effective and efficient at dealing with the pathologies associated with the lower levels of development. The beauty of Wilber's model is that it gives legitimacy to all the schools, psychological and spiritual, Eastern and Western. Every school contains a partial truth. No one school of thought contains the whole truth. Once that is recognised, it is easy to integrate all of the various schools, recognising the value each adds to the developmental process.

Development is not a simple linear progression

According to Wilber (2000a), the human being is a very complex organism. Rather than seeing development as a simple linear progression where one level builds on another (e.g. the individual first has to be well developed cognitively before they can develop spiritually), development should be seen as taking place in relatively independent lines or streams. These lines can develop on different time scales, at different rates and with a different dynamic. So it is very possible for an individual to be highly developed in some lines, and medium or low in others. Wilber's (2000a) argument is that the overall development, what he calls the sum total of all the different lines, does not show any linear or sequential development whatsoever. He points out, however, that research continues to find that the "independent" developmental lines do tend to unfold in a sequential, holarchical fashion. The higher stages of each developmental line tend to build on and incorporate the earlier stages. Furthermore, no stage can be skipped because one builds on the other. In addition, he argues that these stages emerge in an order that cannot be altered by social reinforcement or conditioning.

Wilber supports his argument by pointing out that in *Higher Stages of Human Development* (Alexander and Langer, 1990), a widely regarded collection of the work of 13 "top developmental psychologists", nearly all of them present hierarchical models of human development; and their conclusions are based on "massive amounts of experimental data, not merely on theoretical speculations" (Wilber, 2000a:29). According to Wilber (2000a), there is consensus that no matter how different the developmental lines are, they tend to unfold holarchically. They develop through a physical/preconvention (prepersonal) stage, a conventional (prepersonal) stage and a more abstract postconventional (personal) stage, and finally into higher post-postconventional (transpersonal) stages. It is a complex web of development and there are no guarantees – pathology can enter at any stage of these developmental lines. Hence Wilber often talks of "regression in the service of transcendence": sometimes we have to regress to address or heal lower-order pathologies in order to move forward. The point is not to return permanently to the level where the pathology has occurred, but rather to address the pathology and get back to the higher level of development. If such pathologies are not addressed, they can halt the developmental process and/or hinder the integration processes.

The point is that Wilber's model is not a simple linear developmental model. It is a complex web of developmental lines or streams that are relatively independent. A very good example of this can be found in the Christian tradition. One of the literary classics within Christianity is a book called *The Practice of the Presence of God* by Brother Lawrence, written over 300 years ago. By all accounts Brother Lawrence was a very simple man. His application to join a monastery was continually refused on the grounds that he did not have the necessary intellectual capacity. Due to his sheer persistence, he was eventually allowed into the monastery, although he was never allowed to join the order. His job in the monastery was to wash the pots in the kitchen, as that was all he was considered intellectually capable of. Yet Brother Lawrence had a very highly developed "spirituality". In his simplicity, he developed a method to practise the presence of God, which led to him being a very spiritual man. So much so, that in his later years he became a spiritual director to many monks, priests and bishops. These men were no doubt intellectually far superior to Brother Lawrence, yet in things spiritual he was far more advanced than they were.

Individual and cultural progress

Not only does the individual develop through various stages, but cultures as a whole evolve through similar developmental processes. And more importantly, the individual develops within their cultural context. Here Wilber's thinking is very much in agreement with the theory of complex responsive processes; the individual and the social co-create each other and develop together. Visser (2003) points out that Wilber's earlier thinking was strongly influenced by the work of Jean Gebser, and later by Jürgen Habermas. Wilber found that his stages of individual development corresponded with the stages of cultural development outlined by Gebser. Gebser and Wilber were of the opinion that society as a whole has evolved through four stages: the archaic, magical, mythical and mental. The first stage Wilber called the archaic-uroboric stage/phase. This was the day of primeval humanity. In this phase, people existed in a state of consciousness that was more animal than human, being concerned with pure survival and the search for food.

The second phase, the magical-typhonic, was characterised by a physical-emotional level of consciousness. It was in this phase of development that individuals started to become aware of their mortality. In an attempt to ward off death, magic rituals were devised. In addition, the concept of time started to expand beyond the immediate present, but not much more than that. The most highly developed individuals at this time were the shamans who possessed authentic paranormal powers. We know about this culture because they left traces of tools, settlements and cave paintings.

During the mythical membership phase, about 100,000 years ago, humanity again advanced. Certain social organisations were called for to cope with increased populations. Visser (2003) points out that according to Wilber, the development of agriculture during this phase was of great importance to the development of human consciousness. At this point, humanity became aware of the cyclical nature of time because of their dependence on the rhythm of the seasons. Hence, individuals had to learn to relate to time in a different way; they had to learn to wait for the seasons and manage their crops. It was also at this time that language and writing emerged, in order to record the crops. People began to live together in groups and so the ability to communicate via language developed and cultures flourished. To perpetuate their culture they told stories (hence the term "mythical"). With this development came an awareness of politics or kingship and its shadow side, wars.

The fourth phase, the mental-egoic phase, came into being around the second millennium BCE. It was at this point in the evolution of humanity that ego developed within both individuals and their culture. By transcending the world of magic and myth, mental development started to excel. As a result, time now had a past, present and future. Humans now had a sense of history and modern humanity had arrived.

In his book *Sex, Ecology, Spirituality*, Wilber (1995) developed his thinking on this further, incorporating the work of Habermas. Both believe there is a parallel between the development of the individual and the evolution of humanity as a whole, and both incorporate the ideas of Piaget. Wilber, like Habermas, now divides human history into three main periods.

Visser (2003) points out that according to Wilber, in the first stage culture is magical. Individual identity is associated primarily with the body, thinking is based on images (pre-operational) and the basic orientation is biocentric or egocentric. In the second stage, culture is mythical. Self-identity is associated with the group to which it belongs (the role fulfilled in society), thinking is based on concrete concepts (concrete-operational) and the basic orientation is socio- and ethnocentric. This is very similar to the hypothesis put forward by McGilchrist (2019), that up until a set period in history, culture was developed as a result of the predominance of the right hemisphere of the brain. If you read carefully through the descriptions of the magic and mythical natures of culture, they are functions of the right hemisphere.

The final stage is the current level of cultural development. Culture is rational. And that starts to happen with the dominance of the left brain hemisphere functions, according to McGilchrist's (2019) hypothesis. Here the individual becomes an autonomous individual and ego. Thinking at this stage of development is based on abstract concepts (formal-operational) and the orientation is world-centric. Here Wilber's thinking corresponds to that of Jaques and Clement (1997), where his upper level corresponds to the latter's Fourth-Order Complexity, which is the third level of abstraction involving universals, and task complexity is stratum-VII. This is a world where the level of complexity transcends those levels normally associated with corporate life. Here concepts develop into universal ideas which address ideologies and philosophy. The individual works with the problems of whole societies, and the time-span would be between 20 and 50 years. It is the world of Einstein, Socrates and Plato. This is the complexity level of corporate CEOs working on strategic alternatives for global companies and politicians wrestling with national and global issues. Here the individual starts to operate from a global perspective. Not only do executives and politicians have to deal with the national economy, but with global economics. They have to deal with the complexity of divergent cultures and values, and changing international trade patterns.

The rational level is the upper level of our current cultural development. It is the level of development attained by the average person in the population. Wilber is, however, of the opinion that there are levels beyond the rational. Visser (2003) points out that the absence of scientific evidence of transpersonal stages in culture is due to the relative rarity of these stages in our culture. Yet Wilber (1995) points to the mystics who describe the transpersonal levels; these are people who were not just ahead of their own times, but also ahead of our time. These are people who have evolved to the highest levels of consciousness, levels of consciousness to which society as a whole still needs to evolve. These transpersonal bands Wilber divides into nature mysticism, theistic mysticism, monistic mysticism and non-dualistic mysticism. It is not within the scope of this book to go into detail on these stages. The point is that our history shows that there have always been individuals, for example, Buddha and Christ, who have been more highly developed than the general population. They reach these stages of development long before society as a whole. The tendency has always been for society to try and silence them or to pull them "back" towards the average or median. Just because the median of the population does not experience these levels of development, does not mean that these levels do not exist.

In the corporate world, a similar dynamic is at work. It is not uncommon to find individuals whose development or thinking is way ahead of the average level of development within the company. These individuals are usually under enormous pressure to fit in, conform or leave. Sadly, they often have no choice but to leave the company because it does not support their growth and development. This dilemma seems to be universal. Another example of where this happens is within monastic orders and the church, the very institutions that should be fostering growth and development in people. Pennington (1996) points out that the restrictions of communal service and obedience in the church initially do liberate the individual from attachments and the self-will. But in trying to channel the energies of the spirit, the church can frustrate and stifle human growth and development beyond the median level. In so doing it tolerates "safe", moderate growth and blesses the lack of growth and development. The church therefore tolerates those who do not grow.

This thinking is not unique. Beck and Cowan (2000) express similar views and stages of development in their book, *Spiral Dynamics: Mastering Values, Leadership and Change*. In his book *Integral Psychology*, Wilber (2000a) shows how their thinking can be integrated with his, for the purposes of a more integrated and holistic view of development; but Wilber presents a better framework. Like Jaques and Clement (1997), Beck and Cowan (2000) do a brilliant job of mapping personal levels for the individual and culture. It is in the transpersonal realm where they are found wanting, and where Wilber stands out in the clarity of his thinking. Hence Wilber's model appears more robust and more integrative.

A more integrative approach

Wilber's (1995) model gives us an integrated model of human and cultural development that is open-ended. He points out that human growth and development is a never-ending process with limitless potential. At the same time, however, there are no guarantees that every individual will experience healthy growth. At any stage of the developmental process, individual or cultural, pathologies can develop. These pathologies can be treated and overcome, or they can halt or destroy development completely. The beauty of Wilber's model is that unlike so many New Age fads, he does not call for the destruction of old sciences or the establishment of new sciences. Instead, he shows that every discipline contains a partial truth and no science or discipline contains the ultimate truth. Empirical science and phenomenological science are both valid and we need to honour both. As Wilber (2003) expresses it in his Foreword to

Visser's (2003) book, "integral" means to be more inclusive and embracing; it is an attempt to include as many perspectives, methodologies and styles as possible. Integral approaches are meta-models in that they try to draw together a number of existing, disconnected paradigms into a more enriching perspective.

Critique of Wilber

It is important to note that Wilber's structural-hierarchical model is only one of the major transpersonal paradigms in circulation. An alternative to Wilber's transpersonal paradigm is the dynamic-dialectical paradigm of Michael Washburn (1995), Professor of Philosophy at Indiana University South Bend and one of Wilber's foremost critics. Both models divide human development along triphasic lines (pre-egoic, egoic and transegoic) and both see development as a dialectical movement (thesis, antithesis and synthesis). But Washburn (1995) argues that that is where the similarities end. The dynamic-dialectical paradigm is based on a bipolar conception of the psyche, with human development being interplay between these two psychic poles. At one pole is the ego and at the other pole is what Washburn (1995:10) refers to as the "Dynamic Ground" which is the source of dynamic life (energy, power, spirit). The nonegoic pole is also known as the physicodynamic pole, whereas the egoic pole is known as the mental-egoic pole.

The nonegoic pole includes the dynamic ground (the source of dynamism, libido, energy and spirit) and is involved with instinctuality; somatic or sensual experience; symbolic cognition; and collective memories, complexes and archetypes. In contrast, the egoic pole features the ego (the organising and controlling centre of consciousness) and is involved with reflective self-awareness; self-control, deliberative will and control of impulses; operational cognition; and personal, biographical experience (Washburn, 1995:10).

This bipolar structure is very similar to the division between Jung's ego and collective unconscious. The egoic pole corresponds to the Jungian ego and the physicodynamic pole corresponds to the Jungian collective unconscious. According to Washburn (1995:5–32), triphasic development happens in five stages as a result of a dialectical interplay between the two poles of the bipolar structure:

1   *Original embedment*: The ego is blissfully immersed in the nonegoic or physicodynamic potentials as a result of minimal differentiation. Throughout the pre-egoic stage of development, the infant continues to be drawn into original embedment.

2   *Pre-egoic stage*: The ego slowly starts to differentiate itself from the nonegoic pole. As this is weak differentiation, however, it is easily swayed by the physicodynamic potentials. As a result, the ego frequently returns to original embedment.

3　*Egoic stage*: Through primal repression, the ego achieves independence from the nonegoic pole. As a result, the nonegoic pole is submerged and becomes the deep unconscious. The ego becomes the purely mental or Cartesian ego.

4　*Regression in the service of transcendence and regeneration in spirit*: The ego is regeneratively transformed by the physicodynamic potentials as primal repression gives way. The ego starts to return to the dynamic ground on its way to a higher synthesis within the ground.

5　*Transegoic stage*: The ego is now rooted in, and an instrument of, the dynamic ground. The psyche is an integrated bipolar system and fully developed.

Washburn (1995:36–45) mentions five points of disagreement with Wilber:

1　*The central role of conflict in the pre-egoic stage.* Washburn sees conflict as a primary theme of the pre-egoic stage. This conflict is brought about as a result of the desire for independence in relation to the dynamic ground, as well as the tension between desires for distance and intimacy in relation to the primary caregiver. The Oedipal period and conflict is central, as the child begins to see the father as a rival for intimacy with the mother and a model of egoic independence. Washburn's criticism is that Wilber does not place conflict at the centre of the development stage. In his view, Wilber places the emphasis on cognitive development, which unfolds without serious "countervailing" challenges. As a result, there is no interpolar tension, which is central to Washburn's paradigm.

2　*Are pre-egoic potentials lost or retained in the transition to the egoic stage?* The dynamic-dialectical paradigm holds that the ego resolves the early childhood conflict through primal repression, which submerges the nonegoic potentials into unconsciousness. For the child to continue developing, it must disconnect itself from the original source of its being. To assert its independence, the child has a choice between repression and regression, and in making this choice there is a forfeiture of the physicodynamic potentials of the psyche. Washburn points out that although Wilber does see a forsaking of some pre-egoic structures, these are transitional structures and not basic structures. As a result, the transition to the egoic stage involves a higher reorganisation of the pre-egoic psychic resources, but it does not forfeit them. Washburn believes that the repression and forfeiture of psychic resources is a normal and necessary part of the developmental process; Wilber does not.

3　*Does the mental ego alienate itself from its source in the egoic stage?* Washburn is of the opinion that repression of the nonegoic pole of the psyche during the transition of the egoic stage puts it out of touch with the Ground. This is done through repression. However, once development of the ego is complete, it no longer needs to repress the physicodynamic potentials. It is then that it is ready to reopen itself to the nonegoic pole of the psyche. The structural-hierarchical model, on the other hand, sees the mental ego as remaining in touch with its foundations.

4   *Is it a spiral movement or straight ascent through the stage?* The dynamic-dialectical paradigm sees development as a spiral loop. It is a going back in order to move beyond. There is a regression back into the pre-egoic in order to ascend into the transegoic. Wilber sees it as a straightforward ascending movement to higher levels. Wilber does, however, point out that rather than seeing development as a simple linear progression where one level builds on another (i.e. the individual first has to be well developed cognitively before they can develop spiritually), development should be seen as taking place in relatively independent lines or streams. Washburn, on the other hand, sees this spiral as a regression process in which the ego is disempowered and brought into direct contact with resurging nonegoic life. In so doing, the ego is transformed by the power of the Ground. So, as Washburn points out, none of Wilber's stages require a redeeming of resources that have been forsaken or lost. There is no spiral movement.

5   *Are there two selves or none?* Washburn (1995:43) believes that there is "small-s self", which is one pole on the biopole that needs to be reunited with or transformed by the other pole, the "large-S self". He is of the opinion that with Wilber, the self is seen as an illusion that needs to dissolve; it is merely a transitional structure. That might have been true of Wilber's earlier work, which is the work to which Washburn actually refers. In his later work, however, Wilber believes in the existence of a "self" in the individual which is critical in the developmental process.

Stanislav Grof (1998:89–94) believes that Wilber has a blind spot in terms of the significance of prenatal and perinatal experiences for the theory and practice of psychotherapy, psychiatry and psychology. Grof feels that Wilber does not understand that the perinatal domain is completely different as a logical type to all the subsequent developmental stages. He is also of the opinion that Wilber trivialises the importance of life-threatening situations like birth and death. And as we have seen from the work of Porges (2017), Schore (2019) and Hannaford (2005), our nervous systems have evolved to continuously deal with environmental threats. Any model of human development must therefore take environmental and existential threats seriously. As a result, Wilber's theory cannot make sense of essential features of psychopathology such as the linkage between sexuality and aggression. Grof is of the opinion that Wilber's Pre/Trans Fallacy is too simple and believes it is a complex process in which the personal and transpersonal coexist in a state of interpenetration. So Grof's criticism of Wilber is very similar or close to that of Washburn.

Washburn (1995) has some very compelling arguments and I think his work adds richly to the field. Both Wilber and Washburn are very well grounded in psychological theory, and both provide an understandable framework for transpersonal experience. I had previously argued that Washburn's (1995) model is a very powerful and useful model to use if you are a psychotherapist or psychologist – especially if you have been trained in and understand the conflicts brought about by prenatal and perinatal experiences. I have never been trained in psychology, however, and as a result I do not practise therapy on my clients. After a decade, and with more hindsight, I am now of the opinion that the problem is not in the underlying process but in the languages that all these models use. All models are limited by their language.

Having reworked the material, I can now see the similarities between Washburn's (1995:5–32) five-stage, triphasic development model and McGilchrist's (2019) work on how we experience the world through brain lateralisation. The process explained by McGilchrist is very similar to Washburn's five stages, but they use different words to describe it. And both are describing a dialectical process. According to McGilchrist (2019), the brain must attend to the world in two very different ways and in so doing it brings two different worlds into being. The first is a deeply lived experience of a complex, embodied, continuous flux, interdependent wholes that are constantly forming and reforming; a deeply connected and unique individual world. This is the world experienced through the right hemisphere. Here we experience the world pre-reflectively, holistically, before we divide it into bits. In this world, the subjective and objective are held in suspension and the two poles embrace each other in their togetherness. This is Washburn's (1995) "Original Embedment, Pre-egoic and Transegoic Stage" which takes place in the nonegoic or physicodynamic pole. In the egoic or mental-egoic pole, our experience changes to a "re-presented" version of what is experienced in the right hemisphere. The left hemisphere brings about bounded, separate, essentially fragmented entities that are static and grouped into classes. These can then be used as the basis to make predictions. The left hemisphere makes things explicit, and in so doing isolates and fixes things, making them mechanical and lifeless. Here the subjective and objective appear as separate poles. This is Washburn's "Egoic Stage" which happens in the egoic pole, also known as the mental-egoic pole. This way of experiencing the world through the left hemisphere enables us to know things, to learn, to direct and make things.

The danger is to see this as an antagonistic relationship, where the one hemisphere negates the other, or at worst that they merely complement each other. Both Washburn (1995) and McGilchrist (2019) believe that their incompatibility allows for a dialectical synthesis; it allows for something new to arise. So we are back to the central thesis of McGilchrist's book. Everything new starts off in the right hemisphere, which grounds and integrates the new experience; attention is then shifted to the left hemisphere, where it is manipulated and becomes familiar, and finally it is returned to the right hemisphere. And we see this returning to the right hemisphere happening in the "Regression in the service of transcendence and regeneration in spirit" in Washburn's (1995) model.

Brain lateralisation therefore does allow for interpolar tension, which is central to Washburn's paradigm.

I believe that the criticisms of Wilber by Washburn and Grof are valid. Moreover, I do believe there is a danger in both transpersonal theories that the reader can fall into the trap of believing there is an "ultimate" or "final" state or stage of development that we need to aim for and arrive at. Polyvagal theory and regulation theory have shown me that the state we are in at any point in time is determined by our physiological state. The nervous system, through neuroception, is continuously evaluating the risks in the environment. The nervous system quickly works out whether the situation in the environment or the people in the environment are safe, dangerous or life-threatening. According to Porges (2017), neuroception happens without our conscious awareness because it takes place in the primitive parts of the brain, and it triggers the appropriate behaviours and determines the psychological state we are in. Yet humans need to learn to override these more primitive defensive reactions if they want to create lasting social bonds, and that is what human development is all about. It is a very dynamic process that starts before our birth and ends with death. And during the time we have, we can fluctuate between all these different states depending on which physiological state we are in at any point in time.

No model or methodology is a "silver bullet" containing the ultimate truth; they all contain a partial truth which they contribute to the ultimate truth. Models and developmental theories are a product of how the left hemisphere tries to make explicit what we are experiencing, and they are all limited in their ability to describe reality. Yet it seems to be our human fate that we need these models to help us create meaning from all the sensory input we receive from the environment. Knowing that all models have their limitations, I continue to work with the structural-hierarchical paradigm because Wilber not only provides us with a well-developed theory of human development, but he also gives us an integrated framework in which to think.

The important thing to remember is that all four quadrants are necessary for an integral theory of consciousness. Visser (2003) believes that one of the main advantages of the four-quadrant model is that it enables the identification of all kinds of precise correlations within the various quadrants. As an example, when an individual is capable of abstract thought (upper-left quadrant) due to the fact that the neocortex has developed in the brain (upper-right quadrant) and is a prerequisite for thought, the individual can create a culture (lower-left quadrant) that is rational. And that rational culture can in turn develop industrialised economies (lower-right quadrant).

Given that Wilber has tried to come up with a theory of everything, it is understandable that there will be gaps in his theory. As we know, reality is actually way beyond the conceptual ability of any individual. Wilber (1995) cautions us to remember that any theory is just that – a mere theory. The point is not to know the theory intellectually but to live the reality and to experience it. Not only is Wilber a gifted theorist, he also actually lives what he preaches.

But this is precisely the point Grof uses to criticise Wilber's theory and I tend to agree with Grof:

> Since speculations concerning consciousness, the human psyche, and spiritual experiences represent the cornerstone of Ken's conceptual framework, it is essential to test their theoretical adequacy and practical relevance against clinical data. Ken himself does not have any clinical experience.
>
> (Grof, 1998:88–89)

I believe one of the reasons Wilber's work has not been researched is that he actually does not have an integrated methodology for development. There is no integrated injunction, that is the how-to-do-it. Research into the model can happen only once an integrated methodology for it is developed.

Integrative growth and development

Having an integrated theoretical framework for growth and development is all very well; the question is, of course, how does one facilitate this growth and development within individuals, or in the culture within which the individual lives and operates? Interestingly enough, Wilber does not offer an integrated developmental methodology. Part of the reason could be that he refers to himself as a pandit as opposed to a guru. Wilber (2000b) believes that a pandit does not accept devotees whereas a guru does. Pandits are usually scholars of a tradition and spend their time researching, writing and teaching. They do not engage in spiritual or therapeutic work with individuals; that is the domain of gurus and therapists. To the latter we can also add the profession of coaching. The point is that anybody looking to find an integrated developmental methodology in Wilber's work will be disappointed; they will not find one. Wilber's view is "Work it out for yourself."

Wilber (2000b) does, however, suggest that any individual who wants to grow in an integral way should practise a number of disciplines at the same time – and these disciplines should cover all four quadrants. And many of the integral methodologies that have been developed in response to his work do just that. According to Wilber (2000b), the general idea is to take a practice from each of the levels of being (body, mind, soul and spirit) and exercise all of them to the best of your ability. The aim is to practise them individually and collectively, and to find those disciplines that suit the individual and that are practically possible. In his view, the more categories that are engaged, the more effective they become. The problem is that people tend to concentrate on only one discipline, which leads to individuals not growing in an integrated way. Furthermore, it seems to be a very impractical suggestion for many individuals. In a world that is constantly demanding "more with less", individuals are already having a difficult enough time trying to manage their lives and their time effectively. Multiple practices demand a tremendous amount of time and discipline.

An alternative integrated model

Given the time constraints, resource constraints and the pressures under which most individuals live, it is highly unlikely that Wilber's approach is practicable for these individuals. The question has to be asked whether there is not a more pragmatic approach which can be used to help individuals develop in an integrated way. One possibility is the Diamond Approach developed by A.H. Almaas (2002). Like Wilber, Almaas has been working on an integrated approach to human development which incorporates both Western psychology and spiritual wisdom. In his book *The Eye of the Spirit*, Wilber (1998a) gives a 13-page critique of Almaas's work. His main criticism is that Almaas falls into the romantic notion of the prepersonal being the same as the transpersonal; in doing so he is supporting the Pre/Trans Fallacy. Yet Almaas has been able to develop an integrated praxis, which Wilber has not. And it is because of this that Wilber holds Almaas's work in such high esteem, despite the criticism that he levels against parts thereof:

> in my opinion, the Diamond Approach is a superb combination of some of the best Western psychology with ancient (spiritual) wisdom. It is one type of a more integral approach, uniting Ascending and Descending, spiritual and psychological, into a coherent and effective form of inner work.
>
> (Wilber, 1998a:267)

> This, nonetheless, is an extraordinary achievement, and certainly ranks it as one of the premier transformative technologies now available on any sort of widespread scale.
>
> (Wilber, 1998a:372)

Like Wilber, Almaas is the author of numerous books on human development. He started off his career doing a PhD in physics, but later switched to do his PhD in Reichian psychology. What is interesting is that in his Diamond Approach series, he, like Wilber, articulates a hierarchical view of realisation and the idea that we reach the pinnacle of development, which is enlightenment. But in his book *Runaway Realisation* (2014), he starts to move away from a purely hierarchical view as well. There is the realisation that we never arrive, for as we continue to explore our immediate experience, we realise that experience never ends. It is then that we learn that life is a limitless adventure and we can give up our search for final meaning and striving for an ultimate stage or state of development.

On one level, Almaas's (2002) methodology is very simple, yet at another level it is very complex and involved. It is simple because all that is required of any individual is an open-ended exploration into the immediacy of their own experience. It is about continuously inquiring into one's own personal experience. The beauty thereof is that it is a developmental and spiritual technique that uses the inherent natural capacity of the human consciousness. Human beings are curious by nature and it is just a matter of using that curiosity to inquire into our own experience. All that is required is a certain amount of discipline and desire to want to do it. It is actually so simple that an individual can do it on their own through journalling or silent contemplation, or via engaging in a dialogue with another human being. The inquiry into the experience is then analysed and explored even further by continuously asking open-ended questions. It is about inquiring into personal thoughts, behaviours, feelings and sensations. Like most things in life, it is a discipline that needs to be learnt.

What makes it complex is the language and terminology that Almaas (1998a) uses, which is an inherent problem in all models and methodologies. To really come to terms with this approach, the individual is required to do a tremendous amount of reading or to attend group training sessions to learn the terminology used in this approach. And the terminology is very important because Almaas (1998a) is very precise with the terms that he uses; the words have very specific meanings. The problem, however, is not in the words or the description, but that people who read the words often do not really understand them due to a lack of experience. Almaas (1998a) points out that the usual contention in spiritual literature, that ultimate reality cannot be described, is not accurate. Ultimate reality or "essence", as he refers to it, can be described. The problem, however, is that in describing essence it does not guarantee that someone who has not experienced essence will actually understand it. A person who has had first-hand experience of essence will, however, easily understand what the description is referring to.

As a result of this, Almaas goes to great lengths to describe what he means. For the novice this can be overwhelming. He does, however, make the point that this dilemma applies to anything and all levels of existence, not just essence. A simple example of this dilemma in the organisational context is the word "strategy". Executives use the word freely, believing that when they use it everybody sees the same reality to which they are referring. That reality, however, is often very different. Enough of the concept "strategy" is conveyed for people to have a general or vague idea of what strategy is. The question, however, is whether people are seeing the same picture. Almaas will say no because it depends on the person's level of development and their actual experience. One can return to the work of Jaques and Clement (1997) to see a similar point of view. A person operating at Category B–1 task complexity (stratum-I) will have a totally different view and experience of strategy to a person operating at Category C–3 task complexity (stratum-VII). Hence people at different levels of development often use the same word, but the experience and the worldviews associated with the word are literally worlds apart. To overcome this problem, Almaas has to go to great lengths to develop an appropriate terminology, which can often be confusing for the novice. This is what makes his methodology complex and involved.

On closer inspection, however, it becomes apparent that Almaas (1998a) is actually referring to the prehension dimension in David Kolb's (1984) Experiential Learning Model. His description of the actual experience corresponds to Kolb's (1984) concrete experience and the grasping of knowledge through direct apprehension. When Almaas (1998a) refers to description, he is talking about Kolb's (1984) abstract conceptualisation and the ability to grasp knowledge via comprehension. The beauty of this is that Almaas clearly points out the weakness of working only with the prehension dimension as a source of true knowledge. Some things are simply impossible to pass on via comprehension because it will be distorted and governed by the receiver's actual experience. Hence it is easy to understand why the Christian Church, for example, has often executed or banished its more highly developed saints: although they spoke the same language, they experienced totally different realities. Be that as it may, the point is that Almaas (1998a) is referring to Kolb's (1984) prehension dimension.

Fortunately, Almaas (1998a) does not stop with the prehension dimension. He goes on to say that to be a genuine human being is to be essence. But to be essence is not only an inner experience, it is the inner and outer. Essence is the inner experience in the privacy of your heart and it is the shared outer experiences with others. With a bit of reflection, it becomes clear that Almaas (1998a) is referring to what Kolb (1984) would call the transformation dimension of his Experiential Learning Model. In Kolb's model this is the growth dimension. When Almaas (1998a:82) refers to the "inner and privacy of our hearts", he is talking about Kolb's (1984) concept of transformation via intention. It is the journey inwards and the activity of reflective observation. Reflective observation takes the individual inwards. The danger, of course, is to get trapped in this inner world where it becomes mere escapism. Hence Almaas's (1998a:82) call that reflective observation must be completed or complemented with the "outer and shared experience with others". He is talking about Kolb's (1984) transformation via extension, the going outwards and being engaged with active experimentation. Interestingly enough, the test of true mysticism has always been that the journey inwards is the journey outwards. Both dimensions of the journey have to be present.

It can therefore be argued that at the most elementary level, Almaas's (2002) integral methodology uses inquiry as a developmental tool by making use of Kolb's (1984) Experiential Learning Model. This is not an attempt to simplify a very complex methodology; it is rather an attempt to arrive at a methodology that a novice can use to get started in order to mature into more complex and complicated levels of inquiry. I would therefore argue that Kolb's (1984) Experiential Learning Model can be used as an appropriate starting methodology, which can at a later stage lead to more complex levels of inquiry.

Experiential learning and development

Not only can Kolb's Experiential Learning Model be used as a methodology for learning, but his theory of development can easily be integrated with these various developmental models. Unlike the classical Piagetians who believe that learning is a subordinate process that is not actively involved in human development, Kolb believes that learning is the process through which development occurs:

> It is the process of learning from experience that shapes and actualises developmental potentialities. This learning is a social process ... Thus, learning becomes the vehicle of human development via interactions between individuals with their biological potentialities and the society with its symbols, tools, and other cultural artefacts.
>
> (Kolb, 1984:133)

For Kolb (1984), like Stacey (2010), this learning and development is a social process.

Furthermore, it is apparent that Kolb's (1984) language and concepts are very similar to those of Wilber. Kolb talks about the inner and outer world, personal knowledge and social knowledge. In so doing he is describing Wilber's (1995) four-quadrant model. The last sentence of this quote contains all four quadrants:

> Thus, learning becomes the vehicle of human development via interactions between individuals [upper-left quadrant] with their biological potentialities [upper-right quadrant] and the society with its symbols [lower-left quadrant], tools, and other cultural artefacts [lower-right quadrant].
>
> (Kolb, 1984:133)

The similarities between Kolb (1984) and Wilber (1995) do not end there. They share a very similar view of human development. Kolb's (1984) development model involves the self integrating, via dialectical adaptive modes, increasing complexity and relativism in relation to its environment. The complexity that has to be integrated comprises affective complexity associated with concrete experience, perceptual complexity associated with reflective observation, symbolic complexity associated with abstract conceptualisation, and behavioural complexity associated with active experimentation. In this developmental model, the concept of self starts off being undifferentiated and immersed in the world, in a state that he calls acquisition. The next stage of development is specialisation, where the self is interacting with the world and defines itself in terms of the content with which it interacts. This interaction is seen as mechanical and protects the separate identities of the individual, others and the environment. The final developmental stage, which Kolb defines as integration, is when the self is transacting with the world and sees itself as a process. Transaction implies a more fluid, interpenetrating relationship between the individual, others and the environment, and the relationship essentially changes all of them.

Kolb (1984) sees development as a dialectical process, which requires a confrontation and resolution of dialectical conflicts, and it is marked by increased differentiation and integration. Each developmental stage is characterised by the acquisition of a higher level of development that precedes the stage before it. Yet at the same time, the previous or earlier levels of development remain intact. So the first thing to notice is that Kolb's (1984) model easily accommodates Washburn's model, which sees triphasic development happening in five stages as a result of a dialectical interplay between the two poles of the bipolar structure, and views the dynamic-dialectical paradigm of development as a spiral loop (Washburn, 1995:5–32). Like all models, they are just using different language to describe a dialectical, spiral process. Furthermore, Kolb's (1984) dialectical process is marked by increased differentiation and integration. In this regard, his hierarchical integration is the same as Wilber's (1995) fifth principal that an emergent holon transcends but includes its predecessor(s). Each emerging new holon includes the preceding holons and then adds its own defining patterns. In each case, it preserves the previous holons but it negates their partiality. Kolb (1984) says exactly the same thing, in that each developmental stage is characterised by the acquisition of a higher level of consciousness that precedes the stage before it. Yet at the same time, the previous or earlier levels of consciousness remain intact. So, in Kolb's (1984) model, an adult can display all three levels of consciousness: registrative, interpretative and integrative. Both therefore believe in a developmental hierarchy which evolves towards higher and higher levels of complexity. Furthermore, they both believe that each successive stage of development builds on its predecessor by adding something new, while at the same time preserving the previous stage. Development hierarchies are inherent in Kolb's (1984) experiential learning theory.

Experiential learning theory believes that there are four interrelated developmental dimensions: perceptual complexity, affective complexity, behavioural complexity and symbolic complexity. The important thing is that although these dimensions are interrelated, they can develop separately or independently of each other, or at various rates or speeds. Hence Kolb (1984) differs from Piaget in that he sees individuality not only being manifested in the stage of development, but also in the personal learning style that the person adopts. In other words, it recognises individual differences in the developmental process. And it is not just cognitive development as it is for Piaget. Kolb (1984) sees development as being multilinear and happening in a spiral. Piaget did specify how concepts gain independence from concrete experience in his developmental theory; however, as Kolb and Kolb (2017) mention, his theory does not deal with how these concepts are then reintegrated with the ongoing concrete experience of the individual. Development in experiential learning theory is a continuous learning spiral where abstract cognitive frameworks are integrated with experience. This is very similar to Wilber's idea of separate and independent development lines. Hence both Wilber (1995) and Kolb (1984) break away from the pure linearity of the Piagetian approach, in that they see development as being multilinear. Yet both agree that the more integrated the individual becomes, the more the various lines of development become integrated or converge.

Contrary to the belief that development is an individual internal process, Kolb and Kolb (2017) argue that development results from transactions between the individual and the environment. They are careful to use the word transaction as opposed to interaction. They see the latter as being too mechanical and protecting separate identities. Transaction implies a more fluid inter-penetrating relationship between the individual and the environment, and the relationship essentially changes both. Inherent in their understanding is the concept of people co-creating each other. So it is through our transactions with each other that we co-create each other. Once again, we can see the connection between Kolb and Kolb's (2017) experiential learning theory and Stacey's (2010) complex responsive processes. The theory of complex responsive processes suggests that human action consists simultaneously of private and social responses; the social is the public action directed between individuals, while the private is the private actions directed back at the individual self or mind. More importantly, in this view self and the social are the same process of bodily action. Human consciousness, social interaction and self-consciousness are the same process. Here the individual mind or self, and the social, form each other at the same time. In other words, as a result of complex responsive processes they co-create each other. As a result, for Kolb (1984) there are many specialised and individualised paths to development, as they are all developed in response to the cultural context and social knowledge system in which the individual finds themselves. The environment is not, however, limited to human transactions; it includes transactions like learning a new skill or making tools to solve a specified problem.

Kolb's developmental stages

Kolb (1984) believed that the human development process can be divided into three broad developmental stages: acquisition, specialisation and integration. Acquisition extends from birth to adolescence and it is the stage where the basic learning abilities and cognitive structures are acquired. At the beginning, the self is experienced as undifferentiated and immersed in the environment. As the child develops through the acquisition phase, there is a gradual development of an internalised structure that allows the self to distinguish and separate itself from the surrounding environment. It is at this stage that the discrimination between internal and external stimuli are developed, which matures into the delineation of the boundaries of selfhood. Once again, Kolb (1984) is describing a very similar concept and process to Washburn's (1995) "Original Embedment and Pre-egoic Stage". In original embedment, the ego is blissfully immersed in the nonegoic or physicodynamic potentials as a result of minimal differentiation. Throughout the pre-egoic stage of development, the infant continues to be drawn into original embedment. In the pre-egoic stage, the ego slowly starts to differentiate itself from the nonegoic pole. As this is weak differentiation, however, it is easily swayed by the physicodynamic potentials. As a result, the ego frequently returns to original embedment but eventually separates.

The specialisation phase extends through formal education and/or career training into early adulthood. Given their culture, education and socialisation, the individual becomes more specialised to adapt and master their careers. It is at this stage that the individual will work very intensely with the transformative dimension for the first time, and with the dynamic tension between internal personal and external social forces and expectations. Kolb (1984) points out that during this phase, there is a closer and closer match between self-characteristics and environmental demands. And there are two ways in which this happens; social pressure forces the person to fit in and people tend to select environments that are consistent with their characteristics. Once again, here Kolb is in agreement with Stacey (2010), who sees organisations as a group of interacting people who are interdependent. And it is this interdependence that is the source of power, in that their interdependence both enables and constrains them. At this stage, the self is defined in terms of "content" – professional skills, achievements and past experiences, both good and bad. The sense of self is based on the rewards and recognition received for doing well in a chosen life task. The primary mode of engaging with the world is through interaction. The individual acts on the world and the world acts on them in return through the rewards it gives. Kolb (1984) does point out that although this interaction is bi-directional, neither is fundamentally changed by the other. This stage brings about social security and achievement. And this is the egoic stage in Washburn's (1995) model where, through primal repression, the ego achieves independence from the nonegoic pole. As a result, the nonegoic pole is submerged and becomes the deep unconscious. The ego becomes the purely mental or Cartesian ego.

The integration phase is ushered in with the existential crisis, the conflict between personal fulfilment and meaning versus social demands and expectations. The individual strives more to influence than to be influenced by the environment. There is an exploration of aspects of the personality that was suppressed during the specialisation phase. Hence the concept of the self moves from self as "content" to self as "process". I had previously seen this as a limitation in Kolb's model and mentioned that sadly, this is where Kolb (1984) stops with the stages of development; that he stops his thinking on human development at the highest level of rational development, the existential level.

Based on correspondence with Kolb, I now understand that this is not the case and that he does hint at higher levels of development. And over the years, I have developed a new appreciation for his idea that the concept of the self moves from self as "content" to self as "process". For I now believe that experiential learning and human development is a continuous process that never ends, for we never arrive. At the same time, we are completely immersed in several complex responsive processes where our identities are continually being formed. And this is where we will find the last two stages in Washburn's (1995) model: regression in the service of transcendence and regeneration in spirit where the ego is regeneratively transformed by the physicodynamic potentials as primal repression gives way. The ego starts to return to the dynamic ground on its way to a higher synthesis within the ground. And lastly the transegoic stage where the ego is now rooted in, and an instrument of, the dynamic ground. The psyche is an integrated bipolar system and fully developed.

Integrating the models of Wilber and Kolb

In Wilber's (1995) model, the highest level of rational development is referred to as Vision-Logic and is seen as the transition point into the transpersonal bands. As can be seen from Table 4.2, Wilber (1995) and Kolb (1984) are in agreement on the symbolic complexity via comprehension for the personal bands of development. In short, they are saying the same thing. It is clear that in terms of human development and how it happens, Wilber (1995) and Kolb (1984) seem to be in agreement. The only difference is that Wilber's (1995) model is more integral than Kolb's (1984) model, in that Wilber does not stop at personal levels of development but allows for transpersonal levels of human development. As mentioned previously, however, in my personal correspondence with David Kolb he has made me aware of the fact that although he does not directly address the transpersonal realm, he does allude to it in Chapter 8 of his book. Furthermore, in their later work Kolb and Kolb (2017) do address the biological structures associated with the Experiential Learning Model, which Kolb had not previously done. For that reason, I have incorporated Hannaford's (2005) cerebral neocortex developmental stages into Table 4.2 to create a more holistic understanding of the integration of the two models, and to show how both models of psychological and spiritual development are reliant on the underlying physiological developmental stages.

Furthermore, Kolb and Kolb (2017) start to question the hierarchical stage model with its implied unilinear and unidirectional assumption. An alternative option they consider is the curvilinear idea put forward by Suzanne Cook-Greuter. Firstly, in this model there is an upward separation from the ground of being in early development from the preconventional to conventional stage of development, which would be the specialisation stage in the Kolb (1984) model. Secondly, there is eventually a return to the ground of being with higher awareness in the postconventional stage, which is the integration stage

Table 4.2 Wilber's stages of development in relation to Kolb's stages

Wilber's stages	Wilber's symbolic complexity via comprehension	Kolb's stages	Kolb's symbolic complexity via comprehension	Hannaford's approximate neocortex developmental stages
10. Causal	Experience of emptiness.			Elaboration and refinement of the frontal lobes: 21+ years old.
9. Subtle	Experience of archetypes.			Elaboration and refinement of the frontal lobes: 21+ years old.
8. Vision-logic	Visionary thought.	Integration	Attaching concrete meanings to symbol systems and finding and solving meaningful problems.	Elaboration and refinement of the frontal lobes: 21+ years old.
7. Formal-reflexive	Abstract thought.	Specialisation	Formal hypothetico-deductive reasoning.	Refining cognitive skills: 16 to 21 years old. Increased corpus callosum elaboration and myelination: 9 to 12 years old.
6. Rule/role-thinking	Concrete thought.	Specialisation	Concrete symbolic operations.	Frontal lobe elaboration: 8 years old. Logic (left) hemisphere elaboration: 7 to 9 years old. Gestalt (right) hemisphere elaboration: 4.5 to 7 years old. Limbic system/relationship: 15 months to 4.5 years old.
5. Rep-thinking	Thinking in symbols and concepts.	Acquisition	Object constancy; "ikonic" thought.	Limbic system/relationship: 15 months to 4.5 years old.
4. Phantasmic	Thinking in simple images.	Acquisition	Recognising enactive thought.	Reptilian brain: conception to 15 months old.
3. Emotional-sexual	Life force.	Acquisition	Recognising enactive thought.	Reptilian brain: conception to 15 months old.
2. Sensoriperceptual	Sensation and perception.	Acquisition	Recognising enactive thought.	Reptilian brain: conception to 15 months old.
1. Physical	The physical organism.	Acquisition		Reptilian brain: conception to 15 months old. Reptilian brain: conception to 15 months old.

Source: Adapted from Visser (2003:123), Kolb (1984:152) and Hannaford (2005:93–94).

in the Kolb (1984) model. This is a very similar idea to the one put forward by Michael Washburn (1995), as was discussed previously. And as Kolb and Kolb (2017) point out, it is very similar to Carl Rogers's idea that in the specialisation phase of development, the child's pure experiencing is blocked due to cultural introjections by others. It is only later as the individual matures that the pure experiencing re-emerges. *As a result, they start to move away from the stage models of development and rather start to explore the states described in the stage models. And most critical of all, they do not see these states as necessarily being hierarchical, but rather as modes of adaptation.* That thinking is in agreement with polyvagal theory and regulation theory.

The net effect is that integration and differentiation are no longer seen as broad life stages, but rather as development processes that happen continuously throughout life. The three stages of development are redefined in their new thinking as states of adaptation. These states differ in the way they frame time and space. The adaptive learning state that is confined to immediate time–space they refer to as performance. When the state extends the time–space frame to similar specialised environments, they refer to it as the learning state. The state that covers all life situations and the total life span is called the development state. As a result, the individual's conscious experience is determined by these different states of mind – which, as polyvagal theory and regulation theory have shown us, is a function of our physiological state. At this point, the Kolbs start using the term "consciousness", which can mean many things to many people. My understanding of the term is similar to De Quincey (2005), who is of the opinion that consciousness and experience can be used interchangeably if by "consciousness" we mean "primordial subjectivity/interiority". In the performance state, the experience is simply sensing the results of goal-directed actions; it is registrative. Here experiences can be treated in isolation and singly; consciousness is primarily analytical. An interpretative role is taken on in the learning state. A holistic perspective is added by the integrative consciousness in the development state. It is primarily synthesising in nature, in that it places isolated experiences in context, is more strategic, and is broad in time and space. Furthermore, by carrying forward the flow of experience and centring it, it creates integrity.

Based on challenges from the environment, life circumstances or personal choice, individuals can be in any one of these states at various times and situations. In the same way that they refer to states being associated with various stages, there are different worldviews associated with the different stages in Wilber's model. So, in a sense, the emphasis is moved away from the developmental stages to focusing more on the states or worldviews, which are much more fluid. That in turn makes a lot of sense to me because as have I learnt from polyvagal theory, our experience is determined by which physiological state we are in at any point in time. And those physiological states are not permanent states but fluid states that are continuously responding to demands and threats within the individual's environment. Hence the Kolbs seeing the states as modes of adaptation. I agree with that view while at the same time recognising that those states can contribute to developmental stages. However, I no longer believe that those stages and states are permanent but that they fluctuate based on our physiological state.

In my opinion, Wilber's (1995) model provides a comprehensive framework for integrated growth and development. Wilber's (1995) Integral Model is nevertheless weak in terms of the praxis of human development and it is here that Kolb's (1984) Experiential Learning Model is far superior. Kolb's (1984) model provides a practical, experiential way to learn and grow in an integrated way. To develop an Integrated Experiential Learning Process model, it is suggested that the two models be integrated to form a higher synthesis, as represented in Figure 4.4. By comparing Figure 1.1 with Figure 4.1, it will be clear how Figure 4.4 superimposes the four forms of Kolb's model on the four quadrants of Wilber's Integral Model.

Wilber's (1995) model provides the meta-framework for integrated growth and development, while Kolb's (1984) model provides a practical, experiential way to learn and grow in an integrated manner. Figure 4.4 is an oversimplified presentation of two very complex models, yet it provides a simple framework to explain the synthesis of the two models. An individual will generally experience something concrete in the context of the collective, unless the individual

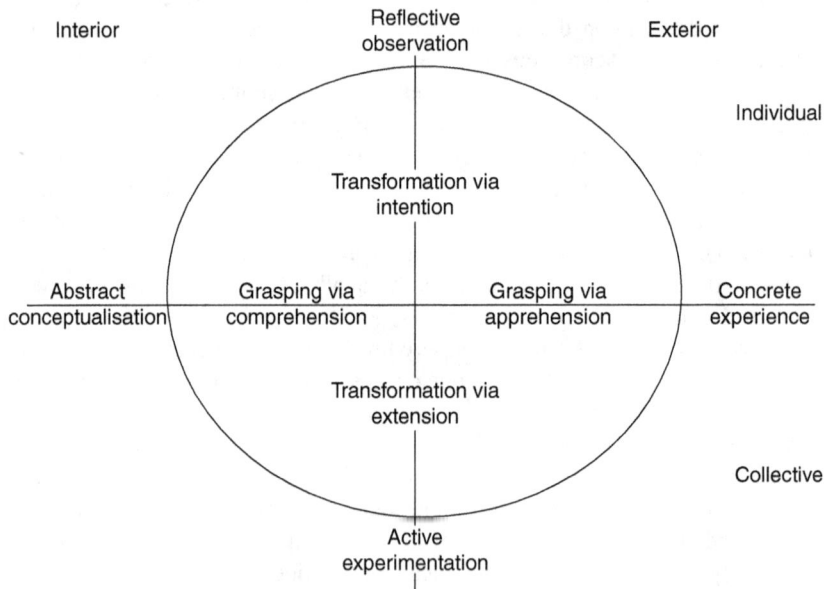

Figure 4.4 Integrated Experiential Learning Process.
Source: Adapted from Wilber (1996:71); Kolb (1984:42).

lives in complete isolation. This is in agreement with the theory of complex responsive processes, in that many of our experiences are interactions with other humans. To make sense of these experiences, the individual needs to make use of the intention dimension, move inwards and reflect on the experience. Having reflected on it, the individual starts to develop some theory or concept about the experience. But abstract conceptualisation is not something that belongs purely to the individual; it is influenced by the culture or system in which the individual finds themselves.

Kolb (1984), like Stacey (2003), Porges (2017) and Schore (2019), conceptualises experiential learning as a developmental process that is the product of both personal and social knowledge. The individual's state of development flows from the transaction of the individual's personal experience and the particular system of social knowledge with which they interact. Here Kolb (1984) disagrees with Piaget, who sees it purely as an individual issue. He agrees with the theory of complex responsive processes, polyvagal theory and regulation theory which have taught us that people learn to cooperate in sophisticated ways through responding to each other's intended actions. Actions in this context means physical movements of the body, constituting gestures to and responses from others. This includes visual gestures in response to facial expressions, emotions which are felt-gesture responses to changes in bodily rhythms and vocal gesture responses to sound. This is fundamentally a communicative process because each gesture will evoke a response in others. Stacey (2003), Porges (2017) and Schore (2019) make the point that humans are physiologically dependent on each other's physiology to regulate their bodies. This is because the biochemical mechanisms for arousal and calming are linked to the actions of separation from and attachment to others. At a physiological level, humans are fundamentally social beings who continuously relate to each other through various processes. Through experience, the individual can learn to act in expectation of responses from other individuals.

In response to these interactive experiences, the individual develops a hypothesis or theory about what is going on; the individual then needs to engage the extension dimension and actively experiment within the collective environment. Kolb (1984) therefore agrees with Stacey (2003), who views human action as consisting simultaneously of the private and social responses. The social is the public action directed between individuals, while the private is the private actions directed back at the individual self or mind. More importantly, in this view self and the social are the same process of bodily action. Human consciousness, social interaction and self-consciousness are the same process. Here the individual mind or self, and the social, form each other at the same time. In other words, they co-create each other.

The beauty of Kolb's (1984) model is that it is independent of context and content. The same methodology can be used to facilitate the learning of meditation, personal fitness training, the design of organisational processes and structures, or learning how to manage people. Done correctly and in a disciplined way, experiential learning will automatically move the individual through all four quadrants and develop all four learning capabilities that are a prerequisite for human growth and development. And the more developed the person becomes, the more integrative the experiential learning experience becomes, thereby facilitating personal growth, development and the transformation of consciousness. At the same time, this model easily integrates and accommodates Washburn's model (1995) as well.

Thus, the Integrated Experiential Learning Process is about facilitating integrated experiential learning in individuals to enhance personal growth and development. It is integrated in that it caters for Schumacher's (1978) four fields of knowledge and Wilber's Integral Model which explores personal development through various levels of consciousness, especially in the personal and transpersonal levels. At the same time, it caters for Washburn's model as well. It is experiential in that it uses Kolb's Experiential Learning Model as the developmental tool or methodology, which is a continuous dialectical process, that is governed and dependent on the underlying physiological state of the individual concerned. In this theory, personal development happens as a result of the individual learning from experience through transactions with the environment, including the social environment. It is important to emphasise that in this theory, the basic physiological structures are the same, that is we all have a lateralised brain with four lobes in each hemisphere and that we all use the four adaptive learning modes of the experiential learning cycle to create meaning. Yet how we do it, and the outcomes we achieve, are unique to every individual. Zull's (2011) work reminds us that the biological foundations might be the same but the resulting mind that develops though experience and nurturing is completely unique and unpredictable in every individual. It is best summed up in the words of Victor Frankl:

> Meaning is relative in that it is related to a specific person who is entangled in a specific situation ... Thus man is unique in terms of both essence and existence. In the final analysis, no one can be replaced – by virtue of the uniqueness of each man's essence.
>
> (Frankl, 1988:54–55)

As a result, no learning style can fully explain the uniqueness of every individual. There is the recognition that our conscious learning happens via the experiential learning cycle. Yet at the same time at an unconscious level, through neuroception, our nervous system is continuously learning from and responding to the environment as well. Yet for Feldenkrais, the more mature we become the more we have conscious control over the latter:

> What I understand by maturity, is the capacity of the individual to break up total situations of previous experience into parts, to reform them into a pattern most suitable to the present circumstances, i.e. the conscious

control effectively becoming the overriding servomechanism of the nervous system.

(Feldenkrais, 2005:196)

Maturity to him is our ability to recognise and accept our uniqueness and to form new responses to our ever-changing environment. Through experiential learning, learn to become aware of what physiological state we are in and learn how to consciously create an appropriate response to the situation, rather than being totally at the mercy of our nervous system.

Furthermore, there is the recognition that although there are developmental stages and states, there is no final stage or state to attain. Life is a continuous flow of energy and experiences, and we can continue to learn from those experiences and create meaning from them until we die. In fact, aiming to reach a certain stage could be self-defeating. Once again, this is eloquently expressed by Frankl:

> Self-actualisation if made an end in itself, contradicts the self-transcendent quality of human existence. Like happiness, self-actualisation is an effect, the effect of meaning fulfilment. Only to the extent to which man fulfils a meaning out there in the world, does he fulfil himself.

(Frankl, 1988:38)

It is through experiential learning within the environment that we find ourselves, and that we all discover how unique we are and what contribution and meaning we bring into the world.

Furthermore, the Integrated Experiential Learning Process is not a purely cognitive way of learning. It recognises that cognition is part of an integrated whole where cognition is impossible without the impulses fired by the nervous system, and the muscles and skeleton that moves because of those impulses. It agrees with Feldenkrais, Hannaford and many other authors that the motor patterns and habits of the cortex are deeply influenced and formed by individual experience. They are movements learnt through experiential learning and are unique to every individual. How we move and how often we move has a direct impact on the quality of cognition. Through experiential learning, we learn to move and improve the quality of our movements and then we use the same process to learn cognitively. Hence movement can improve cognition and cognition can improve movement.

Experiential learning and movement are the two sides of the same coin. Walking upright on two legs and learning is what distinguishes humans from all the other animals. We are given the basic structures at birth, yet our nervous system and brain grow and form as we learn to adjust to the environment we are born into, all through experiential learning. This plasticity of the nervous system, combined with our unique environment, means that we all become who we are through a process of learning. We all learn to walk but we all have a unique gait, a way of walking. We all go through the various stages and states of human development, yet our personalities are completely unique. All because our nervous systems have developed unique patterns on how to respond to the environment through experiential learning. Our personal experiences enable us to develop and form new movement and behavioural patterns in response to our environment. Our nervous system enables us to continuously form new nervous paths, associations and groupings, be that for movement, emotions or behaviours. That is the basis of experiential learning and that is what makes us unique.

As Feldenkrais (2005) reminds us, every emotion or attitude is associated and linked in the cortex with some muscular configuration. Our bodies are therefore as much a part of human development as the emotions and thinking that is associated with every stage or state; they are one and the same process. In fact, if we really apply our minds and reasoning abilities to what this Integrated Experiential Learning Process entails, then we might just agree with Feldenkrais (2019:85) that "objective reality is only a part of subjective reality". For as he points out:

> This is clearly seen in the structure of the nervous system ... out of 3×10^{10} cells only 3×10^{7} at the very most can be informing our interior of the world outside us, which is less than one cell for every thousand cells that manipulate, analyse, and integrate data.
>
> (Feldenkrais, 2019:86)

As a result, the Integrated Experiential Learning Process sees the subjective and objective, the individual and the social as one integrated process.

At the same there is the realisation that because we develop through learning, there is the possibility that our learning can be faulty, or that we learn the wrong or inappropriate response or behaviours. The good news is that through experiential learning, we can unlearn the wrong patterns and relearn a more appropriate pattern or response.

Summary

This chapter explored three meta-theories that influenced the development of the Integrated Experiential Learning Process: the integral theory of Ken Wilber; the integral theory of A.H. Almaas and the experiential learning theory of David Kolb. Finally, the chapter showed how these three meta-theories were integrated or synthesised to develop the Integrated Experiential Learning Process. It is integrated in that it caters for Schumacher's (1978) four fields of knowledge and Wilber's Integral Model which explores personal development through various levels of consciousness, especially in the personal and transpersonal levels. At the same time, it caters for Washburn's model as well. It is experiential in that it uses Kolb's Experiential Learning Model as the developmental tool or methodology, which is a continuous dialectical process, that is governed and dependent on the underlying physiological state of the individual concerned. In this model, personal development happens as a result of the individual learning from experience through transactions with the environment.

Chapter 5

Research methodology

Introduction

Having a philosophy and working hypothesis is all good and well. A working hypothesis without a practical methodology to research it, on the other hand, is of no practical use whatsoever. This chapter deals with the further enhancement of the Integrated Experiential Learning Process by adding a research methodology to the process. This is achieved by integrating it with the transcendental phenomenology of Moustakas (1994), and briefly discussing the research findings. It must, however, be emphasised that this is not *the* research methodology but the one most appropriate to my original doctoral research at the time. We are currently doing further research using other research methodologies.

Phenomenology

A further interesting aspect of Kolb's (1984) experiential learning theory is how well it integrates with phenomenology. Ernesto Spinelli (1998) points out that Edmund Husserl (1859–1938) is credited with developing an investigative approach known as the phenomenological method. Husserl wanted to develop the science of phenomena, a science that could clarify how objects are experienced and presented to consciousness. The task was to explore the subjective experience of individuals. Feldenkrais (2019), as was mentioned previously, is of the opinion that subjective reality is more complex and immensely richer than our experience of objective reality. The aim, as Spinelli (1998:2) points out, was "to expose how our consciousness imposes itself upon, and obscures, 'pure' reality". In so doing, the individual becomes more aware and is able to bracket (or set aside) conscious experience so that a more adequate approximation of reality can arise. Central to phenomenology is the idea of imposing meaning on the world. Phenomenology argues that things exist in the way that they exist because of the meaning that each individual assigns to them, because true reality is unknowable to us:

DOI: 10.4324/9781003356424-6

> Instead, that which we term reality, that is, that which is experienced by us as being reality, is inextricably linked to our mental processes in general, and in particular, to our in-built, innate capacity to construct meaning.
>
> (Spinelli, 1998:2)

Consequently, our reality is a phenomenological reality that is open to a multiplicity of interpretations. What many people take to be objective reality, based on objective laws or truths, actually consists of judgements that are influenced by a consensus viewpoint. This consensus viewpoint is one agreed upon by a whole culture or a group of individuals or professionals; it is an interpretation. It is an interpretation which works and has meaning for the group that has constructed the meaning. Kolb (1984) refers to this consensus viewpoint as the "selectivist paradigm", and it is this higher level of integrated learning which uses the act of purpose (meaning) to integrate the psychological world (feeling, thought, desire) with the physical world (the individual and world as physical/chemical substances). Quoting Von Glasersfeld regarding the selectivist paradigm, Kolb (1984) makes the point that "concepts, theories, and cognitive structures in general are viable and survive as long as they serve the purposes to which we put them" (Von Glasersfeld, 1977:7, quoted in Kolb, 1984:226). The theory, knowledge or construct is viable because it works for us, not because it is in any sense a replica or picture of reality. This does not, however, imply that validity is unique because there could be a host of other constructs as viable as the one constructed. Phenomenology holds that whatever the meaning is, it cannot be concluded to be a true or correct reflection of reality. This is a view held by Jaques and Clement (1997) as well.

Subjective versus objective reality

Does this mean that reality is a purely subjective process – nothing more than mere mental constructs? Not at all. Kolb (1984) speaks about the act of purpose integrating both the psychological (subjective) and physical (objective) world. The problem, as phenomenologists point out, is that we never perceive only the objective world or mental phenomena; we experience the interaction of the two. Hence Feldenkrais (2019:85) points out that "objective reality is only a part of subjective reality". All agree that there is a physical reality, which we have labelled objective reality, that remains free of our consciousness. It is our interpretation of that objective reality that can be questioned. Christian de Quincey (2005) states very simply that the world consists of things and our experience of things, where things are made up of energy, and consciousness is what feels and knows those things. Consciousness is our concrete experience within that context of things. Moustakas sums up the dilemma as follows:

> The phenomenological epoche ... does not doubt everything – only the natural attitude, the biases of everyday knowledge, as a basis for truth and reality. What is doubted are the scientific "facts", the knowing of things in advance, from an external base rather than from internal reflection and meaning.
>
> (Moustakas, 1994:85)

These interpretations or facts, as mentioned previously, are influenced by a whole culture or a group of individuals or professionals; they constitute a paradigm which has been created and in which we operate. These interpretations and this paradigm are therefore open to change, and from history we know that they do change over time.

Phenomenology's fundamental issues

Spinelli (1998) mentions that Husserl focused on two issues in an attempt to examine how we construct our reality. The first is the notion of intentionality as the basis of mental experiences, and the second is the noematic and noetic foci of intentionality which are the shapers of experience.

Intentionality is the basis of all meaning-based constructs of the world:

> As it is employed by phenomenologists, intentionality is the term used to describe the fundamental action of the mind reaching out to the stimuli which make up the real world in order to translate them into the realm of meaningful experience.
>
> (Spinelli, 1998:11)

Human consciousness is therefore always aware of something; the mind is directed towards some entity, whether or not the entity exists. The object can be real or imaginary; it can be a tree, or I can be worried. In the case of the latter, I am still worried about some entity. According to phenomenologists, it would appear that human beings are programmed to interpret an object-based or thing-based world. Thus Moustakas (1994) asserts that intentionality refers to the internal experience of being conscious of something; the act of consciousness and the object of consciousness are intentionally related. The senses respond to unknown stimuli from the physical world, which undergo a translation or interpretation that leads the individual to respond to the stimuli as if they are objects or things. The meaning that the individual ascribes to the object or thing is, however, determined by various socio-cultural influences that have informed the individual's mental framework.

Hence, the knowledge the individual has of the external world is not as a result of their direct access to external reality. That knowledge has undergone a number of complex interpretations that have been influenced by past experience, socio-cultural influences and the level or stage of the individual's development. For this reason, it is possible for two individuals to have exactly the same experience but to experience and interpret it differently. Spinelli (1998) argues that because of the act of intentionality, "ultimate reality" can never be known. As a result, our interpretations of the world and the meaning we ascribe to it are not unique or fixed. Through the act of intentionality, we constantly interpret and assign meaning to our world. In effect, therefore, the phenomenological concept of intentionality is the same or very similar to Kolb's (1984) transformational dimension of experiential learning. Meaning is created through the synergetic role of the dual transformation processes of intention and extension: "Learning, the creation of knowledge and meaning, occurs through the active extension and grounding of ideas and experiences in the external world and through internal reflection about the attributes of these experiences and ideas" (Kolb, 1984:52).

Every act of intentionality does, however, have a noematic and a noetic focus, which are the shapers of experience. The thing that is being experienced is the noema or noematic correlate, and is the object (the "what") towards which we direct our focus. The mode of the experience is the noesis or noetic correlate; it is the "how" we experience an object. As an example, assume two individuals from two different race groups are listening to a lecture on diversity. At the end of the lecture, one individual agrees completely with what has been said, while the other is furious. In Kolb's (1984) terms, both have grasped the lecture via direct apprehension; they had the same experience. The noematic focus is made up of the content of whatever is being focused on or being experienced, in this case the content and arguments presented in the lecture. The noematic focus is the same as Kolb's (1984) concept of grasping via direct apprehension. Yet, although they experienced the same lecture, each individual's experience of the lecture was different. This is due to the noetic focus, which contains the referential elements of the individual, and deals with the various cognitive and affective biases that add more elements of meaning to the experience.

The noetic focus corresponds to Kolb's (1984) concept of grasping via comprehension. Kolb (1984) sees this as a secondary and arbitrary way of knowing. Comprehension is the way in which we introduce order into an "unpredictable flow of apprehended sensations". For as Feldenkrais (2019) reminds us, a complex nervous assembly needs constancy and consistency of environment. Hence the nervous system will look for order and find it, or it will make order where it does not exist. Yet by introducing order, as Kolb (1984) points out, we distort and forever change the flow. In theory, it would appear that we can distinguish between the noetic and noematic foci; in practice, however, the two are not distinct from each other. When it comes to experience, we evoke both foci, the events contained in the experience (noema) and the way we experienced it (noesis). Hence, we see that the noematic and noetic foci of phenomenology are the same as Kolb's (1984) prehension dimension, while the concept of intentionality is the same as Kolb's (1984) transformation dimension.

The phenomenological method

Spinelli (1998) points out that the concept of intentionality, and its noematic and noetic foci, enabled Husserl to develop the phenomenological methodology to help clarify the interpretational factors contained in each experience. The aim of the phenomenological method is to raise an awareness of how consciousness imposes itself and obscures "pure" reality. It is therefore concerned with wholeness, in that it examines experience from many sides, angles and perspectives until an integrated vision of the essence of the phenomenon is achieved. In this methodology, subject and object are integrated. In Wilber's (1995) terms, the methodology deals with the inner (noesis) and external (noema) quadrants, as well as dealing with the individual within the context of the communal, covering both the inner and outer quadrants.

In this methodology, as Moustakas (1994) points out, phenomenology tries to seek meaning and the essence of an experience by reflecting thereon. This in turn leads to ideas, concepts, understanding and judgements. This methodology therefore uses personal experience, subjective thinking, intuition, reflection and judgement as primary evidence for scientific investigation. The phenomenological methodology therefore contains all the elements of the experiential learning processes: concrete experience, reflective observation, abstract conceptualisation and active experimentation. In addition to facilitating learning and growth, experiential learning at a more mature level turns out to be a powerful methodology for scientific investigation as well.

The important thing to remember, however, is that it is always individual experiential learning within a communal or collective context. It is an intersubjective experience, since the world is a community of persons. Moustakas (1994) points out that it is through conversations and dialogues with other people that the individual continuously corrects their interpretation of reality. And at the same time, the individual is participating in complex responsive processes. Other people help us to validate our experiences through the interchange of perceptions, judgements, feelings and ideas. Schumacher (1978) emphasises the same point when he refers to the four fields of knowledge: I-inner, the world (you)-inner, I-outer and the world (you)-outer. He suggests that any individual has direct access only to the I-inner and the world (you)-outer fields of knowledge. An individual can feel what they are feeling and can directly see what the other looks like. But what it feels like to be the other, and what the individual looks like in the eyes of the other, cannot be known directly. To gain access to those fields of knowledge, the individual needs intersubjective dialogue and conversations to help validate their reality. Once again, this thinking is very much in agreement with the principles of complex responsive processes.

Moustakas's (1994) phenomenological research method is known as transcendental phenomenology; it is called "phenomenology" because it utilises only the data that is available for consciousness – the appearance of objects. It is considered "transcendental" because it adheres to what can be discovered through reflection on subjective acts and their objective correlates.

(Moustakas, 1994:45)

It is transcendental because it helps to uncover the ego, for which everything has meaning. It is phenomenological because it transforms the world into mere phenomena. The methodology process consists of four steps: epoche, phenomenological reduction, imaginative variation and synthesis (Moustakas, 1994:84–101).

The epoche process

Epoche is a Greek word which means to abstain from, to stay away from or to refrain from judgement. In our day-to-day lives, we tend to hold knowledge judgementally; that is, we are biased due to our expectations and assumptions. The epoche requires that we bracket as far as possible our biases, understandings, knowing and assumptions, and look at things in a new and fresh way. As Moustakas (1994:33) says, we need to revisit our experiences "from the vantage point of a pure or transcendental ego". This does, of course, assume that the individual has developed a healthy and mature ego that can be transcended. An underdeveloped ego will not be able to do this. The epoche does, therefore, assume and call for a certain level of ego maturity. In so doing, the individual is able to bracket their ordinary thought processes and look at experience from a fresh perspective.

The epoche urges the individual to impose an openness on their immediate experience. As a result, subsequent conclusions drawn about the experience (whatever it may be) would be based more on the immediate experience than upon prior expectations and assumptions. The aim is to see and experience the "experience" in a completely open manner. It is a way of seeing and experiencing before any form of reflection, judgements or reaching conclusions happens. Of critical importance is that in the epoche no position is taken; everything is of equal value. Nothing is determined in advance. Everything is experienced and valued for what it is; it is a fresh way of perceiving and experiencing. This is not an easy state to achieve, and as was mentioned previously, it assumes and calls for a certain level of ego maturity. As Moustakas points out:

> The challenge is to silence the directing voices and sounds, internally and externally, to remove from myself the manipulating or predisposing influences and to become completely and solely attuned to just what appears, to encounter the phenomena, as such, with a pure state of mind.

(Moustakas, 1994:88)

The epoche process therefore requires sustained attention, presence, discipline and concentration. Moustakas (1994) refers to the process as a form of reflective-meditation. In this process, the individual allows prejudices, preconceptions and prejudgements to arise in consciousness and leave freely. The aim is to be as receptive to these phenomena as to the unbiased actions of looking and seeing. Those familiar with the work of De Mello (1990) will immediately recognise that it is all about "awareness", that is just learning to be aware of the phenomena and then to let them go. Eventually, the essence of the experience is seen for what it is. It is impossible to completely bracket everything, but the aim is to become more aware and disciplined in the process in order to experience life and phenomena in a less biased way. With practice, the individual will learn to become more open to their own experience and be more aware of how their biases predetermine and influence their reality.

The epoche process corresponds very well with Kolb's (1984) concept of concrete experience. For a person to learn from concrete experience, they must be able to involve themselves fully, openly and without bias in new experiences. The aim, like the epoche process, is to be open to experience and to move beyond or to transcend personal and social biases. The way of experiencing via the epoche process is the same as Kolb's (1984) grasping via apprehension. Like the phenomenologists, Kolb (1984) is very aware of how using words to put the experience into a concept can take something away from the direct experience:

> Yet to describe these perceptions faithfully in words … is somewhat difficult. It is almost as though the words are vessels dipped in the sea of sensations we experience as reality, vessels that hold and give form to those sensations contained, while sensations left behind fade from awareness.
>
> (Kolb, 1984:43)

Both concrete experience and the epoche process therefore encourage the individual to continuously open themselves in a fresh, nonbiased way to their own experience, free of preconceptions and prejudgements. It is about paying attention to the world through our right hemisphere of the brain. The right hemisphere is heavier, larger, longer and wider than the left. And for McGilchrist, there must be a reason for that. As well as being bigger, the right hemisphere has more white matter (i.e. is more myelinated) than the left. According to McGilchrist (2019), this reflects the right hemisphere's attention to the global picture and to facilitating communication across the regions. It must be open to everything that exists apart from ourselves, trying to avoid preconceptions as far as possible. It does not focus on what it already knows; rather, it is open to pure experience and the novelty it brings. As a result, anything that is new is first presented in the right hemisphere. New experiences tend to come from the peripheral field of vision, and regardless of the side from which they come, it is the right hemisphere that directs attention to what is coming from the edges of awareness. Referring to several imaging and lesion studies, he concludes that the intensity of attention, which involves sustained attention, alertness and vigilance, is reliant on the right hemisphere. It dominates when it comes to global, flexible and broad attention.

Phenomenological reduction

Phenomenological reduction is a process of prereflection, reflection and reduction with the aim of explicating the phenomenon's essential nature. The task is to derive a textural description of what the individual experiences in terms of the external object and the internal act of consciousness, describing the relationship between the phenomenon and the self. The rule is to describe and not to explain. The problem with explaining is that it tries to make sense of the experience in terms of a hypothesis or theory. Spinelli (1998) gives the example of a hypochondriac who has failed to apply the rule of description. Instead of describing the somatic experience in concrete terms, the individual jumps to abstract, disease-model explanations. In so doing, the individual provokes levels of anxiety that reinforce the debilitating situation. Descriptions are derived from the immediate sensory-based experience. Explanations try to make sense of experience within the boundaries of a hypothesis or theory. The aim is to reflect, reflect again and then to describe the experience in terms of textural qualities, varying intensities, special qualities and time references. The experiencing person therefore turns inward in reflection and describes whatever shines forth in consciousness. Whatever stands out and is meaningful for the individual is explored and reflected on. Individual memories, judgements, perceptions and reflections are reflected on and described, as they are integral to the process. The process allows the individual to return to the self, in that the world is experienced from the vantage point of self-reflection, self-awareness and self-knowledge. The more the individual reflects, the more exact the phenomenon becomes. Phenomenological reduction is about observing and describing. In this regard, we can see that phenomenological reduction is the same as Kolb's (1984) reflective observation, which

> focuses on understanding the meaning of ideas and situations by carefully observing and impartially describing them. It emphasises understanding as opposed to practical application; a concern with what is true or how things happen as opposed to what will work; an emphasis on reflection as opposed to action.
>
> (Kolb, 1984:68)

He goes on to discuss how we learn the meaning of immediate concrete experience by reflecting on their "presymbolic impact" on feelings. The issue is that both methodologies call for inner reflection that tries to describe the experience rather than explaining it.

More importantly, reflection is never-ending. Although the individual might reach a point where they consciously stop the reflective process, the possibility for reflection and discovery is unlimited. In phenomenological reduction, this is known as horizontalisation. No matter how many times the individual reconsiders or reflects on the experience, the experience can never be exhausted because horizons are unlimited. Even the final textural description, although completed at a point in time, remains open to further reflection. Another requirement of horizontalisation is that all statements are treated as equal and that the applying of hierarchies of significance should be avoided. By avoiding hierarchical assumptions, the individual is in a better position to examine the experience with less prejudice.

In McGilchrist's (2019) work, this is a movement towards paying attention to the world and experience through the left hemisphere of the brain. The left hemisphere is the domain of selectivity, which involves divided and focused attention, transfers information within regions and prioritises local communication. The dominant attention mode is therefore narrow and focused. The left hemisphere plays a critical role in processing our experiences. It must recognise whatever we experience through certain qualities that we categorise into similar experiences we have had before. And those experiences are associated with certain feelings and beliefs. The advantage is that it gives us the ability to predict and use what we know. It also plays an active role in the next step, imaginative variation, in that it allows us to come up with a hypothesis about what is going on and what to do in response to what has just been experienced.

Imaginative variation

Through the utilisation of imagination, varying the frames of reference, different perspectives and points of view, the individual tries to derive a structural description of the experience and the underlying factors that account for what is being experienced. The aim is to understand the "how" that brought about the "what" of the experience. The question that needs to be explored is how did the experience come to be what it is? By using the textural descriptions, the aim is to derive structural essences of the experience and how it came about. It creates a picture of the conditions that gave rise to the experience and connect with it. According to Moustakas, imaginative variation consists of the following four steps:

- continuously looking for varying and different structural meanings that underlie the textural meanings;
- becoming aware of and recognising the underlying themes that have brought about the phenomenon;
- becoming aware of the universal structures that give impetuous to the thoughts and feelings with reference to the phenomenon. Considering

things like time, space, causality, relation to self and others and bodily concerns; and

• "searching for exemplifications that vividly illustrate the invariant structural themes that facilitate the development of a structural description of the phenomenon" (Moustakas, 1994:99).

In essence, it can be said that imaginative variation is an attempt to develop an understanding or "theory" about how the experience came about. Thus it is very similar to, if not the same as, Kolb's (1984) abstract conceptualisation where the individual is able to create concepts that integrate their observations into logically sound theories.

Synthesis of meaning and essences

The final step in the methodology is the integration and synthesis of the textural and structural descriptions into a unified statement of the experience as a whole. The important thing to remember is that the textural-structural synthesis represents the essence of the experience from the point of view of an individual researcher at a definite point in time and space, and as such it is open to further exploration. The essence of any experience is never totally exhausted. Hence this research methodology is often used for hypothesis-generating research as opposed to hypothesis-testing research. For this reason, it can be seen as a form of active experimentation. It generates a hypothesis that needs to be researched, applied and tested empirically; it is an ongoing experiment. The findings have to be taken further and researched further. This completes McGilchrist's (2019) dialectical process. New experiences are registered in the right hemisphere, and to make sense of an experience we start to reflect on it in the left hemisphere. Finally, the entire process is reintegrated into the right hemisphere.

Integrating transcendental phenomenology with the Integrated Experiential Learning Process

Based on the above logic, it can be argued that Kolb's (1984) Experiential Learning Model integrates very well with Moustakas's (1994) transcendental phenomenological research methodology. It can be argued further that the latter is just a higher or more mature form of learning than the former. In other words, experiential learning matures into transcendental phenomenology. Both can therefore be used as integral developmental methodologies. Transcendental phenomenology is therefore easily integrated with the Integrated Experiential Learning Model, as represented in Figure 5.1.

In applying the Integrated Experiential Learning Process, it is suggested that Kolb's (1984) Experiential Learning Model initially be used as an integrative developmental methodology for learning. As the individual becomes

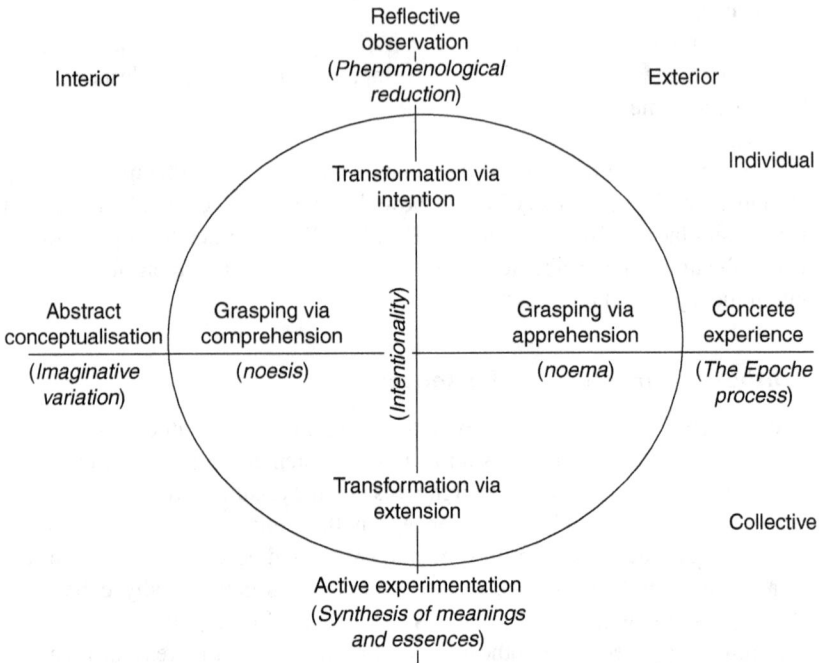

Figure 5.1 Integrated Experiential Learning Process expanded.
Source: Adapted from Wilber (1996:71); Kolb (1984:42).

more skilled in using the Integrated Experiential Learning Process, they will eventually mature and develop into using transcendental phenomenology for their own personal growth and development. Done in a disciplined way, these methodologies could facilitate growth and development right up to the highest rational level, which is Wilber's (1995) Vision-Logic stage and Kolb's (1984) Integration stage. Eventually, if this development continues, transcendental phenomenology will mature into Almaas's (2002) Inquiry method. It is Almaas's (2002) Inquiry method that will facilitate growth into and in the transpersonal bands of development. In fact, it is more correct to say that it facilitates the transpersonal states. The method requires that the individual continuously inquires into their own direct experience. The need to inquire into personal experience is emphasised by Almaas: "To experience the richness of our Being, the potential of our soul, we must allow our experience to become more and more open, and increasingly question who we assume we are" (Almaas, 2002:5).

It is important to emphasise, as Almaas points out, that this is a dynamic, never-ending process in a constant state of transformation, where one experience opens up another. There is no final state or stage at which we arrive, it is just a continuous flow of experience. With that in mind, it can be argued that in

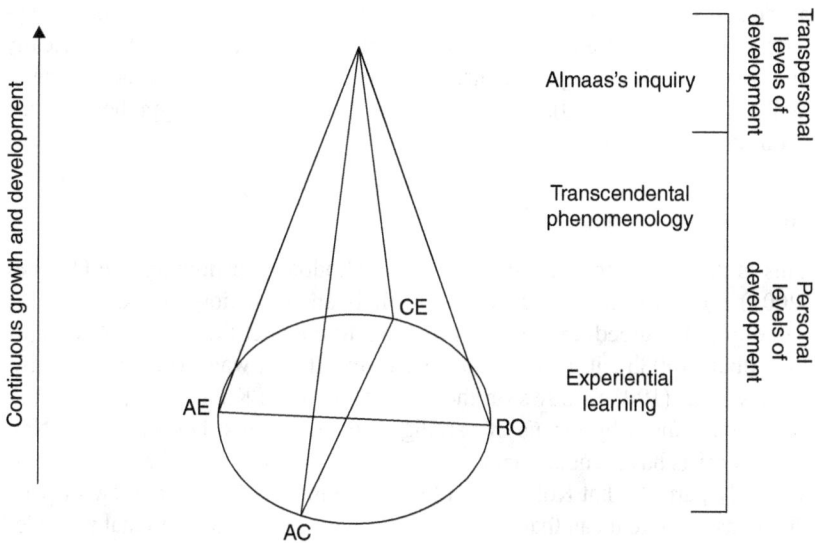

Figure 5.2 The maturity phases of the Integrated Experiential Learning Process.
Source: Adapted from Kolb (1984:141).

the Integrated Experiential Learning Process the experiential learning matures and develops with the individual from experiential learning to transcendental phenomenology to Almaas's Inquiry method. Remembering that this entire learning process is a function of the central and autonomic nervous systems; in this theory of learning, it is recognised that physiology is primary and the cognitive processes are secondary. This process is represented in Figure 5.2.

The strength of the Integrated Experiential Learning Process is that it allows for continuous growth and development in the personal and transpersonal levels, and it provides a practical methodology to facilitate this continuous growth and development. Most Western methodologies tend to stop at the upper levels of rational development; some of them do not recognise the transpersonal levels. The Integrated Experiential Learning Process honours body, mind, soul and spirit, and provides a practical methodology to help facilitate their integration. *It is, however, important to remember that body, mind, soul and spirit are constructs imposed on our lived experience through the workings of the left hemisphere of the brain. Our lived experience is just one continuous flow of experiences, which we experience as different states.*

Valid knowledge

Long-term practice and disciplined application of the Integrated Experiential Learning Process is what moves the individual onto the road to mastery. If the methodology is to become a valid form of empirical and phenomenological research it will, however, have to meet what Wilber (1998b) calls the "three aspects of scientific inquiry" or the "three strands of all valid knowing". Long-term practice is not enough. The methodology must be validated empirically and phenomenologically. The three aspects of scientific inquiry, according to Wilber (1998b:155–160), are instrumental injunction, direct apprehension and communal confirmation (or rejection).

Instrumental injunction

This is the actual practice of doing the methodology or inquiry. De Quincey (2005) refers to this as the Procedure. It is an injunction, an experiment, a paradigm, an agreed-upon set of protocols to conduct the inquiry. According to Wilber (1998b), it always takes the form "If you want to know, do this." Here Wilber (1998b) draws on the work of Thomas Kuhn, who showed that science advances by means of paradigms or exemplars. Unfortunately, New Age theorists have tended to misuse the word "paradigm", in that they emphasise only part of what Kuhn meant by paradigm. The New Age view of paradigm has come to mean that if you want to change something, all that is needed is to change the way you think ("change your paradigm"). By paradigm, Kuhn meant a concept and a way of doing within that concept:

> A paradigm is not merely a concept, it is an actual practice, an injunction, a technique taken as an exemplar for generating data. And Kuhn's point is that genuine scientific knowledge is grounded in paradigms, exemplars, or injunctions.
>
> (Wilber, 1998b:159)

Kuhn, therefore, emphasises the injunctive strand of valid knowledge. Thinking differently is not enough, you must practise the injunction or the methodology. This is the same point Freire (2005) made that reflection without action becomes empty words and is mere "verbalism", just idle chatter, because "there is no transformation without action" (Freire, 2005:87). On the other hand, action for action's sake without reflection is merely "activism". For Freire, dialogue requires both critical reflection and action to develop a true praxis. In the same way, for the Integrated Experiential Learning methodology, the injunction is experiential learning. You need to know the theory and you need to practise the methodology; the one without the other is useless. On one level, Kolb's (1984) Experiential Learning Model is the injunction; but on another level, it is the active experimentation aspect of the Integrated Experiential Learning Process.

Direct apprehension

This is the direct experience or the apprehension of data that is brought about by the injunction. In Kolb's (1984) language, this is grasping the data via direct apprehension as a result of active experimentation. Hence De Quincey (2005) names it the Observation phase, in that the investigator observes and records the data of experience. This is the data of direct and immediate experience. It is what Almaas refers to as basic knowledge:

> Basic knowledge is always direct knowledge in the moment – the stuff of our immediate experience. We usually don't call it knowledge; we call it experience, and if we are a little more sophisticated we call it perception.
>
> (Almaas, 2002:78)

As Wilber (1998b) points out, it is this data on which science anchors all its concrete assertions. Hence Wilber is in agreement with empiricism, which demands that all knowledge be grounded in experiential evidence. The only difference is that he recognises sensory, mental and spiritual experience. That is why Wilber argues that scientific inquiry can be applied to empirical, phenomenological and spiritual research; all are valid fields of scientific inquiry. Experiential learning can be used for empirical learning, such as how to improve business processes or to explore a spiritual practice like meditation. Both levels will generate experiential data via direct apprehension that can be validated or invalidated. Wilber (1998b) goes on to argue that knowledge that is brought forth by valid injunctions is genuine knowledge, since bad data can be rejected. His argument is that paradigms disclose data, they do not invent them.

Communal confirmation (or rejection)

De Quincey (2005) refers to it simply as Reporting. This is where the data or experiences are checked by a community of people who have completed the injunction and the apprehensive strands. In a sense, this is a combination of reflective observation and abstract conceptualisation. Having had the experience and collected the data, an individual will reflect on it, and via comprehension share it with a community who will either validate or invalidate the data. Here Wilber (1998b:159) draws on the work of Sir Karl Popper, whose approach "emphasises the importance of falsifiability: genuine knowledge must be open to disproof, or else it is simply dogma in disguise."

Hence it is important that the Integrated Experiential Learning Process must take place within the context of a community who can validate or invalidate the data. So, for example, if the Integrated Experiential Learning methodology is used to coach business executives, then there must be a community of executives or managers who can validate or invalidate the data. Likewise, if the methodology is used to teach meditation, there must be a community of meditators who can validate or invalidate the data.

In summary, it is argued that experiential learning be used as the injunction in the Integrated Experiential Learning Process in order to facilitate growth and development. The data will then be collected via direct apprehension and validated in the context of a community which has adequately completed the injunction and the apprehension strands.

Research of this theory

At this point, it is important to realise that Grof's criticism of Wilber's theory is just as relevant to the Integrated Experiential Learning Process, namely:

> While logical consistency certainly is a valuable prerequisite, a viable theory has to have an additional property that is equally … important. It is generally accepted among scientists that a system of propositions is an acceptable theory if, and only if, its conclusions are in agreement with observable facts.
>
> (Grof, 1998:88–89)

This criticism was addressed while this theory was researched as the Integrated Experiential Coaching Model for my doctoral thesis, which was completed in 2006. I was awarded the contract to coach 17 middle and senior managers in a large IT firm over a period of 6 months from July 2003 to December 2003. It was agreed with the company that the coaching project be used as part of my Doctoral research programme. I contracted to meet with every coachee for 12 sessions each over the 6-month period. The coaching sessions were usually of 2-hour duration every 2 weeks. Experiential learning is the methodology applied in the Integrated Experiential Coaching Model; participants therefore needed the time in-between sessions to experiment with and assimilate their learning.

The objective of the research was to explore the individual's subjective learning experience, while being coached within the context of the Integrated Experiential Coaching Model, with the aim of using what I learnt to continuously refine or change the Model. It was about exploring and discovering, rather than measuring and explaining; exploring and discovering the meaning and essence of the learning experience while being coached. The research was about obtaining descriptions of experience through first-person accounts via the use of reflective essays. It was about exploring people's inner worlds or dimensions. As a result, it was qualitative in nature and hypothesis-generating, rather than hypothesis-testing. Furthermore, experiential learning and continuous growth lies at the heart of the Integrated Experiential Coaching Model. It was therefore important that the research methodology supported that philosophy and built thereon. As a result, an adapted version of the transcendental phenomenological methodology of Moustakas (1994) was chosen for this study. Traditionally, this methodology involves designing questionnaires and conducting interviews, which means that interviews are the primary source of data collection. This is where I adapted the methodology; instead of gathering the data via interviews, I chose to collect the data by means of reflective essays. That was the only adaptation; apart from this change, I used the methodology as is.

The transcendental phenomenological methodology consists of four steps.

- *The epoche process*: This is about involving oneself in a new experience in a new way. It is about setting aside our prejudgements, biases and preconceived ideas about things. From the epoche, we are challenged to create new ideas, new feelings, new inwardnesses and understandings. It is a way of genuine looking and experiencing that precedes reflection, forming judgements or reaching conclusions.
- *Phenomenological reduction*: Here the task is to describe in textural language just what one sees, not only in terms of the objective reality but also in terms of the internal acts of consciousness, the relationship between the phenomenon and the self. It is called reduction because it leads us back to our own experience of the way things are. The aim is to identify individual themes, and then to develop a composite textural description from the individual themes to arrive at the experience of the group as a whole.
- *Imaginative variation*: Here the task is to derive structural themes from the textural descriptions that have been obtained through phenomenological reduction. The critical question that needed to be explored was how the experience of the relevant phenomenon came to be what it is.
- *Synthesis of meaning and essences*: The final step involved the intuitive integration of the fundamental textural and structural descriptions into a unified statement of the essence of the experience (Moustakas, 1994).

Research findings

A detailed account of the research methodology and the process was presented in my book *Integrated Experiential Coaching: Becoming an Executive Coach* (Chapman, 2010). The research involved a phenomenological exploration of the individual's subjective learning experience while being coached within the context of the Integrated Experiential Coaching Model. Although this research project never set out to test the integrity of the Integrated Experiential Coaching Model, it is worth noting that the research evidence did support the integrity of the model. The research findings generated the hypothesis that the Integrated Experiential Coaching Model facilitated both the prehension and transformational dimensions of experiential learning in individuals. The co-researchers understood and owned some significant behavioural dynamics inside of themselves, as well as between themselves and other significant colleagues. This underlines the possibilities of coaching as a staff development intervention to facilitate self-authorisation by working through one's own unconscious and dynamic behavioural issues. It was hypothesised that coaching presented from this model empowers individual employees to work towards their own cognitive insight, the experience of emotional meaningfulness and taking responsibility for their own growth and career development.

Research implications

Even though all the individuals were coached using the same model, how and what they learnt was unique to each individual. The research results therefore pointed to what Dotlich and Cairo (1999) refer to as the "mass customisation of learning". They point out that we are seeing the de-emphasis of the one-size-fits-all type of training. In their view, this is a trend that will continue to grow as organisations start to realise and value the individuality of their leaders, customers and managers. They point out that training programmes are failing to help individuals deal with change initiatives because change impacts people differently. The point is that these programmes and training initiatives need to account for how each individual deals with change, or they will not work. Given the work of Hannaford, Porges, Schore, Zull and McGilchrist on the physiological development of the central and autonomic nervous system, we can fully understand why we need to account for how each individual deals with change.

This is a significant insight that was critical in the development of Almaas's (1998a) enquiry methodology as well. His insight was, however, not limited to organisational training and development. He looked at teachers whose teachings are timeless and universal, like Buddha, Christ and the Prophet Muhammad. He then asked himself why it is that despite the millions of people who adhere to their teachings, very few actually reach the levels of enlightenment that the founding teachers did. Traditionally, the blame for this lack of enlightenment has been laid at the feet of the student, who was seen as being either too lazy or too undisciplined. Almaas disagrees, in that he sees the problem being due to teachers following a generalised teaching approach:

> We are seeing more and more that teaching cannot be done in a general way. Universal teaching, regardless of how deep and true, must be tailored to the specific needs of the particular individual. Otherwise, the teaching will be ineffective, and it is no fault of the student.
>
> (Almaas, 1998b:15)

Almaas means that the teacher must take into account the unique situation of the student, as well as their level of consciousness: "An effective teacher will handle a situation in a very personal way for the student, taking into consideration the unique situation of the student and his state of consciousness" (Almaas, 1998b:13). Hence Almaas's (1998b) warning that any teaching built around a particular model, or a particular state of consciousness, is bound to be limited. It will be effective only for people who happen to be at that level of consciousness. No model of consciousness can be universally applied to all people. Hence also Smuts's (1973) call for a new science called personology. In his view, psychology works with generalisations and ignores the uniqueness of the individual personality. The same could be said of theology. For it seems to be a pattern that as soon as a discipline or profession matures, it tends to start generalising by trying to apply certain models.

Conclusion

With hindsight, there is the realisation that the power of the Integrated Experiential Learning Process is that it "mass-customised learning" for individuals. Being a multiquadrant, multiple-level-of-consciousness model, it allowed for individuals to apply just-in-time learning. Co-researchers set their own learning agendas and used experiential learning through learning conversations to learn what they had to learn at a particular point. The coach did not come in with a predetermined learning plan or training plan or objective. People learnt what they wanted to learn, based on where they were at that particular time and development in their lives. This meant that the learning was very relevant and meaningful for them, and as a result they took responsibility and accountability for their own learning and development.

Chapter 6

Applying the Integrated Experiential Learning Process to coaching

Introduction

The question that will be explored in this section is: how can the Integrated Experiential Learning Process be applied to coaching? The Integrated Experiential Learning Process is the methodology used to coach, and it is facilitated via a learning conversation. In Lane, Kahn and Chapman (2019), I argued that whenever a model is written up it always appears to be very logical, structured and neat. In reality, a learning conversation can actually be very messy and it is only upon reflection that we structure it into a neat logical process. I find it interesting that whenever I teach this model, students try to apply the model mechanistically. What they soon discover is that when they try and force themselves to follow the experiential learning cycle, the model actually becomes an obstacle. They are so busy trying to do it "right" that they start trying to force the client into the various steps and end up frustrating themselves and the client. When I then encourage them to stop thinking about the model and just have a meaningful conversation with the client, they soon discover, upon reflection, that they would have gone through the experiential learning cycle. This is because the learning cycle is actually a very natural process. We all have experiences and we tend to reflect on those experiences to varying degrees. Based on our reflections, we form a hypothesis or an opinion about what these experiences mean to us and based on that we act.

Learning conversations

A learning conversation, according to Harri-Augstein and Thomas (1991), includes three different levels of conversation over time. Level One is a task-focused learning conversation; for example, a coach is requested to help an individual improve their performance or to learn certain managerial leadership skills. Level Two is a learning conversation about an issue of life relevance, while Level Three is a learning conversation about learning itself.

Every learning conversation, whether it be Level One or Level Three, will always take place within the context of a bigger life relevance situation (Level

DOI: 10.4324/9781003356424-7

Two conversation). It is not uncommon for the conversation to move between Levels One, Two and Three. It might start at Level One (task-focused), but the individual might start questioning their bigger life purpose or the value of doing the particular work that they are doing. In so doing, they move into a Level Two learning conversation. Once that has been dealt with, the conversation might move back to Level One. Learning conversations are therefore very dynamic.

Task-focused learning conversations are intermittent and they can extend over many cycles of task or topic activity. Experiential learning is the basis of these conversations and can be implemented by means of an adapted version of Harri-Augstein and Thomas's (1991) personal learning contract, covering the following key points:

1   Purpose:
    • What is my purpose?
    After taking action (i.e. going and doing):
    • What actually was my purpose?
    • Describe the essential differences.
2   Outcome:
    • How shall I judge and measure my success?
    After taking action (i.e. going and doing):
    • How well did I do?
    • Describe the essential differences.
3   Strategy:
    • What actions shall I take?
    After taking action (i.e. going and doing):
    • What did I actually do?
    • Describe the essential differences.
4   What have I learned from this exercise? (Adapted from Harri-Augstein and Thomas, 1991:151.)

The client will usually come into the coaching session with a real problem or difficulty that they are facing (their concrete experience). In the Integrated Experiential Learning Process, it is very important that the client always sets the agenda. The coach and client will then reflect on the experience (reflection-on-action) together. The client will be encouraged to make sense of what is going on by developing their own understanding or theory as to what is happening (abstract conceptualisation). If needs be, the coach can give some experiential or theoretical input into the conversation. The client will then decide on some course of action that they will experiment with to address the issue (active experimentation).

For learning to happen, it is very important that everything is made explicit, and this is where the personal learning contract is such a powerful tool. It makes the learning experience very explicit. Once the client has decided what they want to do (active experimentation), they fill in the first part of the contract, that is what is my purpose, what is it that I want to achieve? They also specify how they are going to measure themselves to determine whether they have been successful or not. Furthermore, the strategy and the action steps that they will follow are made explicit and written down. The client then goes away in-between coaching sessions and actions what they said they were going to do. This takes care of the active experimentation part of the learning process. Prior to the next coaching session, the client will document what their purpose was, what action they actually took, and how well they did. This teaches them to reflect on their actual concrete experience. They are also required to describe the essential differences between what they said they were going to do and what they actually did, both positive and negative, and explain why those differences exist. In so doing, they raise their own levels of awareness and they start to develop their own theories about why the differences exist. This helps them to improve their abstract conceptual abilities. The coaching session combined with the personal learning contract ensures that the client goes through the entire experiential learning processes in a structured way. It is an iterative process where one contract can build on another.

The main advantage of the personal learning contract is that it makes the learning experience explicit. It thereby facilitates the ability of the client to learn how they learn, which is a Level Three learning conversation. In the long term, learning how to learn is the most important learning that can happen. Initially, the personal learning contract (PLC) gives the learning conversation more structure; as individuals become more comfortable with the process, it is very common for the PLC to fall away and the conversations to become less structured. The more individuals can learn about how they learn, the more independent and autonomous they can become as human beings. The ultimate aim of the Integrated Experiential Learning Process is to help the client become what Harri-Augstein and Thomas term a self-organised learner, the essential characteristics of which are that the individual concerned:

- Accepts responsibility for managing their own learning and is no longer dependent on other people's directives and initiatives. The individual gives personal meaning to the events.
- Becomes aware of how they learn; in other words, they start to reflect on the functional components of the learning processes. They can recognise their need and translate it into a clearly defined purpose. They develop their own strategies to achieve the purpose and are able to recognise the quality of the outcome they have achieved. More importantly, they can critically review the cycle and implement more effective learning cycles.
- Learns to appreciate the dynamic nature of the personal learning process, while at the same time striving for more self-organised learning.
- Learns how to learn by continually challenging their existing partially developed skills, the aim being to transform these skills to achieve higher standards of personal competence.

- Recognises the value of self-organised learning and practises it as a way of life regardless of the social context.
- Redefines self-organised learning in their own terms in such a way that the self-organised learning expertise generates new dimensions of personal innovation and experimentation.
- Constantly strives for quantum improvements in their own ability to learn. The person becomes better at learning on the job, from training courses, from experienced colleagues and from their own and other people's mistakes (Harri-Augstein and Thomas, 1991:89–90).

Harri-Augstein and Thomas (1991) point out that self-organised learning cannot be achieved through direct instruction (provider-centred), as this often leads to complete dependency, alienation and negatively valued learning. On the other hand, to leave the individual to discover how to become a self-organised learner can take too long, hence the need for learning conversations and learner-centred learning. People need support and coaching to learn what Beard and Wilson (2002) call "reflect-on-action" so that they eventually develop the independent ability to "reflect-in-action". The important thing about the conversation is that it starts with where the individual is (i.e. the individual's experience and preferred learning style), and allows as much freedom to learn as the individual can cope with. The client sets the agenda, not the coach. It is a gradual process of expanding the quality and scope of the individual's learning capability. Hence, in the Integrated Experiential Learning Process the coach starts working with and honouring the preferred learning style of the individual, and gradually enhancing the individual's ability to move through the complete experiential learning cycle. This means that the coach must make use of appropriate coaching skills, depending on where the client is at that point in time, in order to facilitate the experiential learning process more effectively. A schematic presentation of the process is found in Figure 6.1.

Brooks-Harris and Stock-Ward (1999) came up with the idea of organising facilitation skills into four quadrants that correspond to the Kolb (1984) learning styles. They referred to these facilitation skills as engaging, informing, involving and applying skills. These four skills apply as easily to coaching individuals as they do to facilitating groups:

- *Engaging coaching skills*: These skills are used to fully involve the client in the learning conversation. Engaging skills are used to activate the knowledge that the client already has, which builds bridges between their past experience and the current learning experience. Due to the reflective nature of engaging skills, individuals with Divergent Learning Style respond well to engaging exercises. Engaging skills include: getting clients to tell their story (narrative); reflecting; paraphrasing; asking for more information to clarify issues; probing; challenging assumptions; brainstorming with the client; and self-disclosure by the coach as and when it is relevant.

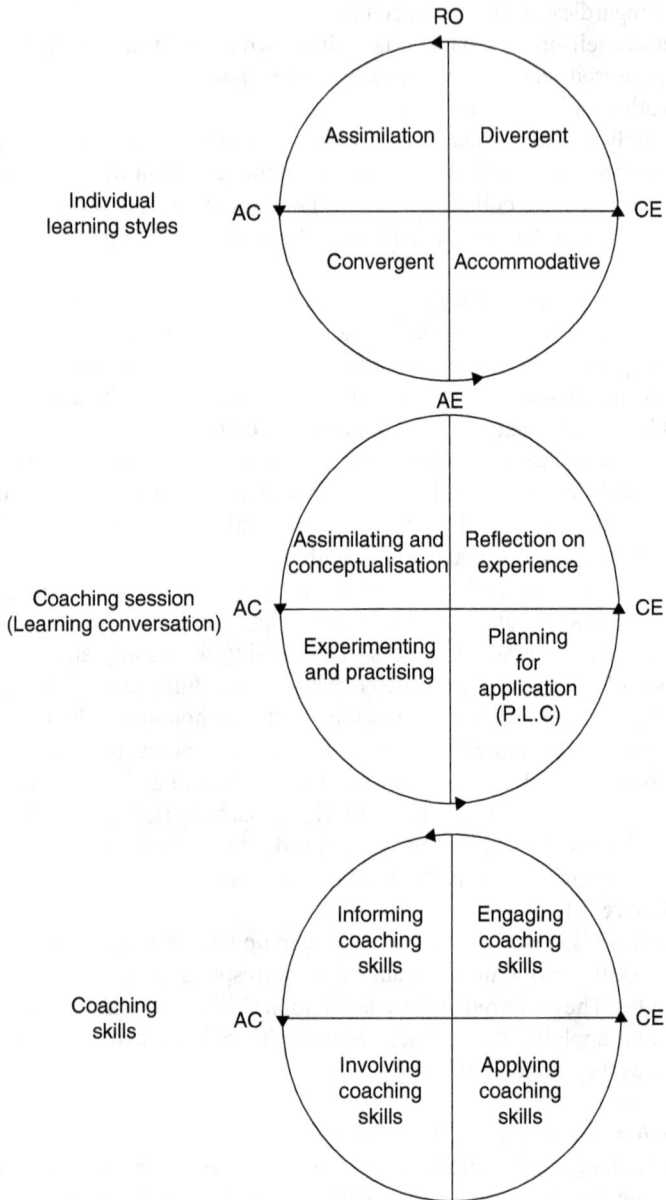

Figure 6.1 Integrated Experiential Learning Process skills.
Source: Adapted from Brooks-Harris and Stock-Ward (1999:16).

- *Informing coaching skills*: Informing involves teaching factual information and allowing the client to gain new knowledge. Here there can be an element of provider-centred learning, in that the coach brings experience and theoretical knowledge to the table. The client learns new information and is encouraged to use the concepts to understand their own experience. What is important to remember is that there is an element of provider-centred learning, but it is within the bigger context of learner-centred learning, which is the primary mode of learning. People with a preferred Assimilation Learning Style react well to informing. Informing skills include: clarifying assumptions; giving factual or theoretical information; answering questions; pointing out what was not mentioned and what was inconsistent; identifying themes; modelling new behaviour; summarising; explaining; and self-disclosure by the coach as and when it is relevant to provide information.

- *Involving coaching skills*: This involves active experimentation, in that it allows the client to play with new knowledge and skills. Learning is encouraged through practising with the new knowledge they have gained. This is hands-on experience, where the client experiments with what works for them. Involving activities and skills work well for people with a preferred Convergence Learning Style. Involving skills include: playing with new behaviour in the coaching session; playing with repertory grids; playing with personal learning contracts; connecting various ideas; interpreting and offering ideas about possible explanations for why the individual is feeling, acting or behaving in a certain way; challenging the client to see and do things differently; helping to make the client's way of learning explicit; concentrating the discussion on the here and now; asking the client what they are feeling to get them in touch with their feelings; and asking for feedback, focusing and getting the conversation back on track.

- *Applying coaching skills*: Here the client personalises what they have learnt by drawing up an action strategy by means of a personal learning contract, the aim being to apply what they have learnt. Because people with a preferred Accommodative Learning Style are highly action-oriented, they respond well to application activities. Applying skills involve: scenario planning; exploring the future; encouraging new behaviour outside the coaching session; pointing out opportunities for application; encouraging action and goal setting; developing personal learning contracts; and self-disclosure that helps and encourages application (Brooks-Harris and Stock-Ward, 1999).

The advantage of this approach is that it caters for the client's preferred learning style, and then aims to help them move through the complete experiential learning process to help them become self-organised learners. This model encourages the coach to use different coaching skills for different clients and different situations. At times it might be very valuable to use engaging skills, but in a different situation informing skills might be more appropriate. Yes, the client will eventually get there if you keep asking questions, but sometimes the coach and client can be up against time constraints. On the other hand, engaging skills could fail with a very strong Accommodator. The person could see the coach as being too fuzzy. Hence there is a danger that some coaching models opt for "a coaching style" and ignore or deny the value of other styles. The Co-Active Coaching Model, for example, has as one of its four cornerstones an Engaging Style:

> The coach does not have the answers; the coach has questions ... This is why we say that the coach's job is to ask questions, not to give answers. We have found that clients are more resourceful, more effective, and generally more satisfied when they find their own answers.
> (Whitworth, Kimsey-House and Sandahl, 1998:4)

Yet at the same time, Whitworth, Kimsey-House and Sandahl (1998) believe that coaching is a learning conversation because it is a conversation that wants to deepen learning, which in turn leads to action. However, it is not a conversation that informs, explains or rectifies. The objective is action and learning, not specific results. What is very clear is that their coaching model is not an experiential learning conversation. They have limited their coaching model to be an engaging learning conversation and decided to ignore the other three aspects of experiential learning. Sadly, even coaches who claim to use experiential learning as the basis of their coaching often tend to limit themselves to an engaging style.

Harri-Augstein and Thomas (1991) suggest that the coach helps the client to externalise the learning conversation (reflection-on-action) in order to improve its quality and to make the conversation as explicit to the client as they learn. As the client's awareness and skill develop, the coach gradually passes control of the learning conversation over to the client. If the learning conversation has been successful, over time there should be evidence of the client moving from dependence on the coach to more self-autonomy. The individual starts to take responsibility for and control of their own learning.

Not only do they move beyond their own preferred learning style to using the complete experiential learning cycle, they even start to identify and challenge their own learning myths. Based on the cumulative impact of past history, every individual brings certain attitudes and assumptions about learning into the learning situation. These attitudes, assumptions and beliefs are personal constructs or myths that the individual holds in regard to themselves, in terms of their ability to learn and how they learn. Based on 20 years of action research, Harri-Augstein and Webb identified the following categories of personal myth about the ways to ensure the most effective learning:

- *Myths about the conditions of learning*: These could cover *physical conditions*, such as the time of day (e.g. in the early morning, or late at night); the place (e.g. small and cosy or large and well-lit); the timespan involved (e.g. short or long); the optimum body position (e.g. sitting or walking); and the most conducive noise level (e.g. quiet or with the radio playing). They could also cover *social conditions* (e.g. alone, in a team or with a friend).
- *Myths about opportunities for learning*: These could cover the *situation* in which learning takes place (e.g. in a lecture, in a laboratory, or in a discussion with a consultant; on the job when everything is running smoothly, or in a crisis; or using a business game or a computerised simulator). Such myths could also cover the type of learning *event* (e.g. a lecture, a week-long course, preparing for an exam, or working on a major project for submission towards a degree). And they could relate to the nature of the *resources* available for learning (e.g. specialist books and academic journals, computerised learning aides, video material or a counsellor).
- *Myths about processes of learning*: These could include beliefs that learning needs to involve listening; repetition and exercises; questioning; feeling; doing; making a mental map; visualising; making patterns; selecting principles; or affirmation.
- *Myths about capacities for learning*: These could include beliefs that learning is easier for those with a memorising capacity; a mind for figures; language skills; brainstorming abilities; colour sense; spatial awareness; manipulative skills; risk taking; long concentration; or sustained commitment.
- *Myths about attitudes, personal characteristics, traits and talents*: These could include beliefs that learning is easier for those with persistence and doggedness; a practical bent; mathematical talent; musical ability; a "sharp eye"; or a "feminine touch" (Harri-Augstein and Webb, 1995).

Obviously, every one of these myths has some truth and relevance about them, that is to say that they might have a physiological base; they do not just exist in the mind as a "myth". As we have seen from the work of Porges, Schore, Feldenkrais and Hannaford, these "myths" have been learnt experientially as the individual transacts with their environment. In fact, given what we know about how the nervous system learns and develops into a free-form information system, it might be more correct to refer to them as learning habits as opposed to learning "myths". Be that as it may, individuals therefore need to continuously challenge their personal learning myths, which may have been valid at a certain age or in a certain context, in order to improve their learning abilities. Part of the learning experience is to make these myths explicit so that the individual can distance themselves from their supposed "limitations". Harri-Augstein and Webb (1995) believe that individuals can distance themselves from their own thoughts, feelings, beliefs and myths only through a process of gradual but deepening reflection on personal learning experiences.

Not only is it important for the client's myths to be surfaced and made explicit, the same applies to the coach. The coach might have their own personal learning myths or habits, as well as myths about the learning of others. Hence in the Integrated Experiential Learning Process, the coach shares their preferred learning style and any personal learning myths of which they are aware. By adopting a learning conversation stance, the client and the coach can work together for personal growth. It is a learning conversation for both parties; both client and coach can grow and develop as a result of the learning experience. Each coaching interaction is in fact a micro-complex responsive process in action. It is an ongoing learning process which should lead to self-organised learning. Harri-Augstein and Webb (1995:46–47) define self-organised learning as "The conversational construction, reconstruction and exchange of personally significant, relevant and viable meanings, with purposiveness and controlled awareness."

It is clear that this definition applies to the client as well as to the coach. If, for example, the coach is bored, and the conversation has no relevance or viable meaning for them, they could hinder the learning process of the client. Learning conversations call for an openness and natural curiosity from both the client and the coach. The coach is an expert in facilitating the learning conversation, but like the client, remains open to the learning process as it unfolds, and is therefore continuously on the journey of self-organised learning. It is a journey that starts with experiential learning and eventually matures into transcendental phenomenology and ultimately Almaas's inquiry method.

Thus the definition of the Integrated Experiential Learning Process can be enhanced by saying that coaching is about facilitating integrated experiential learning in individuals in order to enhance personal growth and development. It is "integrated" in that it embodies Schumacher's (1978) four fields of knowledge, as well as Wilber's (1995) Integral Model, which caters for personal development through various levels of consciousness, especially in the personal and transpersonal levels. It is "experiential" in that it uses Kolb's Experiential Learning Model as the paradigm or injunction, and Harri-Augstein and Thomas's concept of learning conversations as the primary learning tool.

Stages in the coaching relationship

The Integrated Experiential Learning Process, when applied to coaching, follows an adapted version of Kilburg's (2000:80–86) coaching stages. The stages are the same at the macro and micro levels. At "macro level" we mean the contractual coaching agreement, that is from the time the contract starts to the time it ends. At "micro level" we mean that every coaching session will go through the same or a similar process. What follows is a description of the macro-level process.

Stage 1: Establish contact

Stage 1 involves establishing contact with the client. The client could have contacted the coach directly, or the coach could have been contracted by the organisation. In this stage, the coach and the client are introduced and the two parties agree on whether or not they want to work together. In Lane's (1990) Case Formulation Method, which was initially used in cognitive-behavioural psychology and later adapted to coaching, this stage is about trying to define a shared concern that both parties are interested in exploring. This last point is a valuable contribution that Lane (1990) has made to the profession of coaching. It is important that both parties define a shared concern; if no shared concern can be defined, it is better for the coach to walk away from the situation. The coach must be interested in the issue at hand; if not, the coaching relationship is doomed to failure before it even starts.

Stage 2: Present current situation

Stage 2 involves presenting the current situation. Here the client is asked to share their life story. Critically important is that it is the client's story, not the story as told or understood by a third party. The client shares their subjective story. Egan (2002) is of the opinion that helping the client to tell their story is very important and should not be underestimated. He notes that "An important … feature of therapy is that it allows individuals to translate their experiences into words. The disclosure process itself, then, may be as important as any feedback the client receives from the therapist" (Egan, 2002:139–140).

According to Egan (2002), self-disclosure through storytelling can help reduce the initial stress, in that it helps the client to get things out in the open which in turn can have a cathartic effect. It is important to help the client tell their story in as much detail as possible, that is specific experiences, behaviours and emotions. As Egan (2002:140) points out, "Vague stories lead to vague options and actions." Stories are a valuable aid in identifying the client's deficits, as well as their resourcefulness. The aim in the Integrated Experiential Learning Process is to help the client build on their own resourcefulness. This is in agreement with Egan (2002), who believes that incompetent helpers tend to concentrate on the person's deficits. Skilled professionals, although not blind to the person's deficits, capitalise on the person's resources and resourcefulness. Through storytelling, it is possible for the coach and the client to spot and develop unused opportunities.

Stage 3: Explore current situation

In Stage 3, the coach and the client explore the current situation even further. In Egan's model (2002), this stage is about helping the client break through blind spots which may prevent them from seeing their unexplored opportunities, themselves and their problem situations as they really are. In so doing, it is possible to help the client screen or choose possible problems and/or opportunities on which to work.

Lane (1990) refers to this stage as the exploration and testing of hypotheses of cause and maintenance. Every problem and/or opportunity that is selected is a hypothesis. It is a hypothesis because at the time it is the most obvious leveraged problem and/or opportunity with which to work. The hypothesis might change over time and it is therefore an open-ended experiment. It is what Bruch and Bond (1998) refer to as "pseudo-experimenting", because it involves interview logic instead of controlled experiments: the clinical context and experimental rigour of controlled experiments are either not possible or not desirable. In Stage 3, the client and the coach therefore experiment with various options and hypotheses. The first three stages deal with the current reality of the client.

Stage 4: Choose foci

In Stage 4 the emphasis moves on to the desired future. The client is encouraged to spell out possibilities for a better future. According to Egan's (2002) model, this is where the coach helps the client to choose realistic and challenging goals, which are real solutions to the problems or unexploited opportunities identified in Stage 4. Lane (1990) refers to this stage as the formulation of the hypothesis to be tested. It involves getting a sense of the issue with which the client wants to work. Here the client creates a model with which they can go and experiment in the world. It is here that the client defines ways to change that are desirable, feasible and lead to action.

Initially, this is done by means of a PLC. The client defines their purpose (i.e. what they want to achieve), how they will know whether they have been successful (measurement criteria) and the strategies they will implement to achieve their purpose. This is the overarching PLC. It is, however, important to remember that the Integrated Experiential Learning Process does cater for various levels of consciousness and that the clarity of goal-setting will depend on the level on which the client is working. If, for example, the client wants to lose weight or achieve certain business objectives, then it is very important to set clear and realistic expectations and goals. On the other hand, if the client is exploring the transpersonal levels of consciousness, goal-setting can actually be a major stumbling block to their progress.

Stage 5: Implement the working learning conversation

Step 5 involves implementing and going through a number of learning conversations for the specified contractual period. According to Lane (1990), it is the process of applying and experimenting with the new understandings gained in the coaching sessions. In the Integrated Experiential Learning Process, each learning conversation is followed by a 4-week break because this is a methodology based on experiential learning theory and not on a therapy-based philosophy. The time between sessions is used by the client to experiment with and apply what they defined in their PLC. Before the next session, they will evaluate what they actually did, compare it to what they said they were going to do and explain the differences. The sessions can be iterative, in that the PLCs tend to build on each other, or they can fluctuate between the three different types of learning conversation. Sessions generally last for 1 hour.

Stage 6: Closure and review

The final step, Stage 6, is closure and review. Here the coach, client, and if needs be an organisational representative, will review the process and decide on whether to renew the contract or to terminate the coaching relationship. To bring the coaching relationship to closure, each client is asked to write a reflective essay about what they have learnt from the coaching experience. The reason for doing this is twofold: it is a helpful way to bring final closure to the learning experience and the coaching relationship; and it further enhances the ability of the client to reflect on their actions and their own learning.

Case study: How the Integrated Experiential Learning Process is applied

The first thing that needs to be emphasised is how I use the four-quadrant, multilevel part of the Model. The four-quadrant model is the perceptual map I, as the coach, use to try and make sense of the reality that is presented to me by the coachee. It is the tool I employ to make sense of, or manage, the complexities involved with working with the person and the situation. So, for example, if the coachee said to me that they needed help in formulating their strategy for their division or department, in my mind I would see that as being in the social system domain that includes the natural and human-made systems like technology, processes and structures. It is an activity that fits into the rational level of the lower-right quadrant and as such it can be measured. It means we would be working with something relatively easy to measure and the sessions could be more easily structured using a tool that the client is used to working with.

Alternatively, if the coachee said to me that they needed help with time management, in my mind I would see that as fitting into the rational level of the upper-right quadrant, the individual's exterior domain. Once again, it would be a piece of work that could be reasonably well structured and measured. For example, we could use a tool like Covey's priority grid to help the coachee logically prioritise all their activities and time. The measure could be as simple as: "Prior to coaching I could not manage my time and activities effectively; after six months of coaching, however, a noticeable improvement was visible (or not)."

If, on the other hand, the coachee said to me that they needed help with defining a purpose for their lives, I would immediately know that the coaching sessions would be less structured and more "fuzzy" because we would be dealing with the world of inner experience, the upper-left quadrant. Being an existential issue, it means that we would be working with the upper rational level of consciousness and starting to touch on the transpersonal levels of consciousness. Here the coaching would involve more exploration and use of dialogue, and the outcomes could be more difficult to measure. Mentally "mapping" the type and level of work gives me, as coach, a sense of security and ease, which helps me relax and be more present to the client's needs. It helps me to simplify the complexity in my mind. Naturally, as the session progresses, this hypothesis-testing would be going on in my mind all the time, and I would continuously test it with the client.

The coaching sessions themselves involve me as coach facilitating an experiential learning experience for the client; this is best illustrated by means of an actual case, as follows. At the initial meeting, the coachee's immediate manager had raised some concerns that despite having run a very successful business over the years, he was starting to see some cracks appearing in the business for which the coachee was responsible. The coachee's manager was concerned about the quality and sustainability of one specific side of the business (i.e. the problem was manifesting in the lower-right quadrant). In the manager's opinion, the coachee was not as hands-on in the business as he used to be, and the manager wanted to see the coachee take more responsibility for the business and to become more hands-on again. In the manager's mind, the cause of the problem originated in the upper-right quadrant and that is where he wanted the "problem" to be fixed. When the coachee and I explored what he would like to achieve from coaching, he mentioned that he needed help in defining his life's purpose (this was clearly an issue related to the upper-left quadrant). He wanted to discover what his real purpose in life was; he felt that somewhere along the way he had lost the meaning of life. He mentioned that he was no longer so excited about his work. A few years back, he used to enjoy getting out of bed and coming to work; now he found it an effort. He was starting to question whether he was in the right job and whether it was not time for him to make a change. But given that he was a married man with two children, he wanted to make sure what his purpose was before he made any radical career changes. He mentioned that since he had completed his MBA, asset management seemed to be an attractive alternative. These were the issues he was wrestling with; this was his concrete experience, the reality with which he was living.

Having discussed this for some time, we moved into reflective observation. I asked him why he thought that things had changed for him. His response was that he honestly did not know. So we started to reflect on his work and life experience, from which it became clear that he was a very bright and successful individual. For example, he completed his master's thesis in electronic engineering at the same time as his MBA degree. He had an immaculate career track record, having already made a change from the electronics industry to a highly successful career in information technology. He was in his forties, happily married and living in a good house but he could not work out why he was so discontented. As we explored these issues, he realised that there were some aspects of his current job that he still enjoyed but also some that he absolutely hated. He could not put his finger on his discontent, however, or on why he was losing interest in his work.

He then asked me what I thought was going on with him. Was he abnormal? I suggested that there was a strong possibility that he was starting to experience what is generally known as an existential crisis, and that it was common for successful people at his age to experience this. I explained to him that it was a normal developmental process and that he could be starting to make the transition into the transpersonal realms of human development. I also explained a bit of Victor Frankl's logotherapy to him and how discovering our meaning in life gets us through the existential crisis. Immediately he saw how his search for purpose fitted into this theory. In so doing, he realised he was not abnormal and that he was experiencing an aspect of normal human development. The conversation had moved into the abstract conceptualisation aspect of experiential learning. Some theoretical input was interjected into the conversation, which helped the coachee to better understand his current predicament.

We then explored some options with which he could experiment, to help facilitate the process of discovering his purpose in life. The option which most appealed to him was keeping a reflective journal, in which he would reflect on those parts of his job that he found meaningful and energising. I encouraged him to particularly monitor his feelings and energy levels, which parts of his job excited him and gave him energy, and which parts drained him of energy. Using the personal learning contract, we contracted that he would experiment with this approach for a specified time. This step effectively took him into the active experimentation aspect of experiential learning. We were using an upper-right quadrant activity, writing and journalling, to help him discover and explore an upper-left quadrant dilemma, the search for purpose and meaning in his life.

Summary

The Integrated Experiential Learning Process proposes that coaching is about facilitating integrated experiential learning in individuals in order to enhance personal growth and development. It is "integrated" in that it caters for Schumacher's (1978) four fields of knowledge and Wilber's (1995) Integral Model, which analyses personal development through various levels of consciousness, especially in the personal and transpersonal levels. It is "experiential" in that it uses Kolb's (1984) Experiential Learning Model as the paradigm or injunction and Harri-Augstein and Thomas's (1991) concept of learning conversations as the primary learning tool.

Chapter 7

Applying the Integrated Experiential Learning Process in business

Introduction

In the previous chapter, it was proposed that the Integrated Experiential Learning Process facilitates integrated experiential learning in individuals in order to enhance personal growth and development. This chapter will give that meta-theoretical model a business context, in order to arrive at a theoretical executive coaching model. I explain that executive coaching is a one-on-one developmental initiative within the context in which the individual coachee operates.

The Integrated Experiential Learning Process is about working with the behavioural and intentional content of the executive or senior manager, within the context of the social (system) and cultural (world space) in which they operate. By emphasising a more holistic and systemic approach to executive development, the Integrated Experiential Learning Process is in agreement with O'Neill's (2000) systems approach to executive coaching. As was previously pointed out, however, systems approach tends to be limited to the lower-right quadrant; in contrast, this theory is more holistic than a pure systems thinking approach.

Business context

Stacey's (2010) work reminds us that organisations are in essence complex responsive processes. As far back as 1996, Stacey put forward the idea that organisations consist of two subsystems:

- A *legitimate subsystem* which leads to conformity, as a result of all the people in the organisation sharing a dominant schema that engages the current reality. People adhere to the formal processes, structures and share a common culture.
- A *shadow subsystem* which leads to diversity, as a result of the people in the organisation being driven by recessive schemas. People ignore the

DOI: 10.4324/9781003356424-8

official processes and structures and do what they have to do to get things done and to survive.

Business schools are very good at researching and teaching about the legitimate subsystem, but have tended to ignore the shadow subsystem. Stacey believes that it is important for us to study and research the shadow subsystem. Complex responsive processes are at play within both the legitimate and shadow subsystems within any organisation, which adds enormous amounts of complexity to the coaching equation.

Intrapsychic versus person–environment mix

I am in agreement with Peltier (2001), who points out that therapy assumes that the problem is intrapsychic (found in the person), whereas coaching assumes that the problem is found in the person–environment mix. This is a very important insight. When a coach is called in to work with allegedly abnormal temperamental or emotional characteristics of an individual, the question needs to be asked whether the manifested behaviour is really a result of a "flaw" within the individual, or whether the behaviour stems from the structural design and culture of the organisation. More importantly, in the Integrated Experiential Learning Process, physiology is primary and recognises that the central and autonomic nervous systems learn from and respond to the environment. The nervous system will trigger the ventral vagal, sympathetic or dorsal vagal systems in order to make sure the individual survives or thrives within the system. The question therefore becomes: what behaviours are being triggered by the nervous system within the organisation?

An example of this dynamic occurred when I was called in to help coach an individual who had been identified as having an "abnormal temperamental issue". This executive was continually clashing with another executive in the company, and it was seen to be affecting the morale of the entire organisation. As we started to work on the issue, it was discovered that the two executives concerned had actually worked together before, and that previously they had held enormous respect for each other's capabilities. The difficulties started when the "problem" executive, who was responsible for sales, supported the appointment of the other executive to a new role in charge of production. The symptom was that the two executives could no longer get along; in fact, there was an all-out psychological war between them. The real issue, however, was that the other executive's bonus was based on just-in-time production, while the "problem" executive's bonus was based on maximum sales. To maximise his bonus at the end of the year, the other executive closed the production plant in mid-December to ensure that there was no inventory at year-end. Consequently, the "problem" executive could never maximise his bonus because for the first 2 months of the next financial year, there was no stock for his division to sell. The real problem was not with the individuals involved, but with the way the organisation was designed and in the way the reward system actually worked against the company.

Oshry (1999) spent his whole life studying organisations and the behaviours that their systems produced. What Oshry (1999) found was that all organisational systems consist of three types of system, Tops, Middles and Bottoms, and that there are predictable systemic behavioural patterns associated with these three types, irrespective of the individuals involved. In this context, only the Tops and Middles will be dealt with, as executive coaching is normally only aimed at these strata. Tops are collectively responsible for the whole system and these members are regularly confronted with complex, difficult and unpredictable issues with long time horizons. The predictable, cognitive and affective themes of the Top system include:

- *Fear*: They all experience some degree of fear. The question is do they deal with it or run away?
- *Homogenisation and differentiation*: They either share responsibility and information and decide together (homogenise), or they each protect their own turf (differentiate).
- *Differentiation on direction*: Tops have differences with regard to what direction the whole should take. Possible behaviours associated with this dynamic are endless bickering, sabotage, avoidance and/or submergence (Oshry, 1999:59–62).

These behaviours are recognised in all organisations; they are universal to executive teams, which is no surprise given that polyvagal theory and regulation theory have given us the physiological explanation as to why this happens. Unique to polyvagal theory and regulation theory is the assumption that complex behaviours, including social interactions, depend on physiology and how appropriately the nervous system regulates the dynamic autonomic states within any given environment. And as Dana (2018) points out, this provides a physiological and psychological understanding of how and why individuals behave the way they do. The nervous system will trigger the appropriate behaviours to help any individual survive within the given environment.

Given that most organisations are still designed according to functions instead of across business processes, it is not surprising that members of the Middle system are pulled apart from one another, out towards other individuals or groups. The predictable cognitive and affective themes of the Middle system include:

- *Systemic disintegration*: Ideally, members should support one another in the service of a common mission, purpose or function. Given the functional design structures, however, middles spend the bulk of their time handling their individual business, and little or no time supporting one another. There is no incentive for them to support each other and so middles are often in competition among themselves. Who needs to worry about external competition when we design internal competition into our own organisations?

- *Personal disintegration*: If you are not confused as a Middle, you are not paying attention. Middles are being pulled between two very different and conflicting systems (Tops and Bottoms), and there is legitimacy in both systems. Middles can never fully satisfy anyone, and therefore it is easy for them to internalise their dissatisfactions and consider themselves incompetent.
- *Multiplier effect*: In the absence of supportive system membership, each Middle faces these pressures, confusions and self-doubts alone. If Middles try to stay stuck in the middle, their mental health will suffer. They have no option but to choose sides. The question is, "Who do I support, the Tops or the Bottoms?" These are usually the most highly stressed people in the organisation (Oshry, 1999:62–65).

The challenge with executive coaching will always be to work out whether one is dealing with an individual problem (intrapsychic), a systemic design problem or a combination of both. Oshry's (1999) work has shown that a system creates its own behavioural patterns, irrespective of the individuals involved. Yes, at times the behavioural problem can be limited to the individual (intrapsychic); at the same time, however, it is possible that the behaviour results from the system and the way the organisation has been designed. If that is the case, it would be more appropriate to change the system, or at the very least change our relationship to the system:

> Instead of fixing ourselves, we might do better to focus on changing the system by changing our relationship to it. Our feelings of anxiety, anger, frustration, or powerlessness are often clues to the condition of our systems ... we need to change our system by changing our relationships to them.
>
> (Oshry, 1999:9)

The Integrated Experiential Learning Process would suggest that we start with what physiological state the individual is in. It starts with raising awareness of the ventral vagal, sympathetic and dorsal vagal states and how these unconsciously trigger the respective behaviours. As soon as the individual can recognise what state they are in, and how that state has been triggered by their current environment, they can learn to manage the state and try move into a different state. Once an individual is able to recognise and manage their own physiological state, they can start to create an optimal learning state, which enables them to navigate complexity more effectively. In an optimal learning state, it is much easier "to change our system by changing our relationships to them", or to attempt to design more effective organisational systems.

The Systems and Psychodynamics Model

One coaching model that really understands this concept of person–environment mix is the Systems and Psychodynamics Model developed by Kilburg (2000). The systems elements of the Model are familiar organisational concepts such as system structures, system processes, system content, input elements, throughput elements and output elements. The psychodynamic elements are psychological constructs such as the rational self, the instinctual self, the internalised self, conscience, conflict, defence, emotion, cognition, past relationships, present relationships and focal relationships (Kilburg, 2000:23).

The systems elements include the structural elements of the system, which range from tasks to be done to the roles and jobs that individuals do. For Kilburg (2000), these include the traditional elements like hierarchy, departments, degree of centralisation or decentralisation, and the characteristics of the organisational environment, mission, values and culture of the organisation. In his model, the key elements of the organisational processes are contained in the input-throughput-output matrix, and include things like life-cycles of products, change, resource acquisition and allocation, human resource processes, control processes, information systems, motivation, communication, goal-setting, decision-making, followership and leadership. At the same time, it takes into account the key elements of the content of organisational systems, such as research and development, general management, transportation, engineering, manufacturing, marketing, logistics, procurement, finance and safety. Kilburg (2000) is thus very thorough in his approach and covers both the lower-left and lower-right quadrants of the Integrated Experiential Learning Process. The systems focus allows the coach to structure what could be almost incomprehensible, as many of these structures can either be formal or informal.

The psychodynamic aspect of the model provides complex explanations for the motivation of individuals and groups. Kilburg's (2000) model incorporates the major psychological substructures identified by Sigmund Freud. He refers to the ego as the rational self, the id as the instinctual self, the superego as the conscience and the ego ideal as the idealised or internalised self. According to classical psychodynamic theory, these structures exist within the mind of every individual, and have different organising principles and functions, as follows:

- The *instinctual self* is organised around the pleasure principle and its main goals are gratification and reduction of the pressure from biologically based drives and psychological and social needs.
- The *rational self* is organised around the reality principle and its goal is the survival of the individual in biological, social and psychological terms. It helps the person adapt to their environment.

- The *conscience* is organised around the moral principle and its goal is to help the individual maintain social order and cohesion in their world.
- The *idealised self* contains the conscious and unconscious fantasies concerning how the individual would like to be experienced by others. It provides a model of how the individual should behave and live (Kilburg, 2000:27).

Based on the organisation principles and their various goals, it is easy to see how the various internal structures can be in conflict with each other: "The contents or issues of conflict can be varied and complex, ranging from external dangers to internal wishes, demands, emotions, mastery issues, achievement, attachment, separation, control, values and change" (Kilburg, 2000:32). More importantly, these conflicts can occur at the conscious or unconscious level, which adds to the complexity of any situation. This conscious or unconscious conflict can give rise to a host of different psychological defences, including denial, splitting, delusional projection, fantasy projection, passive-aggressive behaviour, dissociation, intellectualisation, repression, detachment, sublimation, altruism, suppression, games, rituals and cognitive distortions. Add to that the complex and varied patterns that are expressed in and through the different social relationships in which people are engaged on a daily basis, especially their roles and relationships at work, and you have a very complex conscious and unconscious environment of various motives for individuals and groups.

The strength of the Systems and Psychodynamics Model is that it sees the psychodynamic and systems approaches as complementary in helping to understand the personal–environment mix:

> Systems theory is useful for its abstractness, general utility and applicability, assistance in organisational and large system assessments, and allowance for prediction and control in some situations.
>
> (Kilburg, 2000:46)

Kilburg (2000) noted that systems theory is not very useful in helping people understand their behaviour internally or when in conflict situations, and that in this regard psychodynamic theory is preferable:

> It is useful in explaining and guiding individuals' behaviour, both internally and interpersonally. It provides useful information about the human side of organisational behaviour, but it is not inclusive enough to assist a consultant or coach with the thorough assessment or diagnosis of organisational operations or human behaviour.
>
> (Kilburg, 2000:46)

I am in agreement with Kilburg about the concept of person–environment mix. But the Integrated Experiential Learning Process adds Schore's (2019) regulation theory and Porges's (2011) polyvagal theory to the equation, which helps to transform psychoanalytical theory from a theory of the unconscious mind to what Schore (2019) calls a "theory of mind/brain/body". Physiologically, the autonomic nervous system and hormonal systems are now part of the unconscious right hemisphere of the brain, thereby inextricably linking in the unconscious system to the body. And the same applies to the conscious mind. Referring to McGilchrist, Schore (2019) mentions that if we mean by conscious that part of the mind that is aware of its own awareness, and brings the world into focus, makes it explicit and allows it to be formulated in language, then almost all that activity lies in the left hemisphere. Integrating an understanding and working of the nervous system into this equation allows for an even more holistic approach to this very complex problem.

More importantly, for me as a person who is not qualified as a psychologist, it is much easier to work with physiological states than psychological constructs. For as Feldenkrais (1977) reminds us, the nervous system is mainly occupied with movement. This is because we cannot sense, feel or think without all the actions initiated by the brain and nervous system to maintain an upright body against the pull of gravity, and to know where and what position we are in. Furthermore, the quality of movement and our physiological state are easier to distinguish. We know more about movement than thinking and emotions like love and anger, for example. It is easier to learn and to recognise the quality of a movement and our physiological state, than the quality of these other factors. We have a richer experience of movement and our physiological state.

Coaching as a sub-discipline of organisational development

Given this level of complexity, it is therefore not surprising that Kilburg (2000) believes that executive coaching is evolving as a sub-discipline of organisational development; it is not psychotherapy in the workplace. According to Jaques and Clement (1997), effective managerial leadership in highly complex environments demands four basic conditions:

1   The individual must have the necessary level of cognitive competence to carry the required role, and they must strongly value the work and responsibility associated with that role. In a sense, this addresses the interpersonal requirements.
2   The individual must be free from any severely debilitating psychological traits that interfere with their ability to work with others. This is a combination of interpersonal and intrapersonal requirements.
3   What Jaques and Clement term "organisational conditions", that is the appropriate business processes, organisational structures and specified

managerial leadership practices, must be in place. These are the systemic requirements.

4   Each individual must be encouraged to use their own leadership style; they must be free to be themselves. There is no "magical leadership" style out there that works for everybody. Every individual is unique and every individual has their own leadership style, depending on their specific competencies and the specified role they fulfil.

Organisational conditions and the design problem

Firstly, let us turn our attention to what Jaques and Clement (1997) term the third condition, or organisational conditions – that is, the appropriate business processes, organisational structures and specified managerial leadership practices must be in place. The reason why so many organisations cannot deliver or implement their strategies is because their business processes and structures do not align with and support each other. Even worse, the structures often prevent the business processes from functioning correctly, or the information technology architecture does not support the desired business processes. There is no alignment between the financial and customer perspectives, the internal business processes, organisational structure, the required competencies and the reward system. If any of these perspectives are missing or not aligned, strategy and its implementation will remain an ever-elusive goal.

Galbraith, Downey and Kates (2002:5) believe that an unaligned organisational design will result in any one or more of the following challenges:

Confusion

If there is no clear or agreed-upon strategy, the consequence will be confusion throughout the organisation. There will be no common direction and as a result people will be pulling in different directions. At the same time, there will be no well-defined criteria for decision-making, and as a result everything becomes a strategic thrust. It is then difficult to decide what is and is not important. In a world of unlimited resources and no constraints, that is not a problem. The reality, however, according to Goldratt's (1990) Theory of Constraints, is that every organisation has some forms of constraint. If that was not true, the throughput for any organisation would be limitless. Given the Theory of Constraints and resource limitations, the art of strategic leadership, according to Perry, Stott and Smallwood (1993), involves the ability to say "no". How can anybody say "no" in the absence of well-defined criteria for decision-making?

Friction

If the organisational structure is not aligned to the strategy, it will result in friction. There is an inability to mobilise resources, which leads to ineffective execution. This in turn leads to lost opportunities for competitive advantage. Jaques and Clement (1997) believe that an organisational structure lies in the pattern of relationships among the various roles that people fulfil within the organisation. Roles set the limits and expectations on the behaviour that is required. Hence all social relationships take place within the context of social structures that are defined by specific roles. If all relationships were totally unstructured, people would not know what to do or how to act. Leadership accountability and authority are therefore defined by specified roles, and not by personal characteristics or traits. That is why they believe that leadership is context-dependent and tied to a role. Using Winston Churchill as an example, they ask whether Churchill was a great "leader"? The answer seems to be that he was a great wartime leader during the Second World War, but not before or after it, leading them to conclude:

> It is therefore no use asking whether a person is a great "leader". The real question should be whether the person is a great manager, or a great commander, or a great political representative, or a great wartime president, or a great peacetime prime minister.
>
> (Jaques and Clement, 1997:6–7)

The right way to go about this is first to define the required role and then to look for a person who has the competencies to fill that role. That is why, in their view, it is so important to get the structure right because it sets the roles and role relationships that specify the types of people needed to fill those roles, and defines how they should behave towards one another. It is impossible to have effective managerial leadership if there is no clear managerial structure.

Not only do you need a clear managerial structure, it has to function effectively. In an attempt to get structures to function more effectively, some management theorists have called for the end of hierarchies and the need for self-organised organisations (*heterarchy*). But, as Wilber (1995) and Jaques and Clement (1997) have pointed out, the problem is not with hierarchies *per se*, but with the pathology within the hierarchy or dysfunctional hierarchies. What Jaques and Clement found was that hierarchical structures are dysfunctional when the roles are not defined and designed correctly. What they discovered was that the level of work in any role can be objectively measured in terms of the target completion times for the longest assignment (tasks, programmes, projects) in that role. The longer the time to complete the task, the heavier the weight of responsibility and accountability. In other words, the boundaries between successive managerial layers occur at certain specific time-spans:

> This regularity, which has so far appeared consistently in over 100 projects, points to the existence of a structure in depth, composed of true managerial layers with boundaries measured in time-span.
>
> (Jaques and Clement, 1997:113)

This discovery has enabled the design of hierarchical structures according to strata, which make it possible to align the nature of task complexity, human nature and capability. In other words, the true organisational layer at stratum-I coincides with the Category B–I in task and cognitive complexity. So at stratum-I you need individuals who follow orders and do what they are told; they proceed along a prescribed linear pathway to a goal. At stratum-III, the task and complexity corresponds to Category B–3; here you need individuals who can work with alternative serial plans. Stratum-VI corresponds to Category C–2 task complexity; here you need individuals who can handle the complexities involved with international trade. In this regard, we can see that Jaques and Clement (1997) and Kolb (1984) are talking a similar language; it is Kolb's concept of "adaptive competencies". According to Kolb (1984), each task or job requires a specific set of skills. The effective matching of task demands and personal skills is what Kolb (1984) calls "adaptive competence". Hierarchies become dysfunctional when individuals are promoted into positions where the level of task complexity exceeds their cognitive ability to manage the task complexity involved.

Gridlock

In the absence of clearly defined business processes, the organisation experiences gridlock and output constraints. Lack of collaboration across boundaries and an inability to share information mean that the organisation cannot leverage best practices. This in turn results in long decision timeframes and long innovation cycle times.

Internal competition

If the metrics and the reward system do not support the goals, it will result in internal competition. The end-result is low standards, wrong results, frustration, high staff turnover and diffused energy.

Poor performance

If people do not understand what they are meant to do, or they are not empowered, it will result in poor performance and low employee satisfaction. Rehm (1997) believes that there are six basic human needs that must be present for human beings to be productive; in fact, he sees them as the foundation for designing effective organisations. In an unaligned organisation, these six criteria will be adversely affected, or they will not be optimised, which leads to lower productivity. The six psychological criteria for productive work are:

- *Elbow-room for decision-making.* People need to know what their parameters are. They need to feel that they are their own bosses and that, other than in exceptional circumstances, they have room to make decisions that they can call their own. On the other hand, they do not need so much elbow-room that they do not know what to do.

- *Opportunity to learn on the job and keep on learning.* Learning is a basic human need and is possible only when people are able to set goals that are reasonable and challenging for themselves, and they get feedback on results in time to correct their behaviour. Without feedback, no learning can take place.
- *Variety.* People need to vary their work to avoid extremes of fatigue and boredom. On the other hand, if people have so much variety due to too much work, they can become overwhelmed, which leads to high levels of stress. This is a common problem in the modern workplace, where the call is for people to continually do more with less.
- *Mutual support and respect.* People need to get help and respect from their co-workers.
- *Meaningfulness.* Meaningfulness includes both the worth and the quality of a product and having knowledge of the whole product and process. The more an individual can see the bigger picture or the bigger process, the more meaningful their work becomes.
- *A desirable future.* People need a job that leads them to a desirable future for themselves, not a dead end. This desirable future is not necessarily a promotion but a career path which continues to allow for personal growth and increase in skills (Benedict Bunker and Alban, 1997:139).

Managerial complexity

In theory and on paper, the process of structuring and designing the organisation is easy to explain. Most executives have no problem grasping the idea or concept of strategy formulation and organisational design. The problem, however, arises with the actual implementation. Why is it that so many companies and executives battle with the implementation or the actual doing of the design? An answer can be found in the work of Jaques and Clement (1997) on stratified systems theory. According to them, the problem has to do with the level of complexity involved. The complexity is not in the formulation of the strategy but in the implementation thereof. Furthermore, the complexity is compounded by the fact that the strategy has to be formulated and implemented within an ever-changing environment. It has to become real-time strategy, constantly responding to the changing demands of the market. And as Goldratt (1990) points out, even the best solutions, including solutions and designs that worked in the past, can actually become the next source of constraints. The problem is compounded further as many individuals tend to underestimate the level of complexity involved, where complexity can be defined as:

a function of the number of variables operating in a situation, the ambiguity of these variables, the rate at which they are changing, and the extent to which they are interwoven so that they have to be unravelled in order to be seen.

(Jaques and Clement, 1997:xvii)

And these variables can be numerous and very elusive, as Kilburg (2000) points out; there can be hundreds if not thousands of variables that contribute to the success or failure of an organisation. Given that these variables interact in both observable and non-observable ways, he argues that "true prediction and control are elusive". He is therefore in agreement with the principles of complex responsive processes. In short, the reason that executives sometimes find it difficult to implement their designed strategies is because they become overwhelmed by the complexity involved with modern managerial leadership, which is a function of complex responsive processes at play.

Add to that the new layer of complexity imposed on organisational design in the post-COVID world. Executives are now faced with the further complexity of designing and managing hybrid organisations which cater for office and/or mobile work. And the evidence seems to be showing that every organisation is going to have to design and manage a hybrid system unique to them and the needs of their workforce.

The challenge all executives therefore face is how to effectively design and implement what Stacey (1996) calls the legitimate subsystem of the organisation in response to the very complex global economy in which they operate. Ideally, a well-designed legitimate subsystem will lead to conformity, as a result of all the people in the organisation sharing a dominant schema that engages the current reality. People adhere to the formal processes and structures, and share a common culture. As Oshry's (1999) work reminds us, however, no matter what structure, business processes and governance processes are designed and put in place, every system creates its own behavioural patterns, irrespective of the individuals involved.

The reason is that, through the process of neuroception, every individual's nervous system very quickly works out which of the three systemic responses must come into play to help that individual thrive or survive in their environment. This in turn determines their behaviour. These individuals then interact with each other. These interdependent groups of people reflect on their current experience, form intentions, make choices and come up with strategies to respond to their current situation. At the same time, however, there are other groups of interdependent people doing exactly the same thing. And what happens or evolves out of this is determined by the interplay between all these groups of interdependent people; it is not simply determined by one group alone. This is the basis of the theory of complex responsive processes, and leads to the formation of a shadow subsystem which leads to diversity, as result of the people in the organisation being driven by recessive schemas. People ignore the official processes and structures and do what they have to do to get things done and to survive.

Individual competencies

Given the complexity of the business environment and the challenge of trying to design a legitimate subsystem and effectively manage the shadow sub-system, what is it that the individual executive needs to do or have to function effectively within that environment? According to Jaques and Clement (1997:44–82), the following competencies are required to effectively manage the levels of complexity involved:

Cognitive power

Cognitive power (CP) is the potential strength of cognitive processes in an individual, and it is therefore the maximum level of task complexity that the individual can handle at any given point in their development. CP is the maximum number, ambiguity, rate of change and interweaving of variables that an individual can process in a given period of time. It is therefore the necessary level of cognitive complexity required to manage the level of task complexity of the specific managerial role. Underpinning CP are the cognitive processes by means of which an individual is able to analyse, organise and synthesise information to make it available for doing work. Jaques and Cason found that it was possible to observe an individual's pattern of mental processing:

> in the manner in which they organised their information, or arguments, in the course of an engrossed discussion or argument in which they were really concerned to set out their point of view and to make themselves perfectly clear to whomever might be listening.

> (Jaques and Cason, 1994:30)

Their research found that there are only four mental patterns or types of mental process that individuals use. The four patterns are:

- *Declarative processing*: The individual explains their position by using a number of separate reasons. Each reason is seen as separate and no attempt is made to connect the reasons. They all stand alone and independent of each other. This processing has a declarative quality.
- *Cumulative processing*: The individual explains their position by bringing together a number of ideas. The individual ideas are insufficient to make the case, but taken together, they do. This processing has a pulling-together quality.

- *Serial processing*: Here the individual builds up an argument through a sequence of reasons, each reason building on the other. The ultimate result is a chain of linked reasons.
- *Parallel processing*: Using serial processing, the individual explains their position by examining several other possible positions as well. The lines of thought are held in parallel, and can be linked to each other, which involves working with various scenarios at the same time. This kind of processing has a conditional quality; not only do the various scenarios link with each other but they can condition each other (Jaques and Cason, 1994).

By combining these observable thinking patterns with the observable levels of information complexity (concrete order, symbolic order, abstract conceptual order and universal order), Jaques and Cason (1994) were able to develop their categories of complexity of mental processing. Using these categories of mental processing, they were able to define an individual's current potential capability by observing and analysing the mental processes being used. Based on their research, they concluded *inter alia* that the complexity of mental processing could be reliably observed when subjects were engrossed in discussions of interest to them. From this they were able to observe the complexity of mental processing being used and make a valid judgement of their current potential. Interestingly enough, these thinking processes were observable only when the topics of discussion were of interest to the subjects; in other words, the study had to take the subjects' concrete experience into account. Having defined the field of interest, the subjects got so involved that the researchers could observe their thinking processes.

Be that as it may, Jaques and Cason (1994) showed that it is possible to identify the amount of complexity any individual could handle at that point of their development by observing and analysing their thinking processes. They concluded that there are categories of complexity of mental processes and that these mature over time. Individuals become overwhelmed by complexity when their cognitive power does not match the level of task complexity demanded of them. This could be due to the individual not having matured into the required cognitive complexity, or they simply do not have the required cognitive ability. Cognitive power is therefore the most critical requirement to handle organisational complexity but it is not the only criterion for success. The competencies listed below are just as important.

Sense of values

A strong sense of values (V) for the required managerial work and for the leadership of others. Even if an individual has the required cognitive complexity, they must want to do the work at hand; that is, they must value the work they are doing. Their personal values have to be aligned with the work they do, so that their mental energy can be focused and unleashed. If people believe in what they are doing, they have much more energy to do the work. The converse is also true; even if the individual is a genius, if the work is no longer meaningful for that individual, mental and physical energy evaporate.

Knowledge and skills

This is the appropriate knowledge and skills (K/S) to do the work. But having the appropriate skills and knowledge is not enough; Jaques and Clement (1997) believe that the individual needs experienced practice in both. Furthermore, when it comes to executive-managerial leadership, it is important to distinguish between technical, managerial and personal skills.

Most individuals start their careers as some form of expert or professional in which they make use of their technical skills. As they move out of being functional or technical experts, they move into management and have to learn managerial skills. If they happen to move into an executive position, personal skills become more important than technical or managerial skills. Technical and management skills are task-based skills, in that they are aimed at addressing a certain task at hand. These skills are usually learnt by making use of Kolb's (1984) prehension dimension of experiential learning. There is a task or a problem that needs to be solved or addressed (concrete experience); people are then trained in various theories or methods by means of abstract conceptualisation on how to apply the theory to the concrete problem or task at hand.

Traditionally, these theories or methods have usually been done via what Beard and Wilson (2002) refer to as *provider-centred* as opposed to *learner-centred* learning. *Provider-centred learning*, which is based on the "banking" model of education as defined by Freire (2005), has tended to be aligned with classroom training and learning, with the emphasis on the immediate acquisition of knowledge and skills required to do the job. The teacher or trainer is the expert, the repository of knowledge, who knows best and therefore has the responsibility and power. The trainer dictates the flow of the learning programme and trainees wait for the learning to be led by the trainer. Trust is low and trainees need continual supervision. The trainer follows a rigid syllabus, dispensing knowledge in pre-determined chunks, but only within their own field of expertise. Passive learning is encouraged and trainees learn by memorising information and using artificial case studies. Learning is monitored, assessed and examined by the trainer.

In contrast, in *learner-centred learning* the emphasis is on promoting deeper, more meaningful learning that affects life behaviour. There are no teacher or trainers, only learners. Learners are considered to have a valuable contribution to make and have joint responsibility for and power over the learning process. Learners continually develop the programme, which is governed by a learning contract and takes place within a climate of mutual care and understanding. Learning is at the pace of the learner. The focus is on fostering continuous learning, on asking questions and on the process of learning itself. The learning provider offers resources to learn, working with the natural curiosity and concerns of the learner, and real issues and problems are used as vehicles of learning. Feedback on self-performance is encouraged (Beard and Wilson, 2002:166).

Unlike technical and managerial skills, personal skills are more environmentally based, such as flexibility, adaptability, intuition and imagination. These types of skill are very difficult to learn in a classroom environment. In a sense, these are the skills that an individual learns from their own experience and are highly dependent on Kolb's (1984) transformation dimension of experiential learning, that is reflective observation and active experimentation. It is the ability to develop and practise what Schön (1983) calls *reflection-in-action*. It is about reflecting and experimenting in a real-time environment. Schön does, however, distinguish between the Technical Rational model of controlled experimenting and what he calls exploratory experimentation:

> The most fundamental question is, "What if?" When action is undertaken only to see what follows, without accompanying predictions and expectations, I shall call it exploratory experiment ... Exploratory experiment is the probing, playful activity by which we get a feel for things.
>
> (Schön, 1983:144–145)

Reflection-in-action therefore makes use of exploratory experimentation to consider the consequences of various actions while one is within the process. Beard and Wilson (2002) argue that reflection-in-action (concurrent learning), as defined by Schön (1983), does not require the support of a teacher/mentor or coach because it happens spontaneously. Over the years, the individual has learnt from his professional practice how to do this kind of reflection spontaneously. To rely on reflection-in-action purely to develop deep learning could, however, be dangerous. Beard and Wilson (2002) point out that, due to time pressure and various constraints, people often do not make the time to reflect on what is happening. Even Schön (1983) admits that in reality, managers do reflect-in-action but they seldom reflect on their reflection-in-action. As a result, their reflection-in-action tends to remain private and not accessible to others.

The inadequacies of reflection-in-action prompted the call for *reflection-on-action* (retrospective learning) by Beard and Wilson (2002), which involves the individual thinking about their previous experience, analysing it and developing their own personal theories of action. Reflection-in-action is an active process of spontaneous reflection, organised by the learner themselves, in order to understand and respond to experience. It usually happens in the workplace, when understanding of the circumstances is necessary and when time is available. In contrast, reflection-on-action is a planned intervention involving contemplation, assisted by a facilitator, to support learning from experience. It usually happens away from the workplace, and is planned for specific times (Beard and Wilson, 2002:198). It is especially in the domain of reflection-on-action that coaching can play an important role to facilitate the development of environmentally based skills. In this respect, coaching is more aligned with the concept of *learner-centred learning*.

Wisdom

The necessary wisdom (Wi) about people and things. Jaques and Clement (1997) believe that wisdom has to do with the soundness of an individual's judgements about the world and people. It is the ability to make good judgements about people and how they are likely to react in various situations. Sensitivity and empathy are central to wisdom, which expresses itself intact. Given that this is a developmental model, wisdom is something that can develop and mature with age. This does not automatically mean that all old people are wise. What it does raise is the interesting dynamic of innovation versus wisdom. In the heyday of the dotcoms, "conventional wisdom" suggested that organisations get rid of the older, wiser members in order to make way for the young innovators. The problem was that, due to lack of experience, many of these innovators did not have the wisdom required to manage a large, complex organisation through its various life-cycles. The reality is that large complex organisations need both wisdom and innovation to be sustainable. Theory without practical experience is not enough. It is very true that experience is a good teacher, in that it teaches new skills and how to improve existing skills; but when it comes to wisdom, experience on its own is not enough. Jaques and Clement (1997) point out that wisdom needs both concrete experience and abstract conceptualisation. They believe that action without sound theory and concepts is unproductive because it distorts our experience and narrows our vision. Theories and concepts determine what we see and what we learn from our own experience. The acquisition of wisdom therefore involves Kolb's (1984) prehension dimension of experiential learning.

Personal qualities and traits: T and (-T)

T is the attempt to define leadership qualities and traits, and (-T) is the absence of abnormal temperamental or emotional characteristics in an individual which disrupt their ability to work with others. According to Jaques and Clement, the focus upon personality qualities and traits is misguided:

> the particular pattern of qualities that constitutes emotional make-up has little effect upon that person's in-role leadership work, unless those qualities are at unacceptable or abnormal extremes and the individual lacks

the self-control to keep them from disturbing his or her work and working relationships with others.

(Jaques and Clement, 1997:79)

This is a very valuable insight which Jaques and Clement (1997) have brought into the business world. As they point out, there are over 2,500 personality variables which most people have to a greater or lesser degree. And how these variables are expressed is often dependent on the situation:

> This huge range of commonly occurring characteristics combines in infinitely varied patterns to give the great richness of differences in personality make-up, all of which may be consistent with effective managerial leadership, and none of which is likely to be better or worse.
>
> (Jaques and Clement, 1997:80)

We have somehow started to believe the myth that there are certain personality traits that make better leaders than others, or – even worse – the belief that there is a correct "leadership style". As anybody with some experience knows, leadership styles come and go along with all other fads. Over the last 30 years, the Gallup Organisation has conducted a systematic study of excellence. This study has so far included two million of the most successful people they could find. In their study, they did discover 34 prevalent themes of human talent, which is what the Clifton StrengthsFinder® is based on. The instrument helps an individual to identify their five dominant talents, where "talent" is defined as "any recurring pattern of thought, feeling, or behaviour that can be productively applied" (Buckingham and Clifton, 2002:48).

Even though the instrument can help an individual identify their dominant talents, how those talents combine in every individual seems to be unique. Buckingham and Clifton (2002) point out that it is highly unlikely for people to have similar signature themes because there are over 33 million possible combinations of the top five talents. It is how they combine in the individual which makes the individual unique. Now imagine the permutations involved with 2,500 personality variables added to that. According to Buckingham and Clifton (2002), innate talents on their own do not lead to strengths. A strength comes into play when you combine innate talent with knowledge and skills. The latter two attributes make up the learning component of a strength.

Buckingham and Clifton suggest that two types of knowledge are required. The first is factual knowledge, which is content, concepts and theories. The second is experiential knowledge. Factual knowledge is the same as abstract conceptualisation and experiential knowledge is concrete experience, the combination of these two being Kolb's prehension dimension. A skill involves putting structure to experiential knowledge. By reflecting on what is required, all the accumulated knowledge is formalised into a sequence of steps that, if followed, will lead to performance. Buckingham and Clifton's (2002) understanding of a skill corresponds to Kolb's transformation dimension of experiential learning.

It can therefore be argued that an individual's natural strengths are a combination of their preferred learning style and their innate talents. According to Buckingham and Clifton (2002), the latter is more constant and enduring, while the former is more dynamic and changeable according to circumstances. Based on this research and on my own personal experience, I have come to the conclusion that Smuts (1973) was right when he said that there is a "creative Holism in Personality". And that even though my body and mental structure can have some resemblance to my parents and ancestors, my personality is indisputably mine. The personality is not inherited; it is a creative novelty in every human being that makes every person a unique individual. Hence Smuts's (1973) argument that psychology does not "materially assist" in the study of personality, since psychology deals with the average or generalised individual; and in so doing, it ignores the individual uniqueness of the personality. Good leadership is the result of an individual using their own strengths in a given context. The message seems clear, stop messing around with people's personalities.

Sadly, many "coaches" have built a practice by focusing on and working purely with the (-T) factor. Unfortunately, due to ignorance, many individuals who market themselves as executive coaches are in fact not coaches but psychologists still practising therapy under another name. Peltier (2001) points out many differences between therapy and executive coaching. For example, therapy is oriented towards treating pathology, the problem being within the person. The client chooses the therapist, is clearly the person with whom the therapist works, and is the one that must feel enriched by the process. In contrast, coaching is oriented towards development of individual growth or skills, any challenges being located in the person–environment mix. The organisation employing the executive being coached may choose the coach, would therefore probably be the "client" paying the coach's fees, and would need to feel accordingly enhanced by the coaching. Therapy works through and aims to resolve personality issues and hence focuses on the past; whereas coaching works around personality issues and focuses on the present and the future. Therapy involves rigid boundaries between therapist and client, sessions take place in the therapist's office, and confidentiality is clear and absolute. In coaching, boundaries are more flexible, coaching sessions may take place in the executive's workplace or elsewhere and confidentiality is complex (particularly if an assessment of an individual's progress must be shared with a more senior executive) (Peltier, 2001:xxvii).

It has to be acknowledged, however, that Peltier's distinctions are not shared by all. Spinelli (2008), for example, does not agree with the past-versus-future orientation. I am sure that there are numerous authors and coaches who will disagree with that distinction. What I do believe is very valid, is Peltier's

(2001) warning that the transition from therapy to executive coaching can be difficult and open to failure. In his opinion, any therapist who does not have significant knowledge of the business world, its bottom-line orientation and its assumptions, is destined to fail. Cavanagh and Grant (2006) make the same argument, pointing out that coaching psychologists need to develop skills and knowledge in areas that are unfamiliar to psychologists. These skills would include management, business, teaching and workplace training and learning. Executive coaching therefore calls for a wider knowledge base. According to Cavanagh and Grant (2006), it is this wider knowledge base, rather than its uniqueness, that is one of the critical distinctions between coaching and other forms of psychological practice.

Therapeutic issues might be raised in the coaching environment and they can be useful. However, as Peltier (2001:xxvii) points out, coaching is growth or skill development oriented, it is not pathology oriented. Referring to managers acting as coaches, Jaques and Clement (1997) see no problem in helping the individual smooth out some rough edges in their temperament; in their view, however, it is not the role of the coach or the manager to try and change the individual's personality. If the coach is a qualified psychologist, they will be able to deal with the problem; if not, the coach has no option but to refer the client for therapy.

If the coach, on the other hand, works only with (-T), it is therapy and not coaching. The emphasis in the Integrated Experiential Learning Process is oriented towards personal growth and skills development, not working with pathology. The Model therefore leans more towards positive psychology, in that it prefers to focus on and help individuals capitalise on their strengths, and help them discover ways to manage around their weaknesses. In this regard, the Integrated Experiential Learning Process is in alignment with the Australian Psychological Society's Interest Group in Coaching Psychology, which defines coaching psychology as an applied positive psychology:

> It can be understood in terms of systematic application of behavioural science to the enhancement of life experience, work performance and wellbeing for individuals, groups and organisations who do not have clinically significant mental health issues or distress that could be regarded as abnormal.
>
> (Lane and Corrie, 2006:150)

Jaques and Clement believe that there are five methods that can be used to facilitate managerial leadership in individuals. The five interventions are:

- *Coaching*, which is an important influence on values and wisdom. It can and should add to the individual's knowledge.
- *Teaching* imparts knowledge to the individual through lectures, practice and discussions. It is focused on abstract conceptualisation.

- *Training*, focused on helping the individual develop and enhance their skills through on-the-job training or simulations. It is focused on active experimentation.
- *Mentoring* is usually undertaken by a manager-one-removed, and helps the individual develop sound judgement and wisdom.
- *Counselling* is applicable when an individual is facing some personal problems and may at times require therapy. It is therefore concerned with personality characteristics (Jaques and Clement, 1997).

Personally, I think that Jaques and Clement have defined coaching far too narrowly; they limit it to working with V and Wi. Any executive coaching intervention could and should work with CP, V, K/S and Wi. Where I do agree with them is that coaching is different to therapy.

More importantly, all of these individual competencies are not given at birth. These are competencies that are learnt and developed experientially over time. Hence the most critical competency to learn and master is how to learn. The Integrated Experiential Learning Process therefore aims to coach executives and managers to develop what Harri-Augstein and Webb (1995) define as self-organised learning. In order to do that, it is critical for them to first learn to become aware of their physiological states. They need to learn about which state they are currently in, be that the ventral vagal, sympathetic or dorsal vagal state. They need to learn how those states actually determine their behaviours and affect the quality of their decision, judgement and learning capabilities. This in turn will trigger certain behaviours in others. More importantly, they need to learn how to manage their different physiological states. For as Feldenkrais reminds us, it is awareness that gives humans the capacity for things like abstract thought, imagination, judgement, differentiation and generalisation. The more we become aware of and can differentiate in which physiological state we are in, the more we can improve the quality of our lives. Awareness and self-improvement help us to develop even more as humans. And for him, development is "the harmonious coordination between structure, function, and achievement" (Feldenkrais, 1977:51). It is the complete freedom from either self-compulsion (being completely at the mercy of the sympathetic and dorsal vagal systems) or compulsion from others (we can regulate our ventral vagal system). Learning to manage their physiological state is therefore the foundation on which all the needed competencies are built.

Executive coaching defined

The executive coaching intervention should therefore be aimed at working with CP, V, K/S and Wi within the system in which the individual operates. In the Integrated Experiential Learning Process, executive coaching is therefore about facilitating integrated experiential learning in individuals, in order to enhance personal growth and development, with the aim of improving individual and organisational performance. It is not therapy. It is integrated in that it attempts to work and think in the context of all four quadrants, and on various levels of physiological state and consciousness. It is always aware that, no matter what tool or method is being used, it is only a partial truth applying to a certain quadrant or level.

Summary

This chapter has highlighted some of the complexities involved when coaching executives in corporations. Clearly, a coach with no understanding or experience of the impact of organisational design and structures on individual and group behaviour would find it very difficult to work in an integrated way with their client(s). In the absence of this knowledge and experience, the temptation, according to Jaques and Clement, will then be to "focus upon psychological characteristics and style that leads to the unfortunate attempts within companies to change the personalities of individuals, or to maintain procedures aimed at getting a 'a correct balance' of personalities" (Jaques and Clement, 1997:28). As they point out, there is no way that effective leadership development is possible unless and until the organisational conditions support it, irrespective of how good the coach may be.

Chapter 8

The Integrated Experiential Learning Process in a team context

Introduction

On completion of the research for my Doctorate in 2005, the client company challenged me to apply the then Integrated Experiential Coaching Model to team coaching. The organisation wanted more people to experience the benefits and improved performance achieved by individuals who had participated in the individual coaching programme. A second reason was purely economic: individual coaching was expensive and they wanted to reap economies of scale. The team model of coaching was subsequently adopted by a major banking group in Africa, where it was refined over a number of years and applied in various organisations internationally. The application of coaching to teams moved the emphasis of the Model to the lower-right quadrant.

Given that the Integrated Experiential Coaching Model was about facilitating experiential learning in individuals, it soon became apparent that the Model could be adapted to teams with the greatest of ease. My working hypothesis has been that Kolb's genius lay in his ability to map out a very natural process, which has been strengthened with the integration of polyvagal theory, regulation theory and the physiology underpinning experiential learning. All that is needed to facilitate learning is to make it conscious and give it some structure. The entire coaching process is therefore about facilitating experiential learning. The first part of the process is highly structured, to allow the team to get to know each other better and to familiarise them with the experiential learning process. It has four simple stages: concrete experience, reflective observation, abstract conceptualisation and active experimentation.

Concrete experience

The first day usually starts with a check-in and expectations exercise. We then start the process by reviewing where the team currently is, that is their concrete experience. The process starts with honouring the team's personal experience. The tool that I use to facilitate this part of the process is the six psychological criteria for productive workplaces. As discussed in Chapter 7, Rehm (1997)

DOI: 10.4324/9781003356424-9

believes that there are six basic human needs that must be present for human beings to be productive; he sees this as the foundation for designing effective organisations. The six psychological criteria for productive work are:

* elbow-room for decision-making;
* opportunity to learn on the job and keep on learning;
* variety;
* mutual support and respect;
* meaningfulness; and
* a desirable future (Benedict Bunker and Alban, 1997:139).

Each individual is asked to rate how they are currently experiencing their job according to the following scales. The rating scale for the first three questions is: –5; –4; –3; –2; –1; 0; +1; +2; +3; +4; +5, where –5 = too little; 0 = just right; + 5 = too much. The rating scale for the last three questions is: 0; 1; 2; 3; 4; 5; 6; 7; 8; 9; 10, where 0 = none, 10 = good. After they have rated themselves, they get together in the big group and share their scores. Team members are encouraged to just listen to their colleagues and they are not allowed to respond. They are allowed to ask clarifying questions but that is all they are allowed to do. The one rule that is applied is that nobody apologises for their experience. The rest of the team are encouraged to honour that experience.

Reflective observation

Having completed that exercise, the team is then split into smaller groups, where they are asked to reflect on what they have just experienced and to answer the question "What did you learn from the previous exercise?" Having explored the question in smaller groups, the big group reconvenes to discuss their learnings.

The big learning which usually arises from this exercise is the phenomenological nature of experiential learning that two people can experience exactly the same situation or phenomenon, yet experience it completely differently. It is not uncommon for problems with structures, processes, procedures and roles to be identified this early in the process.

Abstract conceptualisation

At this point, I usually introduce the theory of the Integrated Experiential Learning Process, how the experiential learning process works and the Clifton StrengthsFinder® (Buckingham and Clifton, 2002). The team is then asked to identify their individual preferred learning style using Kolb's (1984) learning styles inventory. Based on research and clinical observation of the learning styles inventory scores, Kolb (1984) developed descriptions of the characteristics of the four learning styles. I am still very comfortable to work with the four learning styles. If the team feels the need to refine it even more, the updated nine learning styles can be utilised. The four descriptions are:

- *The convergent learning style.* Here an individual prefers to employ abstract conceptualisation and active experimentation. This approach is strong at decision-making, the practical application of ideas and problem-solving. This learning style solves problems through hypothetico-deductive reasoning. People who prefer this style of learning prefer to deal with technical tasks and problems. Social and interpersonal issues tend to be avoided.
- *The divergent learning style.* Here the individual prefers to utilise concrete experience and reflective observation; they tend to like working with people and tend to be more feeling-oriented and imaginative. They love to look at things from many perspectives and tend towards observation rather than action. They are good at brainstorming because of their ability to generate alternative ideas and to think of the implications of these.
- *The assimilation learning style.* This style draws on abstract conceptualisation and reflective observation. Individuals who prefer this style tend to have an ability to create theoretical models, synthesising disparate observations into meaningful explanations using inductive reasoning. The focus is more on ideas and abstract concepts than on people. Theories are valued more for their precision and logic than for their practical value.
- *The accommodative learning style.* Here concrete experience and active experimentation are employed as the preferred learning abilities. It is action-oriented and excels at getting things done, completing tasks and getting involved with new experiences. This style is accommodative because it is best suited for those situations where an individual must adapt to the changing circumstances. These individuals tend to discard plans or theories when they do not suit the facts. Problems are solved in an intuitive, trial-and-error manner. These people tend to rely more on other people for information, rather than on their own analytical ability. Although they are comfortable with people, they can be seen as pushy and impatient (Kolb, 1984: 77–78).

Again, it must be emphasised that these are preferred learning styles. The ideal is for an individual to move through all four learning styles to optimise their learning and growth. The problem, as was mentioned previously, is that individuals tend to get stuck in or concentrate on only one of the four learning abilities, and in so doing limit their own learning, development and performance.

Having identified their own individual preferred learning style, each individual shares this information with each other and the group maps out the team's profile. The team then goes into a discussion of the implications of the individual styles and team profile for the performance of the team as a whole.

Interestingly, Buckingham and Clifton (2002) point out that strength is a combination of an individual's preferred learning style and their natural talent. They point out that a strength needs experiential and factual knowledge (Kolb's concrete experience versus abstract conceptualisation) and a skill, which is a series of steps carried out to do something. Those steps can be things you do (active experimentation) or think (reflective observation). And lastly, you need talents which are naturally recurring patterns of behaviour, feelings or thoughts. Prior to the coaching intervention, each individual would have been asked to identify their natural talents using the Clifton StrengthsFinder®.

The next step of the process asks each individual team member to share their natural talents with the team. At the same time, the rest of the team is asked to validate or question these talents based on their personal experience of and interaction with the individual. At the end of the two exercises, the team will have a reasonable picture of its inherent natural strengths. It is my belief that, given the fast nature of change and the complexity in which large organisations operate, it is vitally important for the coach and the team to identify their natural strengths and learn to put those strengths to work as a team. The Integrated Experiential Learning Process focuses on learning and performance, not pathology. Philosophically, it is on a par with Buckingham and Clifton (2002) in putting the emphasis on maximising strengths and managing weaknesses.

This usually brings the first day to an end. The day is summarised, showing the team that they have completed most of the experiential learning cycle, namely concrete experience, reflective observation and abstract conceptualisation. The day is ended with a check-out process and telling the team that they will engage in another concrete experience after supper.

Storytelling

After supper, the team reassembles for a session of storytelling. (Or for the more academically and scientifically inclined, personal narratives. Personally, I am very happy with the term storytelling.) I discovered the power of storytelling while I was doing my Doctoral research. Storytelling was never designed to be a formal part of the Integrated Experiential Learning Process. I needed something to ground people in their own concrete experience, however, so I asked them to tell me their life stories and I shared mine, so that we could get to know each other better before we started the coaching journey together. To my surprise, the research revealed that people experienced storytelling in a non-judgemental environment as very meaningful. We live in a world where we are continually judged and assessed to death by "professionals" who love to tell us who we are, or what we should be, or what is wrong with us. I have found that people find it very meaningful to tell their own subjective stories because it honours their uniqueness. To me, storytelling is what Jan Smuts (1973) referred to as the discipline of "personology".

Jan Smuts suggested that "personology" should be studied by analysing the biographies of personalities as a whole. This study should be done synthetically, and not analytically as in the case of psychology. This would enable the researcher to discover the materials that can help formulate the laws of personal evolution. Smuts (1973) called this the science of "Biography", or the story behind the uniqueness of every individual. Accordingly, I ask team members to share their chronological life stories with each other. This is not a T-group, so people share what they feel comfortable to share. In my experience as an individual and group coach, storytelling is one of the most powerful tools I have ever encountered. Personally, I am always left with a sense of awe and it has given me an appreciation for the uniqueness of every individual. Teams normally find that in this session, they learn a great deal about their fellow team members. Assumptions are challenged and prejudices are shattered. We all think we know people, when in reality we know very little about each other; yet we still love to label each other, to assign each other to stereotypical boxes. Storytelling, in my experience, tears open all those neat psychological boxes, leaves them in tatters and exposes a unique human being, a mystery that will never be fully known or classified. It gives us the freedom to explore our own unique journey.

Teams as complex responsive processes

On paper, this all seems very simplistic and easy to do. It sounds like a very mechanistic and clearly structured process. The reality is often very different because every team is a manifestation of complex responsive processes, which is a way of thinking in which the individual mind and the team are patterning processes that evolve out of the interactions between human bodies. As a coach, I am learning to become more aware of these complex responsive processes within the team context, and the aim is to make them more conscious so that the team can work with them. In this regard, I have found working with polyvagal theory very helpful.

A good example is a team that a colleague and I have worked with for several years. The MD had asked us to work with the team for 2 days because they had to have a very difficult conversation. Twelve to fourteen months previously, the executive team had decided to engage a well-known international consulting firm to carry out an analysis of productivity in the organisation. Needless to say, this raised major concerns within the organisation about job losses. At the time, the executive team chose to have a town hall meeting in which they reassured all the staff that nobody would be retrenched. At the time, my colleague and I warned them that this was not a thoughtful response and that it could come back to bite them – which of course it did, hence the need for the 2 days to have the difficult conversation. In this case, it was particularly difficult, as some of the executives present were out of the loop and did not even know whether they themselves would still have jobs.

During the first part of the session, we worked hard to create a safe container and space for the intended conversation. A safe enough container was eventually created for one executive to feel secure enough to start questioning and challenging how the process was undertaken. This soon split the group between those in favour of the process and those against it. As this individual became more and more courageous, he challenged the system more and more. After a while, even those who supported him seemed to push back against him. As a result, this individual started to back off more and more, becoming quieter and quieter until he eventually became passive-aggressive. In other words, he stopped participating completely; psychologically, he "checked-out" of the process. The rest of the group, however, had moved from a debate to a dialogue, with very high engagement levels. At the break, I checked in with the MD to see what he thought about the discussion. He expressed his concern that the team had lost this specific individual.

When the team reconvened, I asked them to reflect on their experience so far and how it was going. In response, they described the essence of polyvagal theory, without using the relevant terminology. I then quickly shared polyvagal theory with them, and as I was doing that, I could see the face of the disaffected executive light up. As soon as I had finished, he said that was exactly what had happened to him during the previous session. Once the group had created what he felt was a safe space, he felt safe enough to start asking some difficult questions and to challenge the system; he was in the ventral vagal state. As soon as the group started to turn against him, he immediately went into the fight-or-flight response of the sympathetic nervous state. As a result, he challenged more and fought even harder. When he eventually realised that he was now on his own and that fighting was making the situation worse, he dropped into the dorsal vagal state and psychologically checked-out by withdrawing and keeping quiet. Having made the whole process conscious and depersonalising it, we were eventually able to bring this individual back into the conversation.

The structured first part of the coaching intervention is therefore aimed at creating a safe container, a safe space to allow for the more difficult conversations to happen. And my job as a coach is to continuously observe the physical cues that highlight which physiological states are at play, and how these contribute to complex responsive processes. The aim is to create a space where the ventral vagal system of each individual can be activated as much as possible.

The Ten Components of a Thinking Environment®

A safe space in the team coaching context would include facilitating the Ten Components of a Thinking Environment®. According to Nancy Kline (1999:100–101), team effectiveness depends on the calibre of thinking the team can do, which in turn is dependent on the Ten Components of a Thinking Environment® which are:

- Attention (listening with interest and without interruption).
- Equality (treating the other as a thinking peer; keeping agreements and boundaries).
- Ease (offering freedom from internal rush or urgency).
- Appreciation (a 5:1 ratio of appreciation to criticism).
- Encouragement (moving beyond internal competition).
- Feelings (allowing sufficient emotional release to restore thinking).
- Information (supplying facts; managing organisational denial).
- Diversity (welcoming divergent thinking and diverse group identities).
- Incisive questions (removing assumptions that limit ideas).
- Place (creating a physical environment that says to the other, "You matter") (Kline, 1999).

Attention

The thinking environment cannot be created without attention, the definition of which is listening with "respect, interest and fascination" (Kline, 1999:35). Attention helps people to do their own thinking. It is important to understand that attention is not a technique – it is a way of being with the thinker or the other person. Polyvagal theory and regulation theory have shown that we co-regulate each other's nervous systems unconsciously via the right hemisphere of the brain. We unconsciously know whether we feel safe with the person and whether they really are interested in listening to us. Kline (1999:20) argues that "if you set up the right conditions, people will think for themselves". I would argue that the most important condition is the physiological state in which each person is at that moment. That is why the final characteristic of attention is "physically" showing attention; this is not to be confused with technique. What the other person does with their eyes, face and body while they are listening shows fully focused and concentrated attention. To be physically present, showing interest and respect, the person keeps their eyes on the eyes of the thinker.

Equality

Equality can be defined reassuringly as "You get a turn too." In a coaching environment, the professional coach listens to the client; in the thinking environment between peers, both people have a turn to listen and to speak. When coaching, it is the client who gets the attention but in a thinking environment (particularly in team coaching), each person matters as much as the next person, and each person will have a chance to think equally. It is considerate to discuss some type of time boundary to ensure that all individuals involved are aware of time constraints, so that each has an approximately equal amount of time. One of the assumptions underpinning this component is that, even in an organisation with a hierarchy, each individual can be treated as an equal thinker no matter what their position.

Ease

The definition of ease is "offering freedom from rush or urgency" (Kline, 1999:35). This is to be distinguished from eliminating the rush and the urgency in our own individual external environments. Urgency is actually destructive physically and mentally, whereas ease is creative. As Kline makes clear, "Urgency keeps people from thinking clearly" (Kline, 1999:69). And paradoxically, "When it comes to thinking, the thing on which everything else depends, ease ... actually generates time we don't have if we rush" (Kline, 1999:70).

Appreciation

Appreciation, combined with deep abdominal breathing, is the fastest way to get the heart into a coherent sine wave. The key definition of appreciation is "practising a 5 to 1 (5:1) ratio of appreciation to criticism" (Kline, 1999:35). The most important feature of appreciation is that it needs to be a genuine appreciation of a particular quality in the thinker, and it needs to be communicated authentically. "Appreciation of someone needs to be genuine, succinct and concrete. If you fake it, they will know" (Kline, 1999:63). This links in with research by the Institute of HeartMath showing that the heart moves into a coherent state only when the individual actually feels appreciation, as opposed to thinking about appreciation. The quality of your appreciation for the thinker will come not only through your words but from your tone of voice, the look in your eyes, the position and stance of your facial and body language, the attitude conveyed by all of the above and finally by the enthusiasm and sincerity of the appreciation.

Encouragement

Encouragement is a component of the thinking environment that positively impacts on HRV and stress. Within the thinking environment, the definition of encouragement is "moving beyond competition" (Kline, 1999:35). In the thinking environment, encouragement helps give people the courage to go past the normal boundaries of their thinking, to be creative, to think of ideas never thought of before, to look at the things they would not usually dare to see. It is moving from an attitude of debate to one of dialogue; realising that the world is a very complex place and that no one individual has all the right answers.

Feelings

The definition of feelings within the thinking environment is to "allowing sufficient emotional release to restore thinking" (Kline 1999:35). Feelings are a part of the thinking process and we really mean to say that the thinking (and coaching) environment is essentially a "thinking and feeling" environment. Feelings are sensations triggered by our physiological state; they express and show what physiological state we are in. It is only after we become aware of the sensations as feelings that we think about them and try to name them. Feelings anchor us in the present, whereas thinking can become detached from the present moment and move into a conceptual space that is removed from the "living present". In the thinking environment, the expression of feelings is encouraged; if releasing these feelings helps us to regain our balance, then they are probably useful feelings.

Information

Information as a component of the thinking environment can be defined as "providing a full and accurate picture of reality" (Kline, 1999:35). Further, however, "By information I mean not just the supplying of technically correct information, but also the piercing of denial" (Kline, 1999:82). Information is a difficult component, as the listener has to decide when and whether to supply the facts that have been requested by the thinker. The aim is to help produce what Argyris (2010) calls Model II reasoning, which aims to:

- seek valid information (i.e. information that is testable);
- develop informed choices; and
- vigilantly monitor to detect and correct error (complex responsive processes show that it is very easy in such a complex environment to get things wrong).

In so doing, knowledge can be produced that makes its reasoning transparent and open to public scrutiny where the claims can be robustly tested.

Diversity

Diversity is about difference: in equality, power and worldview. A feature of diversity is that people will think for themselves only when they know that they will be treated with interest and respect even if their ideas diverge from the norm, and that they will not experience reprisal from some sort of authority if they deviate from what is considered normal. Within the thinking environment, diversity recognises that oppression and stereotyping people for their thinking, behaviour and cultures is underpinned by untrue limiting assumptions. These untrue limiting assumptions are not "inherent in the human being" (Kline, 2005). The entire premise of the component of diversity within the thinking process is that these assumptions can be identified, analysed and replaced with more empowering assumptions.

Incisive questions

An incisive question is "any question that removes limiting assumptions from your thinking so that you can think again" (Kline, 1999:54). The key is that, when properly constructed, the incisive question contains all ten components within it. "It has to be a question that accurately identifies the assumption and then replaces it with the exactly right freeing one. The key is listening with precision" (Kline, 1999:55).

Place

Place is composed of two definitions: The first is "creating a physical environment that says back to people, 'You matter'" (Kline, 1999:35). The second definition is treating your body as if it matters (Kline, 2015).

Active experimentation

On the second day, I usually contract with the team about an issue they want to explore in coaching. Once the contracting has been done, we get to work exploring the issue using the experiential learning process. What is the issue we want to work on? (Concrete experience.) Why is it an issue? Why is it manifesting? (Reflective observation.) What are our options? What are the different scenarios? (Abstract conceptualisation.) This is where we formulate our own theory of the problem and how we are going to fix it. At the same time, the team is reminded of what they had learned and experienced about each other on the previous day. So one option is to consider how we are best going to use each other's strengths as a team to deal with the issue at hand. Who is the best person to do what? How can we compensate for any glaring weaknesses that are inherent in the team around the issue at hand? Lastly, we come up with an action plan for the way forward, the next steps, with roles and responsibilities and timelines attached. (Active experimentation.) The second day is concluded by contracting a follow-up coaching session and date (or to conclude the coaching intervention). The final part is a check-out.

Follow-on coaching interventions

Any follow-up intervention will start with a review of how the plan (active experimentation) actually materialised (concrete experience), and a review of where the team is at (reflective observation). The process will then start all over again, by contracting the issue at hand to be explored. It is a process of ongoing experiential learning.

Conclusion

Team coaching using the Integrated Experiential Learning Process is about facilitating experiential learning of the team within that team's particular context. Its major assumptions are that we are all unique, with inherent strengths and weaknesses, and that we can all learn effectively. Experiential learning is a natural process with which we can all identify once it has been made explicit. Combined with our natural talents, it yields strengths that should be harnessed with the greatest of ease to improve team performance. And it does so by consciously making a choice to identify strengths and to use them. It is about harnessing the natural potential of individuals and teams, rather than focusing on what is wrong.

Chapter 9

Coaching presence

Introduction

If there is one thing that I have learnt after all these years of coaching, it is that making explicit what and how I coach is only half of the story. There have been many occasions when I have had fantastic coaching sessions with individuals and groups, when even I have had to wonder what I did. They are those sessions when time just seems to fly by, you are in the zone, and everything comes together and works. Then there are the times when I have coached teams and I am asked, "What exactly is it that you do? You seem to do so little. Yet when you are here, we get things done that we normally cannot do when you are not here." I am sure that there are many good coaches out there who have received similar feedback. Then, of course, there are those times when you seem to do everything according to the textbook, you use all the right techniques and tools at your disposal, and the session just does not work at all. We have all had the experience of listening to some executive or leader of any organisation talking to us, and intuitively we know whether they are telling the truth or lying. My current working hypothesis is that it has to do with physiological presence or state. Does the physiological presence or state of the coach have an impact on the quality of the coaching session? That is the question I would like to explore in this chapter, with reference to what we can learn about this topic from regulation theory and polyvagal theory.

Background

This question around the physiological state of the coach has intrigued me for several years. In fact, it was one of the questions I considered exploring when I first decided to do my Doctoral research on coaching. Eventually I decided to research the coaching model I had developed and this question was put on the back burner. Yet it kept popping into consciousness over the years as I coached. On reflection, I started to notice that when I was calm and relaxed there seemed to be more of a flow in the coaching sessions. When it came to team coaching, I realised that if I managed to stay calm and trust the process of learning, even

DOI: 10.4324/9781003356424-10

when all hell was breaking loose in the room, eventually things would calm down, and in the end the session would work out. Alternatively, if I started to get anxious or disengage, the sessions would head south until I could regain my composure and presence. Intuitively I had learnt this from experience.

During 2010–2011 this question became very conscious for me. At that time, I had met Dr. Gabriell Prinsloo, a medical doctor and coach whom I had met while lecturing on a coaching course. At the time, she was finishing her PhD at the Research Unit for Exercise Science and Sports Medicine at the University of Cape Town. Her area of interest was HRV and using biofeedback devices to help executives manage stress more effectively. Given our common interest around HRV and stress management for executives, we soon became friends. During that time, Gabriell and her colleagues published a journal article entitled "The effect of short-duration heart rate variability (HRV) biofeedback on cognitive performance during laboratory-induced cognitive stress" in which they concluded that:

> the use of short-duration HRV biofeedback intervention resulted in improved cognitive performance. Reaction time was improved and more consistent, and there was a reduction in mistakes made in counting squares during a modified Stroop task.
>
> (Prinsloo et al., 2011:800)

After that, Gabriell and I started experimenting with a beading system that I had developed as an alternative to electronic biofeedback devices, to see whether we could replicate the findings of her research. The results were positive enough for me to approach the university to do research on HRV using the beading system. The Research Unit for Exercise Science and Sports Medicine agreed to the research project but asked if one of their students, Stefano Scribani, could do the research as part of his master's degree. A similar research project was designed using the Stroop task, but in this case the control group simply listened to music while the experimental group used the beading system. The study concluded that

> The changes resulted in overall better performance during the Stroop task, and a subjective increase in MR. Using the beads therefore is useful for increasing HRV, for teaching slow breathing and for causing some cognitive performance improvements.
>
> (Scribani, 2013)

The results of the research did not surprise us because we expected that there would be an improvement, based on Gabriell's research and the experimentation we had done prior to the research being undertaken. What did surprise us, however, was that the improvement was not as great as Gabriell had found in her research. This intrigued us and in trying to understand this discrepancy, we asked Stefano to explain to us how he went about doing the research. The first big difference was that when Gabriell did her research, the clients came to the Sports Science Institute. Stefano, in contrast, had to go do the research at the clients' premises. It was then that the biggest difference became apparent to Gabriell. Because Stefano had to travel to the premises, find the room allocated for the research and set up the equipment, he was actually very stressed every time he did the interventions and collected the data. He told us that he found it very stressful and knew that he was very stressed every time. Gabriell, on the other hand, had made it a strict requirement for herself to use the very same biofeedback device for 15 minutes prior to her engaging any of the research participants. She made sure that she was in a coherent state every time. Gabriell therefore hypothesised that the difference in the research results could be due to the difference in the physiological states of the two researchers. Based on the data and research findings of these two research projects, my working hypothesis since then has been that my physiological state will have an impact on the quality of the coaching session. I had seen the data which confirmed what I had known intuitively that my physiological state will impact the physiological state and the quality of learning of the coachee or team.

That working hypothesis was strengthened even more in 2019 when I helped to design a group coaching intervention for an IT company, which became a research project. The group consisted of the team leaders in the delivery side of the organisation. Forty team leaders were invited to attend the coaching sessions over a 6-month period, and on average 20 members participated. At the time, the executive responsible for the area, Colin Archery, was enrolled for a master's degree in coaching and we decide to use this coaching intervention for his research project. Colin did the coaching during these sessions, and I was there to supervise and stand in for him on the few occasions that he had to step out to deal with pressing organisational issues. At the end of the coaching intervention, team leaders who attended were invited to participate in the research. It was a qualitative study using semi-structured interviews conducted by an experienced, independent interviewer. Twelve members participated in the study.

Not surprising to us were the themes that emerged around learning opportunity, engagement, collaboration, improvements and development as leaders. The one theme that really did surprise us was the theme around the behavioural congruence of the coach and leader. This theme highlighted just how important the behavioural congruence of the coach and leader was to creating a safe space where learning could take place. This finding was in alignment with the essence of what I have subsequently learnt from polyvagal theory and regulation theory. The following quote by one of the participants could easily have come from a book on either of these theories: "So immediately, once he gave his input or suggestion, whatever, and in the mannerism in how he did it and in his tone of voice he did it, you immediately felt safe" (Archery, 2019:45). This research project highlighted to us just how important the physical presence and state of the coach or leader was in creating a safe or unsafe space for learning to happen. In other words, the physiological state of the coach did have an impact on the quality of the coaching.

Coaching presence

As a result of these experiences, and based on the evidence generated by the data, I think I have been on a very similar journey with my approach to coaching to what Schore describes as happening in psychotherapy:

> Neuroscience has legitimised subjectivity in psychology and in therapy. Both science and clinical theory agree that psychotherapy is basically relational and emotional, and so we now think that emotionally and inter-subjectively being with the patient is more important than rationally explaining the patient's behaviour to himself.
>
> (Schore, 2019:256)

His argument is that psychology has placed too great an emphasis on the conscious mind, and the long-held idea that reason must overcome bodily based emotion is now being challenged by neuroscience. It is important for any clinician to have a certain amount of knowledge of psychotherapeutic change processes in order to succeed in what they do. In other words, to pay attention to the therapeutic process from an objective stance, using the left hemisphere of the brain with its dominance of language to explain to the client what is happening in the process. This was the central theme in my previous book, to make explicit via theories and models what coaching was and how it happens. I am still a very strong proponent that a coach should be able to make explicit the theories they use and how they use them. Yet that is only half of the story. For as Schore (2019) reminds us, psychotherapy changes more than just language and overt behaviour, in that it acts on emotions and subjectivity as well. It means paying attention to the process through a subjective perspective via the right hemisphere of the brain.

In fact, prior to me studying towards my Doctoral degree in coaching, that is how I use to work. I used to work, and still do, very easily with what Schore (2019:257) refers to as "intuitive hunches that emerge from the unconscious." I now understand that it is the right hemisphere through which I made coaching contact with the client, and from where these unconscious intuitive hunches originated. It is only later upon reflection, and paying attention via the left hemisphere, that I am able to cognitively explain and understand what emerged. Coaching, like interpersonal psychotherapy, demands that we use both hemispheres of the brain with their different ways of perceiving the world and being therein. As coaches we need to learn to use both our conscious and unconscious minds. For as Schore argues, there are two types of knowledge that underlie psychotherapy change processes, and these apply to coaching as well: broad biological and psychological scientific theories which are explicit knowledge, and "implicit relational knowledge of self and other" (Schore, 2019:258). The latter, as Schore (2019) and McGilchrist (2019) suggest, is a function of the bidirectional communication between areas in the right hemisphere of the brain, which promotes adaptive interpersonal functioning between the client and therapist.

Geller and Porges (2021) argue that the impact of the right myelinated vagus in the regulation of physiological state is consistent with the right-hemispheric bias in behavioural state regulation. One of the central tenets of polyvagal theory is that individuals co-regulate each other's nervous systems and this happens via the ventral vagal system and the right hemisphere of the brain. McGilchrist (2019) points out that due to the right hemisphere being more myelinated than the left, it is more accurate and faster at discriminating facial expressions and interpreting them, as well as vocal intonation and body gestures. It is especially good at understanding the subtle cues that come from the eyes. We get the cues for safety from each other's facial cues and the tone of the other individual's voice. Schore (2019) emphasises that this co-regulation which happens in the right hemisphere of the brain through tactile-gestural nonverbal, auditory-prosodic and visual-facial communication, is the psychobiological core of the emotional attachment bond between the mother and the infant. And as is the case in polyvagal theory, the automatic handling of nonverbal affective cues in infancy is an implicit neurobiological non-conscious joint process operating outside the realm of verbal experience. As Schore puts it, it is the result of the synchronised operation of the mother's right hemisphere interacting with the infant's right hemisphere of the brain. For Schore, this is the foundation for all human communication: "although the emotional contact between humans originates in the mother-infant dyad, it ultimately becomes the way in which individual human beings communicate with other human beings" (Schore, 2019:269).

Exploring emotional relationships from an interpersonal neurobiology point of view helps us to understand how the structure and function of the brain and mind are shaped by these experiences. And to understand these experiences, we need to work with the voluntary behaviour of the central nervous system and the involuntary behaviour of the autonomic nervous system. Hence the idea that a major function of the therapist in this approach is to regulate the patient's autonomic arousal by expanding the concept of containment. So how does one do that?

The constructs of neuroception and the social engagement system from polyvagal theory remind us that there are bidirectional signals regulating our physiological state. There are top-down (brain to body) and bottom-up (body to brain) signals. The neuroception of safety is detectable via physiological markers. Soft facial features, an open posture and deep breathing can all contribute to a feeling of safety. The breathing rate of the therapist or coach can have an impact on the client's physiological state. I mentioned previously how

Gabriell had got her body and mind into a coherent state by breathing at a certain rate using a biofeedback device before she engaged any of her research subjects. Non-defensive social engagements will contribute to a safe environment as well, as Geller and Porges described:

> Through therapists' warmth and prosody of voice, soft eye contact, open body posture, and receptive and accepting stance, the client experiences a calm and safe therapist and further opens in the therapy encounter. The therapeutic environment and clients' growth is thus profoundly facilitated.
> (Geller and Porges, 2021:179)

The therapist has to learn to recognise and regulate their own reactivity to whatever the client raises and to respond in such a way as to keep a safe space. Looking at the client with a warm welcoming face and listening to the client are critical to creating the neural connection between the face, voice and heart that is so important in regulating physiological states. It helps to make the client feel safe and facilitates the neural regulation of the client's physiology. A client who feels heard and safe can drop their defences and feel more present and open. Geller and Porges (2021) maintain that this state allows for deeper therapeutic work to be conducted. Moreover, it is their opinion that this shared biobehavioural state is healing of and in itself. This is a view expressed by Schore (2019) as well, who believes that this shared safe biobehavioural state increases the strength in the therapeutic alliance and the attachment bond, allowing the client to drop dissociative defences and allow for emotions to come online more frequently. More importantly, this happens regardless of what theory or therapeutic approach is being applied. This is congruent with my experience of assessing coaching students on the master's degree programme. For their professional assessments, students use a number of coaching models and techniques, yet despite these models the really good students are able to create a very safe space, by being present, to do very meaningful work with their clients.

The important thing to remember, according to Geller and Porges (2021), is that *it is not the therapist's experience or knowledge that promotes this therapeutic process. Rather, it is as a result of the client's experience of the therapist's presence and engagement.* If the client experiences that presence as positive, it leads to both parties being more present, and the development of relational presence through the co-regulation of each other's autonomic nervous systems. They suggest that the cultivation of safety through developing a relational presence promotes therapeutic effectiveness and positive client growth and change through three mechanisms:

> Relational presence facilitates (a) clients' openness to engage in therapeutic work, (b) strengthening of the therapeutic relationship, and

(c) therapists' being more attuned to the readiness of the client and more able to optimally offer effective and attuned interventions or responses.

(Geller and Porges, 2021:182)

I believe that the same process happens in coaching; the emphasis, however, is not on therapy but on the effectiveness of the experiential learning process. As the coachee reacts (without cognitive awareness) via neuroception to the present-centred coach as safe, the coachee's physiology becomes regulated and calm, allowing for more openness and presence in the client. This sense of safety can in turn further promote a positive coaching alliance and effective experiential learning, despite different coaching models and theories.

Self-awareness of the coach

An interpersonal neurobiology approach to coaching, therapy or any helping profession demands a certain level of self-awareness, self-knowledge and self-regulation. The bulk of that knowledge and awareness is learnt from being with and learning from our clients:

It's what our patients are teaching us, if we are open to it. It's not just about them and the deeper psychological realms within them. It's at the same time becoming more familiar with the deeper core of our own self-system.

(Schore, 2019:258)

It is about becoming aware of my physiological state, as well as that of the client. More importantly, it is becoming aware of how the tone of voice, eye contact, emotional attunement and body posture can make either the coach or coachee feel unsafe and negatively impact the learning experience. This is an interpersonal neurobiology process in which the coachee can trigger unconscious physiological responses in the coach and *vice versa*. The important thing is to realise when this happens and to take corrective action. In my own experience, I have noticed that I can trigger an unsafe space for my clients as soon as I start getting bored and disengaged. At times I have to work very hard on my own coaching presence, or on how to return with full open presence to the client. Thankfully, polyvagal theory has made me aware of the impact of my physiological state on the nervous system of my clients, and how to manage my physiological state more effectively. At the same time, there is the growing awareness of how my clients can trigger my autonomic nervous system and the impact that this has on my coaching presence.

As a result, over the years I have learnt to pay more and more attention to my neurophysiological state before, during and after coaching sessions. I have reached a stage in my professional life in which I am comfortable to ask a client to postpone a coaching session when I am finding it very difficult to regulate my own physiological state. I make it explicit to them that I am not in the right neurophysiological state to add any value to their learning journey on that particular day. Thankfully, it does not happen often. My ongoing professional development at this stage of my journey is about learning to improve my awareness and ability to promote what Porges (2021) calls a "neuroception of safety" for myself as coach and my clients. Central to this process has been learning how to use deep abdominal breathing with long outbreaths to change my physiological state, because exhalation of the breath optimises the influence of the myelinated ventral vagus on the heart. In my previous book, I discussed in depth how to learn to control HRV through breathing by using biofeedback devices. Subsequently, I have learnt how to use my fingers and counting in the moment to control my breath, my HRV, and hence my autonomic nervous state, all of which I have taught my clients to do as well. Cross-lateral and bilateral movements, discussed in Chapter 3, have proved invaluable in improving my ability to manage my neurophysiological state. These movement techniques, combined with deep abdominal rhythmic breathing, have become part of my daily discipline. I have learnt to incorporate them into my coaching sessions as a way to manage the neurophysiological state of both myself and the client. I use it as a way to get into a more present state before and in-between coaching sessions.

These disciplines and practices have helped me to become more present in my coaching. And by present, I mean something very similar to what Geller and Porges refer to as "therapeutic presence", which involves:

(a) being grounded and in contact with one's integrated and healthy self; (b) being open, receptive to, and immersed in what is poignant in the moment; and (c) having a larger sense of spaciousness and expansion of awareness … with (d) the intention of being with and for the client.

(Geller and Porges, 2021:172)

In so doing, I am learning more and more how to be in direct contact with myself, my client and the relationship between us.

Coaching is a complex responsive process

Based on the above discussion and my experience, I am now convinced that coaching is a complex responsive process as defined by Stacey (2003, 2009) and Stacey and Griffin (2005). It is a way of thinking in which the individual mind and society are continuously patterning processes that evolve out of the interactions between human bodies, in this case the coach and the client. Like Stacey (2009), I place the emphasis on the word "continuous", in that it is part of an ongoing process of co-regulation brought about by a preceding history of gestures and responses. Based on what physiological state (ventral, sympathetic, dorsal) Individual A is in, that state will influence their feeling state. The physiological state can be unconscious or conscious, meaning the individual is either aware of the state they are in or completely oblivious thereto. The physiological state will impact the feeling state, which in turn will impact the experiential learning process. As these feelings become conscious (concrete experience), the individual will reflect on the feelings (reflective observation) and hypothesise about what is going on (abstract conceptualisation). In so doing, the individual tries to make sense of the situation and create meaning, and as a result they gesture to the other individual the appropriate response to their hypothesis (active experimentation). Of course, it is very possible that this whole process can be hijacked by the unconscious as well, meaning that the individual's facial gestures, tone of voice and bodily posture contradict what they say.

This triggers essentially the same process in Individual B, who will then respond with what they consider to be the appropriate gesture. The two individuals end up in a dance of continuous co-regulation of each other's physiological states, and trying to make sense of and create meaning about what is going on, as well as the impact of the non-human environment on the context. In other words, they are learning together on what and how to develop the appropriate response to the bigger environment, in order to act in and on that environment. In so doing, the two individuals will affect the context and the environment, which in turn will simultaneously affect them. This process generally plays out within a one-on-one coaching engagement.

What happens in a team coaching context? The same complex responsive process will take place. As more and more individuals are added, however, the process becomes increasingly complex. More and more gestures are added to the situation. Collectively, the group is trying to learn and create meaning together. As a result, a wider range of responses and gestures is introduced, and the individuals need to learn to develop the capacity to take the attitude of the whole group into account. The process of cooperative interaction and co-regulation is therefore much more sophisticated.

Conclusion

One of the criticisms that could have been levelled against my first book and model, the Integrated Experiential Coaching Model, could be that it was leaning towards being a cognitive model of learning. At the time, I tried to address that criticism but was not explicit enough in doing that. In subsequent years, I have paid much more attention to the physiology underpinning that model and the importance of coaching presence. As a result, there has been an evolution away from the Integrated Experiential Coaching Model and towards the Integrated Experiential Learning Process. The Integrated Experiential Learning Process is defined as a complex responsive process involving the mind, brain, body and social relationships, facilitated unconsciously and consciously via the central and autonomic nervous systems in response to the environment. It is much more than a left hemisphere cognitive model of learning.

Chapter 10

Being a scientist-practitioner

Introduction

This book is an ongoing response to the *Dublin Declaration on Coaching*, which noted the importance of research to the professionalisation of coaching, and that coaches are responsible for doing applied research as practitioners (GCC, 2008:11). The lack of books on or examples of how a coach could develop their own practice and coaching model within the scientist-practitioner framework was the idea behind writing this book. This has been a personal account and example of how I developed, researched and refined my own coaching model and practice within the scientist-practitioner framework. This book was not an attempt to present the definitive model on coaching but rather the sharing of a structured thought process, which I hope will enable you, the reader, to get a better idea of how you can develop your own coaching model and practice within the scientist-practitioner framework. At the very least, the book will give you an example of how to go about being a scientist-practitioner as a coach.

As I reflect on my own journey as a coach, and the phenomenal growth that we have seen in coaching globally, I keeping asking myself why coaching has become so popular – what is driving this trend? My current working hypothesis is that it is an evolutionary response to the ongoing development of the human spirit. Could it be that coaching is the new profession of "personology", to which Smuts (1973) alluded as early as 1924 – in that it is a more integrative approach to dealing with the human being? I find it interesting that most of the coaches I respect did not plan to become coaches; they evolved into coaches after they found their own disciplines too limiting to be able to understand and work with individuals. It seems to be a characteristic of the human spirit to defy generalisations and dogma.

Let us take a step back and reflect on the bigger picture for a moment. For centuries, religion was the mechanism which facilitated growth and development in individuals. In the West, this occurred predominantly through Christianity. With the Reformation, however, Christianity experienced a move away from the concrete experience of the individual as being primary,

DOI: 10.4324/9781003356424-11

to abstract conceptualisation as primary. And with that shift came religious dogma. The dogmatic belief system became primary which brought with it the suppression of personal concrete experience. But the evolving human spirit defies dogma and a few centuries later it found expression in a newly developing field: psychology. And the human spirit flourished within this new eclectic discipline; it was open, inquisitive and explorative. The human spirit had broken free of the shackles of religious dogma. Soon there were a number of schools in psychology.

Yet in an attempt to find or define the "ultimate" or "the" school of psychology, psychology too became dogmatic. While religion took a few centuries to become dogmatic, psychology did it in less than a century. I believe coaching has evolved as the next discipline, which is a result of the human spirit's continuous ability to defy dogma. My concern with coaching at the moment is the big rush to try and find and define the "ultimate coaching model". Do we not run the danger of simply becoming dogmatic faster than any other discipline that has gone before? And let us not forget that it is on the shoulders of those disciplines that we are building the discipline of coaching. Coaching, in my opinion, is the next synthesis.

That is why in the beginning of this book, I emphasised that this is not an attempt to outline the definitive model on coaching, but rather to share a model which evolved out of my personal concrete experience. Hence, the model is part art and part science. It is an integration of Wilber's left-hand and right-hand quadrants. Can I claim that it is 100 per cent scientifically correct? Of course not. It has, however, been scientifically researched and it did meet what Wilber (1998b:155–160) calls the "three aspects of scientific inquiry" or the "three strands of all valid knowing":

- *Instrumental injunction.* This is the actual practice of doing the methodology or inquiry; it is an injunction, an experiment, a paradigm. According to Wilber (1998b), it always takes the form "If you want to know, do this." In the Integrated Experiential Learning Process, the injunction is experiential learning and the research methodology is transpersonal phenomenology.
- *Direct apprehension.* This is the direct experience or the apprehension of data that is brought about by the injunction. In Kolb's (1984) language, this is grasping the data via direct apprehension as a result of active experimentation. This is the data of direct and immediate experience that is collected, analysed and synthesised.
- *Communal confirmation (or rejection).* This is where the data or experiences are checked by a community of people who have completed the injunction and the apprehensive strands. In a sense, this is a combination of reflective observation and abstract conceptualisation. Having had the experience and collected the data, an individual will reflect thereon, and via comprehension share it with a community who will either validate

or invalidate the data. In my case, the data were originally written up and presented to the National Centre for Work-Based Learning at the University of Middlesex, and found to meet the requirements for the Doctorate in Professional Studies (Executive Coaching).

I am certainly not suggesting that every coach should do a doctorate. My call is for each of you to develop your own model. Remember that my thinking is very much aligned with the suggestion of Smuts (1973) that every individual is a unique expression of evolution – there will never be another you. And if you take that concept seriously, then you should immediately realise that your coaching model/approach/methodology will be as unique as you are. Coaching is a synthesis of who we are. It is my honest belief that if your coaching methodology or approach is an expression of who you are, you will be coaching with integrity. If we want to develop coaching as a profession, however, then it is imperative for us to at least make our work explicit to our clients and to the coaching community for critical reflection and communal confirmation or rejection.

So how can you go about developing your own model and holding it up for critical reflection? I would suggest Smuts's idea that "personology" should be studied by analysing the biographies of personalities as a whole. In this case, however, it is your personal biography that should be studied. This study should be done synthetically and not analytically as in the case of psychology. This would enable you, the researcher, to discover the materials that can help formulate the laws of your personal evolution as a person and coach. Smuts (1973:262) called this the science of "Biography", and he believed that it would form the basis of a "new Ethic and Metaphysic" which would have a truer spiritual outlook on personality.

I am not the first person to recommend this approach. Dr. Ira Progoff wrote his Doctoral dissertation on the psychology of C.G. Jung. When Jung read the dissertation, he invited Progoff to come and study with him in Switzerland, which he did in 1952, 1953 and 1955. Then Progoff experienced a turning point in his life; he read Smut's *Holism and Evolution*, which had a profound effect on him. He took Smuts seriously and as a result developed the intensive journalling method and a whole new theory of depth psychology based on holism:

> It deliberately refrains from dissecting man and marking him off into compartments. It desires rather to comprehend man in his wholeness and so, when it studies the depth process of personality, it maintains the perspective of man as a unity that is ever in the process of growth.
>
> (Progoff, 1973:4)

I am not going to go into Progoff's work here because it is beyond the scope of this book. (I would, however, highly recommend that any coach who is serious about their own development should study Progoff's (1992) intensive journalling method.) I simply want to draw your attention to the fact that Smut's idea of using a journal to study your own biography is a very powerful tool, as Progoff's (1992) work has shown. It is a very holistic and structured way to journal in order to explore your own evolutionary development. For our purpose, however, I would recommend a simpler, yet very powerful, approach: the four steps of Kolb's experiential learning cycle. The first step is to actively start journalling as a discipline. As you journal over time, you will start to notice your own threads of development. Find a journalling method that works for you: some people like to journal on their PC, while others prefer to have a collection of loose papers. What works for me personally is a hardcover journal and a pen; I find something very cathartic in writing. You might experience the same by typing or even by using a voice recorder.

Concrete experience

Start by recording a chronological timeline of your life. Try to record the period as holistically as you possibly can. Describe both the inner and outer events that come to your mind as you reflect on your life. Try to be as objective as you can and stay open to the experience as you record the events. Like the epoche process in transpersonal phenomenology, do not judge. Remember that epoche is a Greek word which means to abstain from, stay away from or refrain from judgement. In our day-to-day lives, we tend to hold knowledge judgementally; that is, we are biased due to our expectations and assumptions. The epoche requires that we bracket as far as possible our biases, understandings, knowing and assumptions, and look at things in a new and fresh way. Journal whatever comes to mind. And following Progoff's (1992) advice, limit the entries to factual descriptions of your experience. Tell your own story and record it. So, what were the major events in your life that had an impact on you? Moving to a new city; the death of a friend or family member; studying or ending your studies; friends or relatives who had a major impact on you; being retrenched or fired? Write the story of how you got into coaching. Try to keep the events as brief as possible and try and write down as many as possible. The danger here is concentrating on the outer events; remember to record the inner events as well.

Reflective observation

This is the ability to reflect and to observe your experience from many perspectives. The aim is for you to reflect, reflect again and then describe the experience in terms of textural qualities, varying intensities, special qualities and time references. As you reflect on the chronological events that you have recorded, turn inward in reflection and describe whatever shines forth in consciousness. Include individual memories, judgements and perceptions, as they are integral to the process. The process will allow you to return to the self, in that the world is experienced from the vantage point of self-reflection, self-awareness and self-knowledge. The more you reflect, the more exact the phenomenon will become. Whatever stands out and is meaningful for you is explored and reflected on. Reflect in particular on those events that you think contributed towards you becoming a coach.

Was it due to an external event like being fired or retrenched? Was it an internal process of dissatisfaction about your own life? Were you looking for a change in your life? Was the interest in coaching brought about due to research or through reading? Was it through being coached or due to a significant person whom you respected? Was it because you had reached the limits of your current profession? It could be anything. Record those events and describe them in as much detail as possible. More importantly, keep asking yourself why – why this event, or person, or circumstance? The more you reflect and describe, the richer the picture will become.

More importantly, try and reflect on the theories, practices, processes and toolsets that you have used in your coaching practice. Why do you use them and not others? What are the strengths and limitations of the theories, processes and toolsets that you use?

It is important to remember, however, that reflection is never-ending. You might reach a point where you consciously stop the reflective process, but the potential for reflection and discovery remains unlimited. In phenomenological reduction, this is known as "horizontalisation". No matter how many times you reconsider or reflect on the experience, the experience can never be exhausted because horizons are unlimited. Even the final textural description, although completed in a point of time, remains open to further reflection. In my experience, you could find yourself returning many more times to reflect some more. And with every iteration the picture gets even richer. It does not matter whether you do it in one or many sittings. In fact, the more the better.

Abstract conceptualisation

This is the ability to create concepts and to build logically sound theories from your observations. By using your imagination, varying your frames of reference, and adopting different perspectives and points of view, try to derive a structural description of the experience and the underlying factors that account for what is being experienced. Write it up in your journal. The aim is to understand the "how" that brought about the "what" of the experience. The question that needs to be explored is: how did the experience come to be what it is? This is the point where you try to make what you do in coaching explicit. What are you trying to achieve with your coaching? What is its purpose? Are you a life, business, executive, wellness, fitness or financial coach? More importantly, in what context do you or do you not coach? In which niche do you coach?

Next, you need to define what Lane and Corrie (2006:48) refer to as the "perspective" of your model. It is your ability to define what you as a coach bring to the encounter. This would include all the models, values, beliefs, knowledge and philosophies, as well as a sense of their competence limitations. What philosophy and theories underpin the approach? What is your theory about coaching? What makes it so unique? This is where you synthesise all your concrete experience with the conceptual knowledge that you have gained over the years, to develop your own theory and practice about coaching. Describe the philosophy and theories that underpin your work.

Having defined the purpose and perspectives that underpin the work, it becomes possible to structure a process to undertake the work. What methods or tools can be used to help achieve the desired purpose within the constraints of the specified perspective? Why do you use the processes, methods and toolsets that you do? What is the process that you follow when you coach? Why do you use that approach? What are the limitations of the process, methods or tools? I, for example, do not undertake any remedial coaching at all. My model does not cater for this and I personally am of the opinion that a psychologist-coach would be better at that approach.

Active experimentation

This is the ability to use the constructed theories to make decisions and experiment with new behaviours and thoughts. This is where you go and apply your model, and then continuously reflect on what you are doing. It is here that journalling becomes even more critical. Wherever possible, I try to journal every day. Once again, just as in the experiential learning cycle: what was the concrete experience of the day's coaching? Try to explain what you experienced in the coaching sessions. Simply describe it. Then reflect on the experience. Did you stick to your process or methodology? Did you deviate? What worked or did not work? Did you learn anything new? Were you surprised by anything? Are there still some unanswered questions or issues worrying you?

Having done that, try to understand how it happened. Explore various angles and possible explanations. Write down your working hypothesis of what is going on and why it is happening. And then think about what you are going to experiment with in the next session. What will you stop doing, continue doing or try to do differently? Write it down. It will help you to distinguish between the espoused theories and the actual theory.

Conclusion

Journalling is a very powerful tool to make your thinking explicit and to develop your critical reflective ability. I have been asked on numerous occasions how it was possible for me to develop such an integrated theory and practice of coaching. The answer is very simple: I just reread my journals. My experience and thinking have developed over several years but I was fortunate enough to have recorded them in my journals. I have a record of my unfolding journey. For that I am indebted to Reverend Tom Cunningham, my lecturer in Pastoral Psychology. On the day that I completed my theological degree, I went to greet Tom. His parting words to me were, "Lloyd, do you want to continue growing and developing as a human being?" – to which I responded "Yes". Tom then said to me, "In that case, keep a journal from tomorrow for as long as you can" – the best advice I have ever been given. I still journal and my model continues to evolve. You can do the same. Good luck with the journey.

Bibliography

Alexander, C.N. and Langer, E.J. (eds.) (1990). *Higher Stages of Human Development: Perspectives on Adult Growth*. New York, NY: Oxford University Press.

Almaas, A.H. (1998a). *Essence with the Elixir of Enlightenment*. Boston, MA: Weiser Books.

Almaas, A.H. (1998b). *The Elixir of Enlightenment*. Boston, MA: Weiser Books.

Almaas, A.H. (2002). *Spacecruiser Inquiry: True Guidance for the Inner Journey*. Boston, MA: Shambhala.

Almaas, A.H. (2014). *Runaway Realisation: Living a Life of Ceaseless Discovery*. Kindle Edition. Boston, MA: Shambhala.

Archery, C.S. (2019). *An Investigation into the Effectiveness of Team Coaching for Team Leaders in an Information Technology (IT) Company*. Unpublished Research Assignment presented in partial fulfilment of the requirements for the degree of Master of Philosophy in Management Coaching. Stellenbosch: Stellenbosch University.

Argyris, C. (2010). *Organisational Traps: Leadership, Culture, Organisational Design*. Kindle Edition. Oxford: Oxford University Press.

Beard, C. and Wilson, J.P. (2002). *The Power of Experiential Learning: A Handbook for Trainers and Educators*. London: Kogan Page.

Beck, D.E. and Cowan, C. (2000). *Spiral Dynamics: Mastering Values, Leadership, and Change*. Malden: Blackwell Business.

Benedict Bunker, B. and Alban, B.T. (1997). *Large Group Interventions: Engaging the Whole System for Rapid Change*. San Francisco, CA: Jossey-Bass.

Blomberg, H. (2015). *The Rhythmic Movement Method: A Revolutionary Approach to Improved Health and Wellbeing*. Kindle Edition. Morrisville, NC: Lulu.

Bohm, D. (1995). *Wholeness and the Implicate Order*. London: Routledge.

Brooks-Harris, J.E. and Stock-Ward, S.R. (1999). *Workshops: Designing and Facilitating Experiential Learning*. Thousand Oaks, CA: Sage.

Bruch, M. and Bond, F.W. (1998). *Beyond Diagnosis: Case Formulation Approaches in CBT*. New York, NY: Wiley.

Buckingham, M. and Clifton, D.O. (2002). *Now Discover Your Strengths: How to Develop Your Talent and Those People You Manage*. London: Simon and Schuster.

Cambridge University Press (2022a). Agility. In *Cambridge Dictionary*. URL: dictionary.cambridge.org/dictionary/english/agility

Cambridge University Press (2022b). Resilience. In *Cambridge Dictionary*. URL: dictionary.cambridge.org/dictionary/english/resilience

Cavanagh, M.J. and Grant, A.M. (2006). Coaching psychology and the scientist-practitioner model. In Lane, D.A. and Corrie, S. (eds.), *The Modern Scientist-Practitioner: A Guide to Practice in Psychology* (pp. 146–157). Hove: Routledge.

Chapman, L.A. (2010). *Integrated Experiential Coaching: Becoming an Executive Coach*. London: Karnac.

Childre, D. and Martin, H. (2000). *The HeartMath Solution*. New York, NY: Harper.

Dana, D. (2018). *The Polyvagal Theory in Therapy: Engaging the Rhythm of Regulation*. Norton Series on Interpersonal Neurobiology. Kindle Edition. New York, NY: Norton.

De Mello, A. (1990). *Awareness*. Grand Rapids, MI: Zondervan.

De Quincey, C. (2005). *Radical Knowing: Understanding Consciousness Through Relationship*. Rochester, Vermont: Park Street Press.

Devinsky, O. (2000). Right cerebral hemisphere dominance for a sense of corporeal and emotional self. *Epilepsy and Behaviour*, 1(1):60–73.

Dotlich, D.L. and Cairo, P.C. (1999). *Action Coaching: How to Leverage Individual Performance for Company Success*. San Francisco, CA: Jossey-Bass.

Dumas, G., Nadel, J., Soussignan, R., Martinerie, J. and Garnero, L. (2010). Inter-brain synchronisation during social interaction. *PloS one*, 5(8):e12166.

Earls, J. (2020). *Born to Walk: Myofascial Efficiency and the Body in Movement*. Second Edition. Kindle Edition. Berkeley, CA: North Atlantic Books.

Egan, G. (2002). *The Skilled Helper: A Problem-Management and Opportunity-Development Approach to Helping*. Pacific Grove, CA: Brooks/Cole.

Feldenkrais, M. (1977). *Awareness Through Movement: Health Exercises for Personal Growth*. London: Penguin Arkana.

Feldenkrais, M. (2005). *Body and Mature Behaviour: A Study of Anxiety, Sex, Gravitation and Learning*. Berkeley, CA: Frog Books.

Feldenkrais, M. (2010). Mind and body. In Beringer, E. (ed.), *Embodied Wisdom. The Collected Papers of Moshe Feldenkrais* (pp. 27–44). Berkeley, CA: North Atlantic Books.

Feldenkrais, M. (2019). *The Elusive Obvious: The Convergence of Movement, Neuroplasticity, and Health*. Reprint Edition. Kindle Edition. Berkeley, CA: North Atlantic Books.

Frankl, V.E. (1988). *The Will to Meaning: Foundations and Applications of Logotherapy*. New York, NY: Meridian.

Freire, P. (2005). *Pedagogy of the Oppressed*. Thirtieth Anniversary Edition. New York, NY: Continuum.

Fricchione, G. (2004). Generalised anxiety disorder. *New England Journal of Medicine*, 351(7):675–682.

Gainotti, G. (2006). Unconscious emotional memories and the right hemisphere. In Mancia, M. (ed.), *Psychoanalysis and Neuroscience* (pp. 151–174). Milan: Springer.

Galbraith, J., Downey, D. and Kates, A. (2002). *Designing Dynamic Organisations: A Hands-On Guide for Leaders at all Levels*. New York, NY: Amacom.

Geller, S.M. and Porges, S.W. (2021). Therapeutic presence neurophysiological mechanisms mediating feeling safe in therapeutic relationships. In Porges, S.W. (ed.), *Polyvagal Safety: Attachment, Communication, Self-Regulation* (pp. 169–190). Kindle Edition. New York, NY: Norton.

Global Convention on Coaching (GCC) (2008). *Dublin Declaration on Coaching Including Appendices*. Dublin: Global Convention on Coaching.

Goldratt, E.M. (1990). *What Is This Thing Called the Theory of Constraints and How Should it Be Implemented?* Great Barrington, MA: North River Press.

Grof, S. (1998). Ken Wilber's Spectrum Psychology: Observations from clinical consciousness research. In Rothberg, D.J, Kelly, S.M. and Kelly, S. (eds.), *Ken Wilber in Dialogue: Conversations with Leading Transpersonal Thinkers* (pp. 85–116). Wheaton, IL: Quest.

Hanna, T. (1988). *Somatics: Reawakening the Mind's Control of Movement, Flexibility, and Health.* Cambridge, MA: Da Capo.

Hannaford, C. (2005). *Smart Moves: Why Learning Is Not All in Your Head.* Second Edition. Salt Lake City, UT: Great River.

Hannaford, C. (2011). *The Dominance Factor: How Knowing Your Dominant Eye, Ear, Brain, Hand and Foot Can Improve Your Learning.* Second Edition. Salt Lake City, UT: Great River.

Harri-Augstein, E.S. and Thomas, L.F. (1991). *Learning Conversations, Self-Organised Learning: The Way to Personal and Organisational Growth.* London: Routledge.

Harri-Augstein, E.S. and Webb, M. (1995). *Learning to Change: A Resource for Trainers, Managers and Learners Based on Self-Organised Learning.* London: McGraw-Hill.

Hartman, T. (2006). *Walking Your Blues Away: How to Heal the Mind and Create Emotional Wellbeing.* Kindle Edition. Rochester, VT: Park Street Press.

Institute of HeartMath (2001). *Science of the Heart: Exploring the Role of the Heart in Human Performance.* An overview of research conducted by the Institute of HeartMath. Webpage: www.heartmath.org/research/science-of-the-heart-variability.html

Jaques, E. and Cason, K. (1994). *Human Capability: A Study of Individual Potential and its Application.* Arlington, VA: Cason Hall.

Jaques, E. and Clement, S.D. (1997). *Executive Leadership: A Practical Guide to Managing Complexity.* Arlington, VA: Cason Hall.

Johnson, J.M. (2000). Learning strategies for newly appointed leaders. In Goldsmith, M., Lyons, L. and Freas, A. (eds.), *Coaching for Leadership: How the World's Greatest Coaches Help Leaders Learn* (pp. 209–217). San Francisco, CA: Jossey-Bass/Pfeiffer.

Kahneman, D. (2011). *Thinking, Fast and Slow.* New York, NY: Farrar, Straus and Giroux.

Kilburg, R.R. (2000). *Executive Coaching: Developing Managerial Wisdom in a World of Chaos.* Washington, DC: American Psychological Association.

Kline, N. (1999). *Time to Think: Listening to Ignite the Human Mind.* London: Ward Lock.

Kline, N. (2005). *The Thinking Partnership Programme: Consultant's Guide.* Wallingford: Time to Think.

Kline, N. (2015). *More Time to Think: The Power of Independent Thinking.* London: Cassell.

Kolb, A.Y. and Kolb, D.A. (2005). Learning styles and learning spaces: Enhancing experiential learning in higher education. *Academy of Management Learning and Education,* 4(2):193–212.

Kolb, A.Y. and Kolb, D.A. (2017). *The Experiential Educator: Principles and Practices of Experiential Learning.* Kindle Edition. Kaunakakai, HI: EBLS Press.

Kolb, D.A. (1984). *Experiential Learning: Experience as the Source of Learning and Development.* Englewood Cliffs, NJ: Prentice Hall.

Lane, D.A. (1990). *The Impossible Child*, Stoke on Trent: Trentham.

Lane, D.A. and Corrie, S. (2006). *The Modern Scientist-Practitioner: A Guide to Practice in Psychology*. Hove: Routledge.

Lane, D.A., Kahn, M.S and Chapman, L.A. (2019). Adult learning as an approach to coaching. In Palmer, S. and Whybrow, A. (eds.), *Handbook of Coaching Psychology: A Guide for Practitioners* (pp. 369–380). Second Edition. Abingdon, Oxon: Routledge.

Lavie, C.J. and Milani, R.V. (2004). Generalised anxiety disorder. *New England Journal of Medicine*, 351(21):2239.

Levine, P.A. (1997). *Waking the Tiger: Healing Trauma*. Kindle Edition. Berkeley, CA: North Atlantic Books.

Maffetone, P. (2000). *The Maffetone Method: The Holistic, Low-Stress, No-Pain Way to Exceptional Fitness*. Camden, ME: Ragged Mountain.

McGilchrist, I. (2019). *The Master and His Emissary: The Divided Brain and the Making of the Western World*. Second Edition. Kindle Edition. New Haven, CT: Yale University Press.

Mittleman, S. (2011). *Slow Burn: Burn Fat Faster by Exercising Slower*. Reprint Edition. Kindle Edition. New York, NY: William Morrow.

Moustakas, C. (1994). *Phenomenological Research Methods*. Thousand Oaks, CA: Sage Publications.

Mouton, J. (2001). *How to Succeed in Your Masters and Doctoral Studies*. Pretoria: Van Schaik.

Nielsen, R.P. (1998). Quaker Foundations for Greenleaf's Servant-Leadership and "Friendly Disentangling" Method. In Spears, L.C. (ed.), *Insights on Leadership: Service, Stewardship, Spirit and Servant-Leadership* (pp. 126–144). New York, NY: Wiley.

O'Mara, S. (2020). *In Praise of Walking: A New Scientific Exploration*. Kindle Edition. New York, NY: Norton.

O'Neill, M.B. (2000). *Coaching with Backbone and Heart: A Systems Approach to Engaging Leaders with Their Challenges*. San Francisco, CA: Jossey-Bass.

Orlinsky, D.E. and Howard, K.I. (1986). Process and outcome in psychotherapy. In Garfield, S.L. and Bergin, A.E. (eds.), *Handbook of Psychotherapy and Behaviour Change* (pp. 311–381). Third Edition. New York, NY: Wiley.

Oshry, B. (1999). *Leading Systems: Lessons from the Powerlab*. San Francisco, CA: Berrett-Kochler.

Oxford University Press (2022). Resilience. In *Oxford Learner's Dictionaries*. URL: www.oxfordlearnersdictionaries.com/definition/english/resilience?q=resilience

Peltier, B. (2001). *The Psychology of Executive Coaching: Theory and Application*. New York, NY: Brunner-Routledge.

Pennington, B.M. (1996). *Thomas Merton, My Brother: His Journey to Freedom, Compassion, and Final Integration*. New York, NY: New City.

Perry, L.T., Stott, R.G. and Smallwood, W.N. (1993). *Real-Time Strategy: Improving Team-Based Planning for a Fast-Changing World*. New York, NY: Wiley.

Piaget, J. (1952). *The Origins of Intelligence in Children*. New York, NY: International University Press.

Porges, S.W. (2011). *The Polyvagal Theory: Neurophysiological Foundations of Emotions, Attachment, Communication, and Self-regulation*. Norton Series on Interpersonal Neurobiology. First Edition. Kindle Edition. New York, NY: Norton.

Porges, S.W. (2017). *The Pocket Guide to the Polyvagal Theory: The Transformative Power of Feeling Safe*. Norton Series on Interpersonal Neurobiology. Kindle Edition. New York, NY: Norton.

Porges, S.W. (2021). *Polyvagal Safety: Attachment, Communication, Self-Regulation*. Kindle Edition. New York, NY: Norton.

Prinsloo, G.E., Rauch, L.H.G., Lambert, M.I., Muench, F., Noakes, T.D. and Derman, W.E. (2011). The effect of short-duration heart rate variability (HRV) biofeedback on cognitive performance during laboratory-induced cognitive stress. *Applied Cognitive Psychology*, 25:792–801.

Progoff, I. (1973). *Depth Psychology and Modern Man*. New York, NY: McGraw-Hill.

Progoff, I. (1992). *At a Journal Workshop: Writing to Access the Power of the Unconscious and Evoke Creative Ability*. New York, NY: Tarcher/Putman.

Ratey, J.J. and Hagerman, E. (2008). *Spark: The Revolutionary New Science of Exercise and the Brain*. Kindle Edition. Boston, MA: Little, Brown.

Rehm, R. (1997). *Participative Design*. Unpublished paper. Chicago, IL: Loyola-Chicago University.

Roberts, B. (1993). *The Experience of No-Self: A Contemplative Journey*. Albany, NY: State University of New York.

Schön, D.A. (1983). *The Reflective Practitioner: How Professionals Think in Action*. New York, NY: Basic Books.

Schore, A.N. (2019). *Right Brain Psychotherapy*. Norton Series on Interpersonal Neurobiology. Kindle Edition. New York, NY: Norton.

Schumacher, E.F. (1978). *A Guide for the Perplexed*. New York, NY: Harper and Row.

Scribani, S.L. (2013). *Physiological and Psychological Measurements During Cognitive Stress: Comparing the Effectiveness of Two Stress Intervention Techniques*. Unpublished MSc (MED) Thesis in Exercise Science. Cape Town: University of Cape Town.

Smuts, J.C. (1973). *Holism and Evolution*. Westport, CT: Greenwood.

Spinelli, E. (1998). *The Interpreted World: An Introduction to Phenomenological Psychology*. London: Sage.

Spinelli, E. (2008). Coaching and therapy: Similarities and differences. *International Coaching Psychology Review*, 3(3):241–249.

Stacey, R.D. (1996). *Complexity and Creativity in Organisations*. San Francisco, CA: Berrett-Koehler.

Stacey, R.D. (2003). *Complexity and Group Processes: A Radical Social Understanding of Individuals*. Hove, East Sussex: Brunner-Routledge.

Stacey, R.D. (2009). *Complex Responsive Processes in Organisations: Learning and Knowledge Creation*. Abingdon, Oxon: Routledge.

Stacey, R.D. (2010). *Complexity and Organisational Reality*. Second Edition. Abingdon, Oxon: Routledge.

Stacey, R.D. and Griffin, D. (2005). Experience and method: A complex responsive processes perspective on research in organisations. In Stacey, R.D. and Griffin, D. (eds.), *A Complexity Perspective on Researching Organisations: Taking Experience Seriously* (pp. 13–38). Abingdon, Oxon: Routledge.

Tucker, D.M. and Moller, L. (2007). The metamorphosis: Individuation of the adolescent brain. In Romer, D. and Walker, E.F. (eds.), *Adolescent Psychopathology and the Developing Brain: Integrating Brain and Prevention Science* (pp. 85–102). New York, NY: Oxford University Press.

Van der Kolk, B. (2014). *The Body Keeps the Score: Brain, Mind, and Body in the Healing of Trauma*. Kindle Edition. London: Penguin.

Vardey, L. (1995). *Mother Theresa: A Simple Path*. London: Random House.

Vernikos, J. (2016). *Designed to Move: The Science-Backed Programme to Fight Sitting Disease and Enjoy Lifelong Health*. Kindle Edition. Fresno, CA: Quill Driver.

Visser, F. (2003). *Ken Wilber: Thought as Passion*. New York, NY: State University of New York.

Von Glasersfeld, E. (1977). The concepts of adaptation and viability in a radical constructionist theory of knowledge. Paper presented at the *Theodore Mischel Symposium on Constructivism* at the 7th Annual Meeting of the Jean Piaget Society, Philadelphia, May 19–21.

Washburn, M. (1995). *The Ego and the Dynamic Ground: A Transpersonal Theory of Human Development*. New York, NY: State University of New York.

Watt, D.F. (2003). Psychotherapy in an age of neuroscience: Bridges to affective neuroscience. In Corrigall, J. and Wilkinson, H. (eds.), *Revolutionary Connections: Psychotherapy and Neuroscience* (pp. 79–115). London: Karnac.

Whitworth, L., Kimsey-House, H. and Sandahl, P. (1998). *Co-active Coaching: New Skills for Coaching People Toward Success in Work and Life*. Palo Alto, CA: Davies-Black.

Wilber, K. (1995). *Sex, Ecology, Spirituality: The Spirit of Evolution*. Boston, MA: Shambhala.

Wilber, K. (1996). *A Brief History of Everything*. Boston, MA: Shambhala.

Wilber, K. (1998a). *The Eye of Spirit: An Integral Vision for a World Gone Slightly Mad*. Boston, MA: Shambhala.

Wilber, K. (1998b). *The Marriage of Sense and Soul: Integrating Science and Religion*. New York, NY: Random House.

Wilber, K. (2000a). *Integral Psychology: Consciousness, Spirit, Psychology, Therapy*. Boston, MA: Shambhala.

Wilber, K. (2000b). *One Taste: Daily Reflections on Integral Spirituality*. Boston, MA: Shambhala.

Wilber, K. (2001). *No Boundary: Eastern and Western Approaches to Personal Growth*. Boston, MA: Shambhala.

Wilber, K. (2003). Foreword. In Visser, F., *Ken Wilber: Thought as Passion* (pp. xi–xv). New York, NY: State University of New York.

Zohar, D. (1997). *Rewiring the Corporate Brain: Using the New Science to Rethink How We Structure and Lead Organisations*. San Francisco, CA: Berrett-Koehler.

Zull, J.E. (2011). *From Brain to Mind: Using Neuroscience to Guide Change in Education*. Kindle Edition. Sterling, VA: Stylus.

Index

Note: Page numbers in **bold** indicate tables; those in *italics* indicate figures.

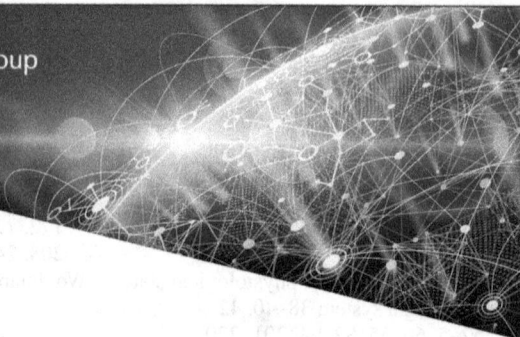

For Product Safety Concerns and Information please contact our EU
representative GPSR@taylorandfrancis.com
Taylor & Francis Verlag GmbH, Kaufingerstraße 24, 80331 München, Germany

www.ingramcontent.com/pod-product-compliance
Lightning Source LLC
Chambersburg PA
CBHW061143220326
41599CB00025B/4337

9 781032 411361